Unwanted Daughters

Unwanted Daughters

Gender Discrimination in Modern India

Editors
T.V. Sekher
Neelambar Hatti

RAWAT PUBLICATIONS
Jaipur • New Delhi • Bangalore • Mumbai • Hyderabad • Guwahati

ISBN 81-316-0323-7

Published by
Prem Rawat for **Rawat Publications**
Satyam Apts, Sector 3, Jawahar Nagar, Jaipur 302 004 (India)
Phone: 0141 265 1748 / 7006 Fax: 0141 265 1748
E-mail: info@rawatbooks.com
Website: www.rawatbooks.com

New Delhi Office
4858/24, Ansari Road, Daryaganj, New Delhi 110 002
Phone: 011 2326 3290

Also at Bangalore, Mumbai, Hyderabad and Guwahati

Typeset by Rawat Computers, Jaipur
Printed at Chaman Enterprises, New Delhi

In memory of
P.N. Mari Bhat

Contents

Foreword

P. Padmanabha

Former Registrar General and Census Commissioner of India

The issues relating to the declining sex ratio in India have been of concern since many years but have invited concentrated attention only after the publication of the results of the 2001 Census of India. In particular, the tabulation of the sex ratio in the age group 0–6 years has brought home to us the magnitude of "missing girls" and the implications that this has for us as a society.

Here, I will refrain from presenting data, since these are well known. I would rather deal with the factors that influence this sex ratio adverse to female children. Let me, at this point, confess that I am not a professional demographer, much less a social scientist, but am a concerned citizen.

In the larger context, discrimination of women has been a feature of our society since ages. Many reasons, or social settings, have over the decades institutionalized this discrimination—property and inheritance rights, son preference, the dowry system, daughters leave for other households, and the like are repeatedly recognized as possible causes. Son preference, in particular, is recognized as strongly influencing the sex ratio among children. Recall the Vedic benediction to the bride in marriage—may you have a hundred sons!

There are strong cultural forces that result in son preference. Among these are the rigidly and rigorously imposed traditions that only a son can perform the last rites among Hindus, and that sons provide social security in old age. A change in such strong traditions would need the active and sustained exhortation of religious leaders, especially those of the large religious orders. This is not forthcoming and they have played no significant role as catalysts of change.

The social and family pressures on the woman for early pregnancy after marriage and for a son can be stifling, often leading to violence, neglect and personal criticism. The long-term psychological and health effects on a woman due to these pressures, and particularly if she does not ultimately have a son, could be disastrous. Therefore, when we consider this issue of an adverse sex ratio among children, we should also ask ourselves if women have much choice in the matter.

Generally, and unfortunately so, many women themselves subscribe to the view that having a son is an assurance of respect in the family and their social group. I recall reading the response of a woman in a field study that having a son was "izzat ki bat hai"! This is probably particularly so in the richer rural agricultural families and in some strata in the urban setting too. The responses in the NFHS–2 to the question of what sex is preferred if one were to have an additional child is interesting. Nearly 47 per cent of the women preferred a son, only 11 per cent a girl, with 27.5 per cent expressing no preference and 14.7 per cent leaving it to God.

There seems to be little appreciation of the biological fact that it is the male partner that determines the sex of the child, and that if anyone has to be blamed for not having sons it is the father! This fact needs to be built into all information, education and communication programmes relating to health and also in the RCH programmes. The concerned manuals do indicate this but it needs to be widely advertised.

As mentioned, discrimination against girls—as part of the discrimination against women—has unfortunately been practised since long. In 1789 the British Resident in Banaras recorded that female infanticide was prevalent among Rajputs in his Division. Similarly, female infanticide was reported in Gujarat in 1817. In the 1921 Census reports, for example, there are references to female infanticide and castes were listed as those with a tradition of female infanticide and those without. References to female infanticide are made in various other documents as well. The sex ratio has been adverse to women over decades.

The reality is that sex discrimination has been a feature of our society since decades, and therefore it is not necessarily a result of modernization. What seems to be true is that modernization has aggravated the problem, with rights to greater wealth and property, social compulsions of conspicuous display of wealth in weddings and family functions, increase in the practice and quantum of dowry beyond reason, and the like. At least in this context, this is not "modernization" at all!

The issue regarding the sex ratio in the age group 0–6 years adverse to girls is important for many reasons. It includes a human rights issue and indeed the right to live of the girl child. Also, it results in a serious demographic disadvantage with social consequences. It reflects weak governance, combined with lack of sensitivity, with regard to both human rights and gender issues.

Medical technology has, in recent times, unfortunately provided the tools for enhanced sex discrimination. Despite the Prenatal Diagnostic Techniques Act, now called the Preconception and Prenatal Diagnostic Techniques (Prevention of Sex selection) Act and the Medical Termination of Pregnancy Act and the safeguards they provide, technology has aggravated the problem. All social classes, or rather all economic levels, seem to practise sex discrimination in varying degree. The adoption of technology for exercising a choice in family composition is not viewed as a crime. Both the professionals involved and their clients are fully aware of the law, but this discrimination is internalized as necessary for the economic and social well-being of the family. The larger social and demographic implications are of no significance to them.

At this point we would do well to remember that it is not just discrimination even before birth of girls through sex determination tests followed by abortions that skews the child sex ratio. There is discrimination even during the childhood years of 0–6. This discrimination is reflected in various ways—neglect in medical attention of the girl child except in serious situations, harder household work, and often-decreased food and nutrition inputs. The decreased medical attention and nutrition by themselves are not proximate causes of mortality of the girl child, but they result in increased morbidity leading to eventual and early mortality. Within the family, as in the case of the adult women, there is less leisure and periods of rest and health care for the girl child. Therefore, female infant and child mortality rates also have impact on the sex ratio. For example, the SRS (1997) indicates that in Karnataka the age-specific death rate in the age group less than 5 years is 11.3 among male children and 13.2 among female children. The corresponding all-India rates are 21.8 and 24.5. This would bear further investigation and study.

It is important to note that the sex ratios even in the higher age groups among children are adverse to the girl child. The NFHS–2 indicates that the sex ratio in the younger age groups is 937 in the age group 0–4 years, 916 in 5–9 years and 918 in 10–14 years. The girl child is at a disadvantage not merely at birth but even in adolescence. Anaemia and malnutrition are contributory factors for this skewed sex ratio adverse to girls in these age groups.

The son preference could also slow down the transition to low fertility. Families with strong son preference may not limit their families. In the 1992–93 NFHS, the response was high that women wanted 50 per cent more sons than daughters. The states in which this response was highest included Punjab, Rajasthan, Uttar Pradesh, Bihar and Gujarat. It has been estimated that fertility at the national level would decline by 8 per cent if there were no gender preference. Also, the NFHS results indicate that while literate women have much lower fertility levels than illiterate women, the influence of son preference on fertility levels is higher among the former. It is doubtful, therefore, whether just improvements in literacy and economic levels of women would have a major impact on the sex ratio. A concerted multidimensional social movement would seem necessary.

The implications—social and demographic—of the decreasing sex ratio among children are serious and are interrelated. The imbalance in the number of men and women has obvious social implications, particularly in the states where the sex ratio in the age group 0–6 years is highly skewed such as Delhi, Gujarat, Haryana and Punjab. It is already becoming obvious—one reads of brides being sought from other states, increased crimes against women including young girls, and the like.

The data are in abundance, the facts are known and the implications for the nation and society understood. The question is what does one do to mitigate the adverse sex ratio among children and in the population too. How does one bring about social change that would alter attitudes and mindsets? One could consider the possible measures for initiating this social change on two levels. The first is the legal framework and the second the enforcement of the laws.

The laws prohibiting sex determination, prohibition of dowry payments and related issues in themselves would seem adequate. However, the laws relating to property inheritance and rights for maintenance of the elderly and other categories of relatives that now discriminate against daughters would need a hard look and amendments to provide for equal rights for both men and women would be necessary. How far the laws need changes for mitigating the existing social and economic factors that induce discrimination would need study. This would be a useful exercise in itself.

The other issue would be the enforcement of the laws. In essence, one is talking of effective systems of licencing, monitoring, inspection and prosecution—good governance in brief. There is, of course, the need for constant and intensive programmes of dissemination of information and educating the community. Good governance presumes the interest of the community and that of both the political and executives wings of government in these issues.

There is obviously clear understanding of the issues and their implications within government and a large part of the community, but there is a reluctance to rigorously enforce the laws or to insist that they be enforced. We are all aware of the reasons. These range from corruption to political reluctance to induce rapid social change. There are political advantages in maintaining the status quo, which I feel is the reason for lack of concerted efforts to improve literacy levels too. However, one hopes that the recent changes in policy with respect to primary education would alter this dismal scenario.

Incidentally, the 2000 National Population Policy does not express any concern with regard to the adverse sex ratio. The implications of the results of the Census of India, 2001 would necessarily have to be built into the population policy.

Unfortunately, social issues that call for sustained action on a long term do not attract the powers that be—like primary education, public health, gender issues and the like. There is no glamour in activities with a long haul, since, to use a recently popular word, 'shining' results would not be apparent. Both effective governance and accountability are missing.

Closely associated with the re-examination of the relevant laws and the systems for their effective implementation, is the consideration of the feasibility of self-regulation of medical professionals. Surely, anybody of professionals would do well to institute systems of monitoring and self-regulation, but in the case of medical professionals these would seem essential. What systems could be developed for this purpose?

Apart from the stricter implementation of the relevant laws and self-regulation of the medical profession itself to the extent this is feasible, there are sectors within government that together influence the sex ratio in the age group 0–6 years. These would include compulsory primary education in conjunction with the mid-day meals programme, the examination of children as an essential part of the school health programme, nutrition programmes such as the ICDS, and the like. These programmes, taken together, enhance the well-being of the child. These programmes are closely linked, or should be implemented in a linked manner, and influence both attitudes towards the girl child and ensure her health. The current systems of coordination between the departments concerned need to be constantly reviewed, to ensure that they remain effective.

In this process, what could be the role of the Panchayati Raj institutions? Could they be vehicles of change? In particular, the role of the village panchayat, which is the local authority closest to the community, would need emphasis. But, the fact remains that they are essentially political organizations. Nevertheless, they should be assigned a major role in the process of social change in their local area. This could include dissemination of information, communication and education on this issue. Also, being in charge of the development sectors such as health, primary education, and the other associated programmes, it would be useful to carry out systems studies to determine how their involvement could be enhanced to ensure effective results. In other words, it would be useful to consider the possible mechanisms that would help in transforming these bodies, specially the village panchayat, into vehicles of social change. How they could assume a leadership role would need to be explored.

Equally important is the induction of local community organizations in information, communication and educational activities with regard to this issue. These would include Mahila Mandals, Youth Clubs, Farmers Associations, Self-Help Groups and similar organizations. In particular, women's organizations would need to be energized and assigned a major role in this effort.

The sex ratio is not just a demographic index. It is an indicator of gender discrimination and reflects society's attitude towards women. It is significant that even with increasing education and access to information of other societies, the sex ratio has remained at disturbingly adverse levels. In fact, the reverse seems to be true—education does not seem to have a noticeable impact on traditional mindsets and affluence seems to have aggravated the problem as evidenced by the decline of the sex ratio from 955 in 1921 to 933 in 2001. What is of particular concern is the decline in the ratio in the age group 0–6 which has serious implications for the future.

The papers presented in this book seek to analyze the nexus of economic, social and cultural factors that underlie daughter discrimination in Indian context. I would urge that the functioning of the systems of administration and implementation that are concerned with this issue receive due emphasis, so that policy suggestions emerge with regard to the parameters that influence the sex ratio. On most of these parameters we have enough data—it is their interrelationships and the morphing of the latter into action points that would now seem important.

I congratulate the editors of this volume, T.V. Sekher and Neelambar Hatti, for bringing together a set of scholarly and well-researched papers for wider dissemination.

Acknowledgements

Human rights are the rights, which every individual is entitled to enjoy and which protect the dignity of human beings. Unfortunately in our country, and elsewhere, many unborn girls are aborted merely because they are girls, thus denying them the fundamental right to be born and live. The parents who opt for aborting female foetuses are far from ignorant about what they are doing. To discuss the issues relating to the problem of "missing girls" of India, the editors had organized a workshop at the Institute for Social and Economic Change (ISEC), Bangalore in 2005. The workshop was funded by Swedish Research Council, as part of a collaborative research project on gender discrimination.

The collection of essays in the present volume has seen the light of the day in the midst of such a trend of sex-selective abortion, which has had, and continuous to have, serious economic, social and demographic implications. The book would not have been possible without the efforts of many concerned researchers and social scientists who took part in the workshop. The volume comprises of papers presented in the workshop which are based on extensive fieldwork from different parts of India dealing with various aspects of this social epidemic. We are thankful to Shri P. Padmanabha, former Registrar General and Census Commissioner of India, for writing a foreword for this publication.

Our thanks are due to many who were involved in organizing the workshop and to those who participated. In particular, we would like to mention late Prof. P.N.Mari Bhat for his encouragement and inspiration. He attended the workshop and delivered the valedictory address, highlighting the implications of sex-selective abortion. He was an outstanding and highly innovative demographer. We dedicate the volume to his memory.

T.V. Sekher
Neelambar Hatti

Contributors

Sutapa Agrawal, Assistant Professor, Indian Institute of Health Management Research, New Delhi.

Mumtaj Begum, Associate Professor, Lady Doak Collage, Madurai.

Preethi Bhat, Research Associate, Institute for Social and Economic Change, Bangalore.

P.N. Mari Bhat, Former Director, International Institute for Population Sciences, Mumbai.

Pernille Gooch, Senior Lecturer, Human Ecology Division, Lund University, Sweden.

Neelambar Hatti, Emeritus Professor, Department of Economic History, Lund University, Sweden.

William Joe, Research Scholar, Centre for Development Studies, Thiruvananthapuram.

Ravinder Kaur, Professor, Indian Institute of Technology, New Delhi.

S. Khanna, Associate Professor, Oregon State University, USA.

Mattias Larsen, Research Scholar, Goteborg University, Sweden.

Tulsi Patel, Professor, Delhi School of Economics, Delhi University, Delhi.

C.P. Prakasam, Former Professor, International Institute for Population Sciences, Mumbai.

S. Irudaya Rajan, Professor, Centre for Development Studies, Thiruvananthapuram.

Priyajit Samaiyar, Research Scholar, Centre for Development Studies, Thiruvananthapuram.

T.V. Sekher, Associate Professor, International Institute for Population Sciences, Mumbai.

Christianna Singh, Lecturer, Lady Doak Collage, Madurai.

Roma Srivastava, Researcher, University of North Carolina, Greensboro, USA.

S. Sudha, Associate Professor, University of North Carolina, Greensboro, USA.

Sayeed Unisa, Professor, International Institute for Population Sciences, Mumbai.

A.J. Francis Zavier, Programme Officer, Population Council, New Delhi.

Introduction

Unwanted Daughters: Gender Discrimination in Modern India

T.V. Sekher and Neelambar Hatti

During the last two decades, considerable debate has taken place, particularly in India, on the imbalance in sex ratio and the question of 'missing women'. The Indian subcontinent is one of the few regions in the world where there are more males than females in the population. In a significant article titled as "More than 100 million women are missing", Amartya Sen brought to focus the increasing gender discrimination by analyzing the male-female ratio (Sen, 1990). He argued rather convincingly that the problem of missing women is clearly one of the momentous and neglected problems facing the world today. Barbara Miller, in her pioneering anthropological study of the neglect of female children in north India, illustrated the strong relationship between culture and mortality. It is the cultural bias against females in north India, which brings into play neglect and mistreatment of unknown numbers of girl children. According to her, the solution to this problematic future lies "in giving high priority to achieving gender equality in economic entitlement and increased awareness of the social importance of equal health and survival of males and females" (Miller, 1981: 214).

In general, the sex ratio can be considered as a direct indicator of women's status and welfare.[1] There have been a number of studies, which have attempted to illustrate how the decline in fertility will affect gender bias and more imbalances in juvenile sex ratios (Clark, 2000; Croll, 2002; Bhat and Zavier, 2003). A substantial decline in fertility presupposes a desire for fewer children and the means to limit the family size. Both these conditions can be achieved with increase in social and economic development. It is generally accepted that the pace of demographic transition is closely associated with the levels of socio-economic development. However, there are evidences to show that, even in the poorer regions, substantial decline in fertility has occurred through political interventions, in the form of family planning programme. However, the social and economic development and governmental interventions do not ensure any substantial change in the cultural ethos of the society. One important factor (both cultural and economic) that determines the level of fertility transition is son preference. In developing societies, it is believed that a major barrier for decline in fertility was the prevalence of strong son preference, irrespective of socio-economic development. It is also argued that with the increase in welfare and economic development, the influence of son preference would decline gradually. These assumptions are being questioned by some studies indicating that there has been an increase in son preference during the years of fertility decline (Das Gupta and Bhat, 1997). These occur not only in poorer communities but also in populations where women have taken the education, employment and have achieved considerable social status. The existence of strong son preference has resulted in the desire to prevent the birth of daughters by carefully balancing the desired family size and desired sex composition of the children. In other words, the decline in fertility partly explains the raising masculinity of many populations. It is hypothesized that as fertility declines, two opposing forces could affect the child sex ratio, what is called as 'parity effect', which leads to a reduction of sex bias and 'intensification effect', which increases it. Considering this dimension, there is a need to examine the influence of the mirror image of son preference, namely, the daughter discrimination. Does a strong son preference ultimately result in deliberate discrimination against daughters? Miller has stated "the problem is that son preference is so strong in some areas of India and amongst some classes that daughters must logically suffer in order that family's personal and culturally mandated needs are fulfilled" (1981: 25). Logically, this would mean that stronger the son preference, more marked the daughter discrimination.

Rather than going through repeated pregnancies bearing daughters in an attempt to produce male progeny, small family and reduced fertility seems to imply that unborn daughters are the first to be 'sacrificed'. Generally, both infanticide and fatal neglect of female children seem to have been supplemented by sex identification and sex-selective abortion, to achieve the desired family size and gender composition. Better opportunities for women's education, increasing labour force participation and an enhanced exposure and freedom do not guarantee equal status for daughters as that of sons. In many Indian communities, daughters are associated with a double loss. Firstly, a daughter leaves the natal family after her marriage and the benefits from investments made on her upbringing accrue to the new family, constituting a loss to her natal family. This is further compounded by the burden of expenses for her marriage, particularly dowry. Sons, on the other hand, are considered as assets worthy of short and long-term investment. In India, the birth of a boy is thus a time for celebration while a birth of a girl, especially second or subsequent one, is often viewed as time of crisis (Bumiller, 1991). Apart from this economic considerations, there are cultural factors that support son preference. All these factors put together contribute to the assumption and firm belief that daughters cannot substitute sons. A common explanation for the existence of son preference and daughter discrimination is that sons can provide old age support. In India, a majority of the old parents live with married children, who, to an overwhelming majority, are sons. Indian context characterized by high levels of uncertainty, where no institutional alternative to the family as a source of social insurance has emerged, parental decisions are likely to be powerfully motivated by their concerns about their own security in the old age. The existence of such an understanding and commitment between parents and sons, called as inter-generational contract, is one of the factors that appear to have remained unchanged through overall socio-economic changes. Sons are also important because they alone are entitled to perform the funeral rituals of the parents. Added to this, most women have limited or no possibility to contribute towards their parents' welfare. This creates an apparent dichotomy between the value of a girl to her parents and that of a woman to her in-laws. It has also become more costly to raise children as education has become more important and a necessity irrespective of the sex of the child. The increasing cost of education and marriage of girls is a major drain on the household resources, which acts as a strong disincentive to have daughters.

The underlying causes of female discrimination are undoubtedly highly complex. However, a number of broad factors have been identified which together create a situation where sons are preferred and daughters are neglected. The patterns of inheritance are typically patrilineal in India with property passing from father to son (Miller, 1981; Das Gupta, 1987; Kabeer, 1996; Sekher and Hatti, 2007). Upon marriage the bride leaves her natal home to live with the family of her husband. In this exogamous lineage system women are left out. They become dispensable essentially because they count for very little as individuals. There is a double loss of a daughter leaving the family together with the fact that the benefits from investments made in a daughter's upbringing will accrue to the new family. In other words, even though a woman's status might improve, it does not change the nature of the social order, as it does not directly correlate to a change in her position within it. While valuing adult women's contributions to the household, the system generates strong disincentives to raising daughters.

In recent years, a major factor directly influenced the imbalance in child sex ratio is the widespread use of sex determination technologies and sex-selective abortions. In India, the Medical Termination of Pregnancy (MTP) Act was enacted in 1971 as a health measure to protect women. The revised MTP Act of 1975 allows medical termination of pregnancy (abortion) for any of the reasons such as:

(a) the pregnant woman has a serious medical disease or condition that would endanger her life if the pregnancy were to continue;
(b) continuation of pregnancy would entail a substantial risk of physical and mental handicap to the new-born child;
(c) the pregnancy resulted from rape;
(d) the socio-economic circumstances of the mother would endanger the health of the new-born child; and
(e) the pregnancy occurred because of failure of a contraceptive method.

The last reason legalizes abortion on demand, in effect. Despite legalization of abortion, more illegal abortions are being performed in India than legal ones. While government statistics estimate legal abortions at about 0.6 million annually, illegal abortions are estimated to be 8 to 11 times as high as legal abortions. Birth histories collected during the National Family Health Surveys (first in 1992–93 and later in 1998–99) show an unusually large proportion of male births in some population groups, which suggest that female foetuses are being aborted. Sex-selective abortion is a two-step process involving determination of the sex of the foetus followed by abortion if the foetus is not of the desired sex. During the last two decades, prenatal diagnosis technologies have proliferated rapidly in India primarily used to avoid the birth of daughters, as there exists a strong preference for sons. Couples who have achieved their desired family size may not stop having children if they have not reached their desired number of sons. Soon after the introduction of the sex-determination tests, advertisements began to spread both in urban and rural areas by private practitioners motivated by high profit margin in providing abortion services: "Pay Rs 500 (US $ 10) now rather than Rs 5,00,000 (US $ 10,000) later". These attractive advertisements specifically addressed prospective parents to abort female foetuses in order to avoid future dowry expenses. Daughters are considered as a 'liability' for the family by these advertisements and in a way they exhort women to avail themselves of the services of the clinic to escape the future financial burdens arising from getting the daughter married.

Misuse of sex determination tests has been a subject of media attention for many years. Health activists and women's organizations voiced their concern forcing the government to act. In 1994, the Government of India banned the tests at the national level, with the Pre-natal Diagnostic Techniques (Regulation and Prevention of Misuse) Act, popularly known as PNDT Act. As per this new legislation, only government registered clinics and laboratories may employ prenatal diagnostic procedures that could be used to assess the sex of the foetus. The new Act also specifies that no prenatal diagnostic procedures may be used unless there is a heightened possibility that the foetus suffers from a harmful condition or genetic disease. It also states, "no person conducting prenatal diagnostic procedures shall communicate to the pregnant women concerned or her relatives the sex of the foetus by words, signs, or in any other manner". This Act was again amended in the light of the newer techniques of pre-conception tests and the amended rule came into effect from February 2003. Now, the Act is renamed as the Pre-conception and Pre-natal Diagnostic Techniques (Prohibition of Sex-selection) Act, 1994.

Even after all these restrictions and campaign against this practice, the business of sex determination is thriving in all parts of the country. This perverse use of technology is encouraged and boosted by money-minded practitioners. Ultrasound is considered by many couples to be a good investment in order to save many times that sum in future dowry payments if the foetus is a female. The prenatal diagnosis technologies have been misused intensifying the oppression of women, particularly in cultural settings such as in India, where women already have a low status.

Female foetuses are liable to victimization on the basis of their sex alone even before they are born. Only far-reaching social changes that aim at increasing female autonomy, female economic power and the value of the girl child are likely to make a significant impact on the demand for sex-selective abortion. Interestingly, there is no reliable statistics available on sex-selective abortion at the state or national level in India. An indirect estimate using the data from two rounds of National Family Health Survey (NFHS) indicates more than 1,00,000 sex-selective abortions in India every year (Arnold, Kishor and Roy, 2002). The evidence of substantial sex-selective abortion in states such as Punjab, Haryana, Delhi and Maharashtra is consistent with the high rates of use of ultrasound and amniocentesis (Retherford and Roy, 2003).

The 2001 Census has set off a debate on the sex ratio issue and focused attention on juvenile sex ratio of children aged 0–6 years. This has generated widespread concern particularly among the gender experts and NGOs working for improving the status of women, resulting in legislation. However, the legislation has been a miserable failure in preventing the couples seeking sex determination and the medical practitioners performing them. Enforcement of legal procedures alone will not reduce these incidences unless there are significant changes in the attitudes and social life.

At the national and state levels, we have reasonably good idea about the levels of fertility decline, the extent of son preference, and the magnitude of gender discrimination based on the analysis of large-scale data from various demographic and health surveys. But, how this really manifests at the village level, and on certain rural communities, particularly in the context of widespread and easy availability of sex-selection techniques? Given this scenario, a research project was undertaken with financial support from Swedish Research Council to probe various dimensions of gender discrimination. By studying villages and communities from different parts of India with varying levels of socio-economic development and at different stages of fertility transition, we attempt to understand how these factors interplay at the micro level, with changing attitudes and preferences. In general, the project study addresses the following issues: Why millions of girls do not appear to be surviving in India despite an overall improvement in development and many governmental measures to enhance the status of women? Why are female children still at risk and why is daughter discrimination on the increase despite progress in female literacy and participation of women in economic and political activities? Is there any significant shift from centuries old 'son preference' to new forms of 'daughter discrimination' at the household level? How the village communities perceive the changing status of women and the value of girl children in the fast changing socio-economic milieu? Whether the socio-economic changes and the forces of globalization and modernization have influenced our attitude towards children, particularly girls? How far have the fertility transition and new reproductive strategies aided by advancement in medical technology influenced the gender composition of modern family?

The recent discourses in India have changed the focus from 'missing women' to 'missing girls', highlighting the precarious situation of female children before birth (their chances of being born at all), at birth and during childhood. In this context, it is necessary to understand the nexus of economic, social and cultural factors that underlie daughter discrimination. What are the social and economic impact of the declining feminity and the consequent policy implications? At the final phase of the project, a workshop was organized at Bangalore to discuss these issues in detail as well as to find out the findings and observations of similar studies carried out in different parts of India. The workshop, attended by sociologists, demographers, gender specialists, NGOs and others, provided a multidisciplinary perspective to address this complex issue. Twelve papers were presented in the workshop, which generated productive discussions. The keynote address by Shri P. Padmanabha (former Registrar General and Census Commissioner of India) and the valedictory address by Prof P.N. Mari Bhat (then Director, International Institute for Population Sciences, Mumbai) raised many pertinent issues for discussions and also for further research. In this volume, we have included selected papers from the workshop that cover various aspects of gender discrimination from different socio-geographical locations of India.

In India, girls are aborted on a massive scale simply because they are girls. The threat of not being allowed to take birth or to fade away if born, is increasingly becoming a commonly raised issue. Sociologist Tulsi Patel, in her interesting paper titled as—"Risky Lives: Indian Girls Caught between Individual Rationality and Public Good"—explores the savvy couple that exercises reproductive choice and makes informed and careful reproductive decisions. In being in control of their lives, couples act what is in their best interest. The question this paper is trying to address is how does one understand the logic that individual rational action leads to public good? Patel, based on her extensive fieldwork in northern India, illustrates how changing family and community characteristics influence the gender equations within the family as well as the fertility decision-making of the household. Couples may not be certain of outcomes of raising daughters but they try to asess some probabilities of taking or averting the risk of having to raise one or more daughters.

In their paper, Mattias Larsen, Neelambar Hatti and Pernille Gooch, "Inter-generational Interests, Uncertainty and Discrimination: Declining Child Sex Ratios in India", deal with the continuing decline in child sex ratios despite improvements in general welfare and of female status in the society and point to deeply rooted structures of gender inequality. This paper builds upon the recognition that the declining child sex ratios are a result of an ongoing societal change. At the centre of the factors concerning the problem of daughter discrimination stands the family. The problem of 'missing girls' can be ascribed to social, economic and cultural factors, which together create incentives for son preference and disincentives for raising daughters. However, it is within the family that the decision-making takes place. Hence, it is of importance to analyze the relationships between these factors with a focus on the family. In order to understand why female children are at risk and why there is an increasing discrimination against girls in India, it is particularly important to consider the intra-household allocation of resources. The parents, as a reaction to the uncertainty that those very changes produce, 'fall back' on traditional norms regarding gender and domestic roles. This makes the bargaining situation and the criteria for the allocation of resources highly adversarial for girls, creating a structure in which there is little space for daughters. Looking at areas both in the north and the south of India, which have shown significant decline in the child sex ratios in the last two decades, the paper draws on from recently conducted field studies in the rural areas of Karnataka in the south and Uttaranchal in the north.

There is an increasing conflict between preferred family size and preferred sex composition of children in many societies undergoing fertility transition. A substantial decline in the fertility presupposes a desire for fewer children and the means to limit the family size. The widespread use of advanced technologies for sex determination and sex-selective abortion has given a new means for parents to achieve the desired gender composition of their children. In communities where son preference co-exists with discrimination against daughters, stronger the son preference, more intense is the daughter discrimination. The paper entitled—"From 'Fertility Control' to 'Gender Control'? Evidences of Gender Discrimination in Rural South India" by T.V. Sekher, Neelambar Hatti and Preethi Bhat—attempt to examine whether fertility decline has led to an increased elimination of daughters. This paper, based on two village studies carried out in low fertility regions of Karnataka and Tamil Nadu states, provides useful insights into the emerging forms of gender discrimination. Through household surveys, interviews and focus group discussions, the study analyzed the changing attitudes of the peasant communities of the district. It was observed that rapid fertility decline, not accompanied by changes in the cultural values and gender inequality, was in a way responsible for a deliberate attempt to get rid of the girls. In other words, the strong son preference, the increasing pressure on limited land, and the spiraling costs of marriage and dowry compel the couples to avoid having daughters. The observations from the villages indicate an intensification of gender bias along with the drastic decline in fertility, and the increasing preference for sons has manifested in a deliberate discrimination towards daughters.

In an interesting paper, P.N. Mari Bhat and A.J. Francis Zavier analyze the effect of PNDT use on the sex ratio at birth. Data from 2001 Census reveals that the sex ratio at birth may have increased by 6 percentage points in India since 1985 and in some parts by 20 per cent points. According to their analysis, the effect of PNDT use on the sex ratio at birth is found to be contingent on whether women are in the male-selection situation or not. While income and education are found to increase the use of PNDT, their misuse is more governed by cultural factors and the sex composition of children already born. Although the use of PNDT is now fairly common in many parts of India, only a minority of couples who use these techniques misuses it for aborting female foetuses. The higher sex ratio at birth observed among more educated and higher income groups is mainly because of their better access to these techniques rather than from their greater misuse.

C.P. Prakasam's paper deals with the imbalances in sex ratio in one district of Tamil Nadu ("Imbalance in Sex Ratio in Rural Tamil Nadu: A Case Study of Salem District"). Among the districts of Tamil Nadu Salem district shows low sex ratio (680 females per 1,000 males). Research investigations are made to explore the reasons for this gender disparity in a state otherwise known for its significant progress in socio-economic development. An attempt was made to find out the variation in sex ratio in Salem district and the prevalence of sex-selective abortion contributing to imbalances. To know the prevalence of sex-selective abortion, data were derived from a survey conducted in Salem district during 2003. The survey covers 1,565 currently married women in the age group 15–49 who have experienced at least one delivery. Reproductive history of the currently married women and the reasons for undergoing repeated abortions have been examined. Besides these, case studies have been conducted to elicit information on the practices of infanticide and foeticide. Qualitative data analysis revealed that female foeticides and infanticides are very much in practice because of the prevalent dowry system and existing poverty in some communities.

The paper on "Traditions in Transformation: Emerging Son Preference Attitudes among the Nairs of Kerala" by S. Sudha, Sunil Khanna, S. Irudaya Rajan and Roma Srivastava, examines the changing gender preferences among the Nair community of Kerala state in southern India—whether preconditions for gender bias (preference for male children) have emerged among this group and whether gender bias is expressed, either verbally or in the uptake of modern reproductive technologies for prenatal sex selection. Kerala has been lauded in the demographic literature for high achievements: 'normal' sex ratios, near total literacy, long life expectancy, low fertility and good health service coverage—all at a low level of economic development. The status of women is considered to be high in Kerala, attributed to the matrilineal kinship systems historically practised by several groups in the state, including the Nairs. However, matrilineal kinship had been dismantled over the previous century; and high female unemployment, dowry custom, domestic violence, and other negative features are widespread in Kerala today. The authors conducted interviews using rapid ethnographic assessment methods among three generations of Nair men and women living in the Thrissur urban area. The results show that patrilineal kinship and family organization, changes in marriage customs, spread of dowry, and gender-based division of labour in the household and at work have penetrated into the Nair community. Verbal expressions of gender bias are widespread. Modern prenatal sex-selection techniques appear to exist on a very small scale and are not in wide evidence as in northern parts of India. This interesting study is a unique contribution to the existing literature on female deficit in India as it examines a community never before researched from this perspective, but which has a cultural background assumed to protect against gender bias.

Improving the status of women through varied policies and programmes will automatically improve the status of girls in the family and society, has proved to be ineffective. Even in countries where women enjoy high status, girls are less preferred to boys. There are basically three factors of son preference in India, viz., economic utility, socio-cultural utility and religious functions. The studies indicate that sons are more preferred than daughters to provide labour, earn wages, and as old-age support for parents. Upon marriage, a son, in the form of his wife, makes an addition and asset to the family providing assistance in household work and brings an economic reward through dowry payments, while daughters get married off and merit an economic penalty through dowry charges. The socio-cultural utility factor of son preference implies that, in India's patriarchal system of families having at least one son is mandatory in order to continue the familial lineage, and many sons constitute additional status to families. The paper authored by Mumtaj Begum and Christianna Singh ("Status of the Girl Child and Son Preference in Madurai") examines the effect of socio-economic characteristics on the actual probability of having sons through a maximum likelihood logistic estimation in a city such as Madurai with its strong traditional bind. Primary data collected through a survey of 300 samples drawn from varied strata is used. Since the perceived cost of the girl child is higher, the preference for sons is stronger. When the perceived cost of the girl child is reduced, her status is improved and son preference weakened. Awareness is the prime tool to achieve this, and according to authors, formulating strategies for empowering girls are the beginning of women's empowerment.

In the context of declining sex ratio, it is important to examine its implications on marriage squeeze and marriage pattern, which has a serious bearing on quality of life and status of women in India. In demographic literature 'marriage squeeze' is understood as imbalance in the sex ratio in the marriageable age group. When there is increase in the supply of females, it is termed as the female marriage market squeeze and vice versa. The study by Priyajit Samaiyar and William Joe ("Implications of Declining Sex Ratio on Marriage Squeeze of India)" examines the marriage squeeze through the measurement methods involving sex ratio and age distribution of marriage. Marriage pattern can be understood as the variables like delayed marriage, age gap between the spouses, and the proportion never married in the population over different marriage cohorts and periods. The analysis carried out using the National Family Health Survey (NFHS), National Sample Survey Organization (NSSO) and census data discusses the socio-economic correlates of marriage squeeze in terms of examining the relationship of marriage squeeze with the selected indicators of marriage pattern. The study demonstrates how the government policy of promoting two-child norm without giving consideration to the problem of sex-selective abortions can actually aggravate the problem of sex imbalance in the country. This declining sex ratio has direct and serious consequences on the marriage market.

Sutapa Agrawal and Sayeed Unisa, in their paper, "Active and Passive Elimination of Girl Child: Findings from Rural Haryana", highlight the sex-selective discrimination in terms of active and passive elimination of girl child in different socio-economic conditions as a life course approach. The study has used primary data collected from 329 ever-married women in five villages of Haryana. Active elimination has been seen in terms of abortion according to the sex of the surviving children, pregnancy order, women's childhood experience, autonomy status and marital instability. Autonomy, education and exposure to mass media have negative impact whereas co-residence with in-laws and no male child have significant positive impact for active elimination. In-laws play an important role in abortion under the umbrella of son preference. In logistic regression results, sex of the children ever born and autonomy were found to be significant factors. The quantitative as well as qualitative data shows that there exists extreme sex-selective discrimination against the girl child in the rural society through conception to their rearing and bearing. Woman who herself had a worst childhood experience (in terms of discrimination in all spheres including childhood status, food, education, mobility, etc.), had less autonomy in various dimensions, and felt high instability in her married life, is more responsible for the discrimination against girl child leading to a vicious cycle of gender deprivation and discrimination.

The implications of the low sex ratio for future marriages have as yet been little studied in India. It is obvious that less and declining number of girl children, as revealed by the 2001 Census, will lead to a larger 'bride shortage' that is already being experienced in certain northern states of India. This paper by Ravinder Kaur ("Across-Region Marriages: Poverty, Female Migration and Sex Ratio") addresses the less explored question of how society deals with this socially and culturally created demographic imbalance. Given that marriage is socially valued and physically/economically necessary, what is the range of responses and solutions devised by society in order to meet the shortage? Do these solutions (e.g., across-region marriages, polyandry and forced bachelorhood) differ in different regions and over different time periods? Related to these questions are the implications for society of the excess number of bachelors, the impact of shortage of brides on dowry values, and the changing contours of the marriage market. This sociological study first establishes the parameters of 'bride shortage' at present and in future in India. Second, based on primary ethnographic research in selected districts of Haryana, U.P. and West Bengal, it explores the strategies adopted by 'needy' men and their families to address the shortage of brides.

In general, the collection of the papers in this volume, based on extensive research from different parts of the country, provides us a multidisciplinary perspective to understand the varied facets of increasing gender discrimination in contemporary India. Though researchers vary considerably in their views regarding the causes and consequences of female deficit, all of them underline the pressing need for a change in the socio-economic attitudes of Indian society towards girl children as a lasting solution to this social epidemic.

Note

1. It should be borne in mind that under-enumeration of females, typically encountered in many South Asian countries, also makes census sex composition more masculine. In view of this, the census data should be interpreted with caution because improving the quality of age data on children can produce a spurious trend of falling sex ratios at certain childhood ages (Bhat, 2002).

References

Arnold, Fred, Sunita Kishor and T.K. Roy (2002). Sex-selective Abortions in India, *Population and Development Review,* Vol. 28(4), pp. 759–85.

Bhat, Mari P.N. (2002). On the Trail of 'Missing' Indian Females (I and II), *Economic and Political Weekly,* 37(51 and 52), pp. 5105–18 and 5244–63.

Bhat, Mari P.N. and Francis Zavier (2003). Fertility Decline and Gender Bias in Northern India, *Demography,* 40(4), pp. 637–57.

Bumiller, E. (1991). *May You be the Mother of a Hundred Sons: A Journey among the Women of India,* Penguin Books, New Delhi.

Clark, Shelley (2000). Son Preference and Sex Composition of Children: Evidence from India, *Demography,* Vol. 37(1), pp. 95–108.

Croll, Elisabeth J. (2002). Fertility Decline, Family Size and Female Discrimination: A Study of Reproductive Management in East and South Asia, *Asia-Pacific Population Journal,* 17(2), pp. 11–38.

Das Gupta, M. (1987). Selective Discrimination against Female Children in Rural Punjab, India, *Population and Development Review,* 13(1), pp. 77–100.

Das Gupta, M. and P.N.M. Bhat (1997). Fertility Decline and Increased Manifestation of Sex Bias in India, *Population Studies,* 51(3), pp. 307–15.

Kabeer, Naila (1996). Gender, Demographic Transitions and the Economics of the Family: Population Policy for a Human-centred Development, Occasional Paper 7, UNRISD.

Miller, B.D. (1981). *The Endangered Sex: Neglect of Female Children in Rural North India,* Cornell University Press, Ithaca, NY.

Retherford, R.D. and T.K. Roy (2003). Factors affecting Sex-selective Abortion in India and 17 Major States, National Family Health Survey Reports, No. 21, Mumbai, IIPS and Hawaii, East-West Centre.

Sekher, T.V. and Neelambar Hatti (2007). "Vulnerable Daughters in a Modernizing Society: From Son Preference to Daughter Discrimination in Rural South India", in I. Attane and C.Z. Guilmoto (eds.), *Watering the Neighbours Garden: The Growing Demographic Female Deficit in Asia,* CICRED, Paris.

Sen, A. (1990). More than 100 Million Women are Missing, *New York Review of Books,* 20 December, pp. 61–66.

ONE

Risky Lives

Indian Girls Caught between Individual Rationality and Public Good

Tulsi Patel

Highly skewed sex ratios in India, especially for young children between 0–6 years of age, are now well known in academic as well as other circles. Amartya Sen (1990) had raised the alarm a while ago. Hatti et al. (2004) have analyzed the risk faced by the girl child in India. Overall, at 865 girls per 1,000 boys in the age group 0–6, Delhi, in fact, has the dubious distinction of ranking third among the states with low sex ratio. Punjab tops this list, followed by Haryana. National Sample Survey data (1999–2000) shows that the child sex ratio among the poorest 5 per cent of the households in rural areas is 946, while among the richest 5 per cent it is 804. The corresponding figures for urban areas are 903 and 819 respectively. Clearly, there is a stronger bias against girl children among the rich and the urban Indians. For example, Delhi with a child sex ratio (CSR) of 865 in 2001, and below 900 for each of its nine districts, the lowest (845) is in southwest Delhi, which is one of the most prosperous districts. Since urban health indicators are known to be better than rural health indicators across sexes, this fall in CSR in the more affluent areas cannot be taken to mean a higher mortality in the rich. Sudha and Rajan (1999) found an increasing masculinization in sex ratio using reverse survival methods to estimate sex ratio at birth for several parts of India (see Table 1). Delhi had an accelerated fall in child sex ratio, which has declined from 915 in 1991 to 865 in 2001 (see Table 2).

Table 1

Trends in FMR and 0–6 Year Sex Ratios in Some Selected States of India

Zone	*State*	*1971 FMR*	*1981 FMR*	*1991 FMR*	*2001 FMR*	*1971 0–6 yr*	*1981 0–6 yr*	*1991 0–6 yr*	*2001 0–6 yr*
North	Punjab			882	874	892	908	875	793
	Rajasthan	911	919	910	922	931	954	916	909
	Uttar Pradesh	876	862	876	898	899	935	928	916
South	Andhra Pradesh	977	975	972	978	986	992	974	964
	Karnataka	957	963	960	964	968	975	960	950
	Tamil Nadu	978	977	974	986	964	967	974	939
	Kerala	1016	1032	1036	1058	972	970	958	962
West	Gujarat	934	942	934	919	956	947	928	878
	Madhya Pradesh	920	921	912	920	944	978	952	931
East	Bihar	957	948	907	921	958	981	959	938
	Orissa	988	981	971	972	984	995	967	950
	West Bengal	891	911	917	934	1007	981	967	963
India		931	935	927	933	954	962	945	927

Sources: Census of India, 2001; Banerjee and Jain, 2001.

Table 2

Declining Child Sex Ratio in Delhi

Districts	*Child sex ratio in the age group 0–6 years*		
	1991	*2001*	*Change in points*
Northwest	913	854	–59
Southwest	904	845	–59
West	913	858	–55
North	920	870	–50
East	918	868	–50
Northeast	917	867	–50
New Delhi	919	882	–37
Central	937	902	–35
South	912	886	–26
Entire state	915	865	–50

Source: Office of the Registrar General and Census Commissioner of India, 2003.

The distortion in the sex ratio was brought out starkly also by an analysis of the data from the second National Family Health Survey (NFHS) conducted in 1998–99, undertaken by Arnold et al. (2002). They showed that at all-India level, the male to female sex ratio of the last births was 697 girls for every 1,000 boys, among currently married women who did not want any more children, which was much lower than the sex ratio of 935 girls for every 1,000 boys for all the other births. However, there were significant variations in inter-state sex ratio for last births and in the states of Haryana, Punjab and Gujarat, which ranged between 570 girls for every 1,000 boys to 460 girls for every 1,000 boys. Underreporting of girls in the censuses, migration effect and natural propensity among Indians to produce more boys were said to be the major reasons in Visaria's (1971) sound work on sex ratio. Infant mortality differences by sex and consistently low sex ratios at birth by birth order of babies are clearly contributing towards the skewing of sex ratios to the extent of 0.5 million missing female births every year in India calculated by Jha et al. (2006) based on a large sample of 1.1 million households' special survey of fertility and mortality in 1998–99. Tables 3 and 4 show sex differences by infant and child mortality and by birth order respectively.

Table 3

Infant Mortality Rates and Death Rates in 0–4 Age Groups by Gender

Year	*Infant Mortality Rate*		*0–4 years death rate*	
	Male	*Female*	*Male*	*Female*
1905	231	218	—	—
1936	170	153	—	—
1955	99	91	—	—
1964	76	72	—	—
1972	132	148	—	—
1984	104	104	39.6	43.1
1993	73	75	22.7	24.8
1999	71	73	22.2	25.6

Sources: Premi, 2001; Agnihotri, 2000.

Table 4

Sex Ratio at Different Birth Orders in Punjab and Haryana

Sex ratio (females per 1,000 males)	*Haryana*	*Punjab*
First order	890	698
Second order	787	830
Third order	743	664
Fourth order and above	577	96
Overall	787	458

Source: Bose and Shiva, 2003.

The Delhi and Chandigarh Study

The question this paper raises is how does one understand the logic that individual rational action leads to public good. It explores if and how does the individual/couple rationality at the micro level of the household reconcile with that at the macro, i.e., regional/national levels. It tries to explore the considerations, constraints, reasons and rationalizations behind the rising risk to a girl's life, rather than that of the female foetus in India.

It is important to mention that not every female foetus is considered undesirable and subsequently aborted in India. The paper acknowledges that with modernization and development, Indians are using ultrasound technology to find the sex of the foetus and aborting female foetuses. Technology has given couples a handle to streamline the composition of their children. The desire for more sons and at the most one daughter is well known for India in the KAP surveys conducted through the 1970s and 1980s. One daughter is not considered as causing a crisis in the family, but a second is seen to be so. If we take for a probability calculation, a sanitized example of 100 pregnant women, the probability is for 53 to have sons and 47 to have daughters. For those who have had sons, it makes little difference what the sex of the second baby is as they have fulfilled the basic requirement. But for the 47 women who have had daughters, life is not easy unless they produce a son. Lived predicaments arise for them in the application of the concept of ideal composition of one's children in this specific context. The declining sex ratio at birth by parity is affected by the mothers having daughters who are not likely to want another daughter, while the 57 who had sons are likely to produce not more than 24 daughters assuming that they do not care what the sex of their second baby is or at least its sex does not pose a serious predicament for them. The 47 women with a first-born daughter are likely to get ultrasound tests and also abort if the foetus happens to be a female. Most middle class Indian couples today consider two children as an ideal number for them. The depleting sex ratio is a consequence more of this calculus derived from the general desire for a certain kind of composition of one's children, which is the social optimum, i.e., to have only two children—one son and one daughter.

The paper draws on ethnographic data collected through focus group discussions from women who are housewives, gynaecologists, ayurvedic doctors, and college teachers in Delhi and Chandigarh in 2003, 2004 and 2005.

Punjab was the first to start the commercial use of sex determination test as early as in 1979. The advertisement in the newspaper regarding the New Bhandari Ante-Natal SD Clinics in Amritsar wooed customers to come for such test. It put forward a very simple calculation in terms of cost and benefit both in the short and long run. The advertisement was culturally imbued soliciting customers to spend Rs 500 and save Rs 50,000 twenty years later (implying the latter amount was the cost for a daughter's wedding). Like most educated and professional Indians, the doctors at this clinic were proud to contribute towards efforts at population reduction through abortions following the sex determination test (see Jeffery, Jeffery and Lyon, 1984).

College teachers in Chandigarh saw rural and small town women at clinics in Chandigarh. Private medical care is more commonly accessed in Punjab than is government medical care. Anuradha described what she often sees at clinics in Chandigarh. There is something odd about the scene to suspect that clinics engage in sex determination tests, an illegal practice in India since 1994 when the PNDT, i.e., Pre-natal Diagnostic Techniques (Regulation and Prevention of Misuse) Act was passed. Anuradha pointed to one of the women would confidently go in the doctor's cabin jumping the queue, but she did not look like a staff of the clinic. She had been conversing casually with some of the women waiting outside. She seemed like the mediator for sex determination tests to Anuradha. This kind of site is not uncommon at clinics.

A college teacher from a women's college in Delhi meaningfully asked me, "Do you know that usually miscarriages are of female foetuses? Women don't seem to miscarry boys, it is only girls". Miscarriage and induced abortion in India entitles a woman working in the formal sector to three to six weeks of leave (this facility is part of the population control attempt of the Indian state). Those in the informal, especially the unorganized, sector are not able avail much or any paid leave benefit from miscarriages. None of my informants during 2003–2005 claimed to have indulged in the sex determination and female foeticide act themselves or knew someone personally for having done so. Nevertheless, ultrasonography is so popular that a family of doctors near Delhi said, "It is like going to a pharmacy or a beauty parlour. It is treated as very casual. You don't think twice to visit a clinic for the purpose. Everyone in the family expects you to get the test done. When they learn of the pregnancy they inquire if the test has been done". "It is like going for a blood test for malaria".[1] The doctors interviewed went only as far as stating that they get suspicious, from the body language of the pregnant woman, and feel that something was wrong somewhere when approached for an ultrasound test or just for abortion.

In one case in Delhi, the woman narrated, on promise of anonymity and refused to divulge the doctor's name or her clinic's address/location, the following story. She is an educated employed woman in a public undertaking in Delhi. She has most of her relatives living in Delhi. Most of the family's child deliveries have been conducted by their family doctor, a gynecologist and obstetrician. "The doctor knows the family well and also understands what people need (in terms of sons and daughters)". She had confided that their family doctor would never let out the family members secrets to one another or to any outsider. This case came to my notice by chance and not for the explicit purpose of the study. "I had gone for routine check up during my second pregnancy and wanted to know the sex of the baby as I already had a daughter. She knew very well what I wanted to know. She had conducted my first child delivery earlier; though she knows us for long I had to pay something extra for knowing the baby's sex. She hinted to me in a way that I got the hint to abort. I went in for abortion at her clinic and rested for a few weeks as I could get leave from my office for miscarriage". Such cases are chance cases and not easy to find. Doctors have their own norms about not divulging their patients' details to others, and if these happen to be related to matters that are not overboard, all the more reason to be secretive about them. A relative undervaluing of girls in the family has been observed historically in some caste groups through the practice of female infanticide.

Discrimination and the Ultrasound

Gender discrimination, especially in terms of access to the right to live, has been analyzed through persistent excess female child mortality (Kishor, 1993). Earlier studies on discrimination of young girls were done by Basu (1989), Chen, Huq and D'Souza (1981), Das Gupta (1987) and Miller (1981). With NRTs (new reproductive technologies, especially amniocentesis and ultrasonography) that made inroads into the Indian medical scene since the late 1970s and early 1980s, the elimination of the girl child has been advanced from that after the birth to before the birth. There is mounting evidence from across the country that with increasing affluence, female infanticide is being transformed into female foeticide! (Swaminathan et al., 1998).

Evidence for this is available both through child sex ratio and sex ratio at birth figures. As mentioned above, female foeticide was first advertised in Amritsar in 1979 soliciting customers through the temptation of saving rupees fifty thousand later by spending five hundred now. The spread of ultrasonography and depletion of sex ratio was spotted first in North India. There has been no looking back in this regard since then notwithstanding the protests from women's groups and the eventual promulgation of PNDT Act, 1994. The tussle between private interest and the public objection against it goes on in this regard. The girl child is at most risk in this matter, caught between the household's economic calculus and the persistently adverse sex ratio statistics.

The sex ratio, measured by the ratio of female population to male population in India and vice versa in rest of the world, is the most common and oldest measure of gender inequality. There are various other measures of inequality in the literature on gender and development issues. Other gender sensitive indicators proposed in the UNDP Human Development Report, 1995 are concerned with gender equity: the gender development index (GDI) and the gender empowerment index (GEM). In India, the desirable is the baby boy and the unwanted is the baby girl, especially after the first one. The result is obvious. The 2001 Census results have revealed that with sex ratio of 927 girls for 1,000 boys, India had deficit of 60 lakh girls in age group of 0–6 years, when it entered the new millennium. Sex ratio as a space signifies much more than mere numbers and remains the focus of this paper. It makes intelligible various considerations that go into not only the making of adverse child sex ratios that have become a glaring feature of the Indian society, but has also thrown itself open to a variety of overlapping and complex arguments and considerations around the practice of female foeticide.

The threat of not being allowed to take birth often as a replacement of being killed or allowed to fade away if born, is increasingly becoming common with inroads made by NRTs (new reproductive technologies; in this paper NRTs mean amniocentesis and ultrasound tests/sonography). This paper explores the savvy couple's reasoning in their exercise of reproductive choice and in making informed and careful reproductive decisions, a call made louder since the ICPD in Cairo, 1994. The freedom of the individual in democracy is at issue. Having a sense of being in control of their lives, couples act in accordance with what they think is in their best interest. The notion of risk is linked with the model of a rational investigating individual. How do people trade off their liabilities against their costs? What are the feelings of what is acceptable and/or tolerable? What are the reward expectations for taking risks or, more aptly for the case at hand, for averting risks?

Risk and Uncertainty

For Giddens (1991), risk is essentially a feature of modern society. It is a society "taking leave of the past, of traditional ways of doing things, and modernity is seen as opening itself up to a problematic future". Giddens talks about the universalizing of risk and putting of science claims at risk most forcefully in the most intimate arenas of life. The calculation of risk opens up the possibility of insurance, and a 'colonization' of the future towards which society is now oriented. Risk taking is pathological and risk aversion is rational in modernity. The work of Giddens, and Beck (1992), is a grand theory, a meta narrative of late modernity, it is universalistic. My work on female foeticide is about reproductive couples in households who are positioned within the broadly modern processes of the globalizing Indian society but deals with the micro processes of managing risk, of raising and marrying off daughters. Their risk-averting strategies are tied with forging marital alliances with other families and with the macro processes of society that seem to operate at the level of the family. Unlike Giddens' and Beck's assumptions that risk is precisely not managed in a society in late modernity, my study tries to show how it is attempted at the micro level of the family-household, through modulating reproduction.

The work of Mary Douglas (1992) situates risks in their social and moral environment. The risks each society singles out for particular attention are indicative of its values and must be understood in the context of the wider social structure. Perhaps the most useful aspect of Douglas' work is, however, the fundamental point that people do not treat risk as a matter of calculable probabilities. Rather, risk is a social matter. Human's experience of their environment is mediated by conceptual categories formed in their social intercourse. The perception of risk is held by issues and ideas of equity and fairness. Distribution of risks is related to power and status and in turn to the issue of justice. Risks are normally not taken in isolation, but after consultation with friends and relatives. Moral obligations, values and relationships are taken into account in decisions about risk taking. In a recent volume, *Risk Revisited* (Caplan, 2002), contributors draw attention to the cultural and the social settings in which risks are evaluated and negotiated. This kind of work is different in orientation from the universalizing theories of a global 'risk society'. However, here individual and collective choice in decision-making has to be introduced to take leave of methodological individualism. This paper takes on the task of recontextualizing risk in the cultural understandings and micro-level interactions between individuals situated in family-households in communities. Here some of the health-related research on risk is also pertinent. Luker (1975), for example, describes the process of contraceptive risk taking, where earlier approaches had attributed unintended pregnancy to lack of information or psychological resistance. Luker shows how an understanding of the local meanings of contraception, sex and motherhood, people's relationships, and the influences most prominent at that particular time for that individual are important considerations which reveal the decision to take risks with contraception. Such a decision is to be rational on its own terms (see also Bujra, 2000 on HIV prevention).

Is Raising Children a Rational Choice?

Briefly moving away from Douglas and company mentioned above, we take a look at the micro-economic view of rational action. For several decades now, economists have brought the grubby material view of human nature on the institution of the family, especially to workout how people choose to allocate their scarce resources to achieve their ends whether material or spiritual. Economists such as Winch (1964) have attempted to solve the puzzle of having children. Winch noted that a child is a net financial liability but that people continue to have children and to accord children, especially child bearing a high status. He finds this a puzzle because much of his analysis revolves around the material resources produced in and introduced into the family. If the cost of something rises people will be less likely to do it. To some extent, in this logic, the economist is evading the question by saying that what exactly are considered as benefits is a matter of tastes. He is only concerned with the reaction of a consumer with given tastes to changes in prices and incomes. Economic theory accepts the underlying tastes and preferences for children as given—as it does for all other goods which are the subject of choice, and analyzes the effects of changes in costs and benefits.

Talking of family's rationality appears as an oxymoron. The household is a benefit producing unit, an insurance against sickness and unemployment. Ideally, the family as an institution is the site of emotion, love, affection, attachment but even violence. As feminist studies have revealed, the family is a site of micro-politics and conflicts and not purely an emotional aggregate of equal members (see Patel, 2005 for elaboration). Many seemingly irrational decisions are taken in the family. For example, until the end of the 20th century, beginning from the II World War onwards, those in the population establishment in the developed world who advocated for smaller families criticized parents having high fertility in the developing world as irrational. Surprisingly, the advocates themselves may seem less than rational given that the estimated cost incurred by a middle class urban family in raising a child to the age of 18 years was nearly a quarter of a million US dollars. The cost of raising a child to the age of 18 in urban middle class family in India today is at least 25 lakh rupees. After parental time and energy is spent in raising children, children are increasingly leaving the parents when they are grown up. Is this parental success, an economic decision, a rational choice? Children clearly are an economic liability. In Malthusian terms, economic ideas are applied to the family. Becker (1981) was awarded the Nobel Prize in economics in large part because of his extension of the traditional economic thinking based on rational economic theory into the emotional and irrational area of the family, fertility relative with consumption.

The research inspired by Becker's 'new home economics' approach, treats the family as a homogenous block with all its members having identical interests and choices, therefore identical decisions. When applied to Becker's famous example of parental choice between a baby or a car, it is the couple who is assumed as an individual unit making a common and rational decision. But if we were to bring forward the earlier estimate of a very high cost of raising a child, it seems that the parents' decision is not rational even if one assumes that they have decided on the case as a single husband-wife couple unit. Here we also need to bear in mind unlike Becker that a couple spending time and energy to raise a child to fly out of the nest is considered not only reasonable but also successful. How does parental success get defined and who defines it? Of course, the larger society consists of many more couples and families that consider success as reward in raising children to leave their parents after a certain age. They share the meaning of being successful parents among themselves even if doing so is economically speaking, irrational. The typical difficulty in this case is the reconciliation of the contrast between economic rationality and social norms and their shared meanings.

Is Public Good also Individual Profit?

If each couple acts to maximize profit by making the choice between fertility and consumption, i.e., between a baby and a car, how is it that couples would still choose to have babies thereby following social norms? Doesn't having a baby limit individual choice and the ability to maximize profit? One must hasten to add the relevance of diminishing marginal utility that the new home economics approach of Becker (1981) relies on. In order to get to the depth of the choice making exercise we need to extend the logic to the social sphere. Rational choice implies some ordering of alternatives in terms of relative desirability. What is it at the societal level that inspires and motivates the individual couple to do something, which may not be profit maximizing? Conversely, we may ask, how is public good seen as individual profit? Let us take the example of marriage in dealing with this case. Incest taboo is intrinsically tied with marriage. It is apparently seen as a proscription in simple terms as it clearly means denial of sexual ties between the kin of opposite sex, such as a mother-son, father-daughter, brother-sister, and often also extends to a set of cousins, and often parents' siblings, etc. Is this denial of sexual access to women who are close at hand a rational choice? Though it is a denial, is it simply to be seen as denial of sexual access alone? Or is it to be seen as a denial at all? Levi-Strauss (1969) in *The Elementary Structures of Kinship* sees this denial as a means of organizing one's marriage and sexual relations. By restraining oneself from sexual intercourse with one's female kin and sacrificing them by giving others sexual access to them, one gains other women for sexual intercourse. Thus, one's sexual life is organized through avoiding sex with mother, sister and daughter. Exchanging these women for other women is a sort of kinship rationality, where kinship encompasses political, economic and jural domains. It is in this sense a cultural rationality. Through acquiring brothers-in-law, men enlarge the scope of their political and economic influence in society, and also their symbolic capital. A range of sanctions is imposed for violations of the incest taboo. How is social organization constituted in the interdependence between actors in the everyday life, contracts, rights, authority and norms? Personal benefit, through the incest taboo logic, is defined in terms of providing for others' benefit in matters of marriage towards social, economic and political organization of the society. In a similar vein parental success is defined through spending time, energy and money in raising children to leave later. This logic does not find accommodation in instrumental rationality.

Going back to our first example of the highly expensive venture of raising a child and the second one of incest taboo, the contrast between economic rationality and cultural rationality arises. Does economic rationality exist in its own right in matters of childbirth and raising children. Social organization is constituted in the interdependence between actors, contracts, rights, authority and norms. This interdependence between actors and norms is played out in the reproduction of structure. Informed by cultural and everyday practice, predispositions direct actors to reproduce the structure and enhance simultaneously their symbolic, cultural, social and economic capital. Large-scale structural forces may appear external but they get their energy from people who are continually generating and regenerating the social system from within their own experiential realms. The major experiential mediator between the individual and the society is the family-household—the primary context through which both are reproduced. The household has its partial autonomy, while it is a manifestation of general principles, be they religious, political or economic. All are sequiturs of the same principle. It is easier to study the individual than social groups and institutions, especially when studying problems regarding aggregates of individuals and normative behaviour. But we are dealing with individuals belonging to households, families, castes, communities etc. So, the effort is to see structures being deployed by individuals in their routine activities of living, which in turn recreates social structures.

As members of individual households in a community, parents are clearly not selfish inasmuch as they choose to have a baby, an exorbitantly expensive venture. Parents make choices that are at once economic as well as social in preferring to have a baby. It is into the social meaning of having children that their economic calculus is woven, unlike theoretical economic rational calculus. How does this logic work when the sex composition of a couple's children is introduced is the crucial question? Parents do not see offspring as a blanket category but see sons and daughters as belonging to separate categories. It is the size, sex composition and birth order of offspring that together appears as a family size category that is already sub-divided in the parents' mind (Patel, 1994).

The Principle of Gender: Uncertainty and Logic of Risk Aversion

Danger is certain but risk is uncertain. It is in this light that risk has been traced to gambling before it was writ large onto modernity. How has the idea of risk got associated with a daughter? The promulgation of the PNDT Act, 1994 has led to two outcomes: under-grounding of the actors and their actions, and increased cost of each operation. Poorer slum dwellers and wage workers in Delhi often go through an ordeal to collect the requisite amount of fees for the sex determination test rather than let go. The widespread trend in the country engulfing the poor and what is called the 'northernization of southern India' in adverse sex ratio for females, I see also as attributable to half a century of the family planning programme in India (see Patel, 2005 for more). The anti-natalist population policy's small family norm fed through the economic rationality argument for fifty years seems to have impacted couples to arrest their fertility. It is indeed a successful social engineering exercise. Kishor (1993) quotes what in population studies is the commonly prevalent family size norm, i.e., people stating two sons and a daughter and/or one son and one daughter as the ideal family size. Both Chinese and Indian couples have become what is called, economically savvy (rational), with regard to raising children. But the parents' economic rationality is certainly not gender neutral. Nor do they see any link between micro-household decisions and macro-national level sex ratio figures (see Patel, 2005 for details). The macro-level implication of curtailing fertility is an economically rational outcome both for the parents and the nation. There should be no mismatch between the familial and the social calculus or that is at least what has been the central message of the family planning programme for half a century. The growth rate of the population has fallen below 2 per cent during 1991–2001 after being over that figure for a few decades. The unintended consequences of reproductive choices made at the micro level however are not happy when disaggregated by sex of the children at the macro level. Is it possible to claim couples' behaviour as economically irrational? The logic used for eliminating female foetuses frequently evokes economic rationality of exorbitant dowries parents of daughters are obliged to arrange at their weddings. Such reasoning makes it essential to combine the economic with the socio-cultural logic into a single frame as marriage and dowry are not merely economic costs for parents. They enable parents to establish affinal ties and gain social and symbolic capital through them. They have very deep and emotive meanings with social assessments and bonds. Nevertheless, matters of marriage are also monetary matters.

Patel (2003) highlighted the enormously higher social and cultural costs of raising a daughter in comparison with a son, notwithstanding increasingly higher educational expenses on daughters in middle and upper class families. Expensive weddings and prohibitively large dowries make daughters an avoidable choice—perfect economic rationality. And further, increasing expenditures on marriage and dowry are socially approved outlets for flaunting and enjoying them, no matter even if dowry is illegal in India. Marriage exists to regulate sexuality. Control of daughter's sexuality prior to marriage rests with the parents and is rather demanding on the family. The reciprocal act of woman exchange, a definitive cultural bond holding societies together, is critically linked with virginity. A daughter's/sister's virginity, among other things, is closely guarded to make her a desirable bride and keep the honour of the household and the men she is related with untarnished. Affinal bonds through children's marriages do provide desirable social links, but being bride-givers rarely accords the same status as that of the honourable bride-receivers. Besides, there is always the risk of not being able to get the best suitor for one's daughter(s). For women and their parents, marriage is a time of particular risk. Brides traditionally move to their husband's home, and so are conceptualized as vulnerable. The parents are oppressed by the burden of ensuring their daughter's safety and happiness in the choice of a responsible, trustworthy, reliable and protective husband and a caring family into which she moves upon marriage. The attempt is at the same time to marry off a daughter up the social scale. Hypergamy has been historically known to be associated with high dowries and female infanticides (Vishwanath, 2000). Hypogamy is proscribed even among the lower castes.[2] The question then arises, is a daughter as expensive as a son or more expensive or is she more risky to raise? The physical safety of a daughter is only one dimension among a number of others.

Is it just dowry that makes girls more expensive to marry off or is raising them and finding a desirable husband more risky? Clearly, the fear and uncertainty about a daughter's future is felt to be far higher both while raising a daughter, which in India usually means not only food, nutrition, medication, caring and educating but also marrying her off and investing material and social resources into her conjugal family to ensure her marital stability and her acceptance into her conjugal family for several years after her marriage. In fact, intermittent obligatory gifts and visits by bride-givers to bride-receiver families strengthen and keep the ties warm between the families. These long drawn gift-giving customary practices enhance the social standing of all those concerned in the kin circle and the community. In this sense, having a brother who will fulfil the obligatory gift-giving responsibility for his sister and her children after the parents' death is highly desirable. "Raising a daughter" is said only in the manner of speaking. It communicates a whole complex of emotional, economic and socio-political considerations and calculations when one says: "it is not easy to raise a daughter" or "it is not easy to marry off a daughter". Parents harbour fears and uncertainty associated with raising children, especially daughters and finding grooms for them. This is becoming more risky with increasing migration and gradual erosion of the geographical proximity of kin and relatives who exerted moral pressure on one another in family and marriage matters by their sheer presence in the vicinity and frequent interaction amongst them.

NRTs and the Social Organization of Prestige Economy

The introduction of NRTs has not transformed people's circumstances or the Indian social organization. The prestige economy includes among other things, good education, potential to earn a very high income, and acquire all gizmos in the world modern technology produces. The aspiration of an ideal family is to emulate the model of "consumer is the king". A great more is now spent on travel for education, employment, marriage, and affinal purposes, expensive newer consumer items that hit the market with rapid speed and in turn make the earlier ones seem old or obsolete. A competition to possess the latest consumer goods engulfs people commonly. Marriageable children, sons with high earnings in particular, command desirability as prospective grooms. The marriage and family structures in India remain intact, as cultural goals. Weddings have been becoming prohibitively expensive as signifiers of high status. Wedding rituals and feasts are conspicuously displayed and exhibited, and set off a competition to outdo the other. Each wedding is talked about and compared with some other one for some time after it is over for many of the extravaganzas, arrangements, invitees, and expenses. Eligible girls have to come with pots of money and grand wedding festivity and party to get into a family with money, influence and power. Also, the series of rituals and number of parties around wedding rituals has increased. I am told that Bollywood films like *Ham Aapke Hain Kaun* are models for weddings not only among Indians, but also among the Indian diaspora in Western countries.[3] Even among the most poverty stricken, the bride-givers are expected and known to acknowledge their own obligations and fulfil them.

The social ideal of one son and one daughter to a family is acceptable to socially concerned social analysts, but if the second foetus happens to be a male to parents who already have a son, it only signifies that lady luck is smiling over the family. It feels like winning a lottery in the prestige economy. But if the second foetus happens to be a female after the first daughter, abortion is a wise step. It is fear and uncertainty in having more than one daughter that micro-level economic rationality sees no adverse unintended consequences at the macro level. The fall out is only making life more fearsome and murkier for the girls and not raising the value of girls as would any other scarce good in the world of economics. Thus, the question about risk here is turning more into that of meaning, of honour rather than of choice based on economic calculus. Each couple clearly benefits in striving towards the family's goal of prestige maximization, i.e., enhancing economic, social, cultural and symbolic capital by avoiding the odds of having more than one daughter and securing potentially greater benefits by having a son if not two.

Couples Locked in the Prisoner's Dilemma: Looking Beyond

In averting births of female babies in the face of fear and uncertainty in raising and marrying off a daughter, the parents (who see themselves as bride-givers) are locked into the prisoners' dilemma with other parents. The prisoner's dilemma is a Russian story of two persons accused of the same crime. Both were denying having committed that crime. The judge decided to offer an incentive for telling the truth and none for telling a lie. If one of the two confessed to have committed the crime his imprisonment would be for five years and the truthful person would be freed. If neither confessed, the imprisonment would be for seven years in each case. And if both confessed, each of them would be imprisoned for ten years. Both had no communication with each other. The judge's pay off set off a complex scenario in their minds. Assuming that X was guilty, and if he confessed, he would get the highest imprisonment, but a heavier one by maintaining the lie of innocence. The dilemma for the truthful Y is greater if X continued to lie (behave irrationally), Y's punishment would be for seven years. Y's imprisonment could be reduced if he lied (behave irrationally) but only if X continued to lie.

For if X confessed while Y decided to confess too both would get the highest imprisonment, i.e., each would get a ten-year term. The success of the silent movement of foeticide may be attributed more to the Xs and Ys continuing to contemplate about their confessions in the hope that each gets a better deal this way. The rules of the game, the trade offs and pay offs are clear to couples who play the game, whatever may the judges think. Are their strategies morally right or wrong is another matter.

Each rational choice of a couple influences some other couple's rational choice decisions whereby they mutually benefit only by being truthful, hypothetically speaking in the prisoner's dilemma game, of which neither is certain. By being truthful in not averting female births they are both better off at a macro level, though unequally, and in their minds after sliding lower down the social and economic capital ladder at the micro level. In case both stick to their stand both are bigger losers. One's action influences another. Such an interdependent state of affairs shifts the issue from individual couple's calculated risk taking to a social and moral question. Micro foundations of the interrelated family-household dynamics are constituted in the social calculus at the back of people's minds as social actors. People learn from past experiences. Their past is constantly present in their contemporary considerations about their future. The environment of the actors is knowable irrespective of the decisions they take. Further, the environmental variables hold some values for the actors. Decisions are taken in the light of the parameters of the environment, and the rewards depend on one's choice in relation with others' rewards and choices. What kind of trade offs and pay offs are the couples expected to experience? When the choice of averting a birth or vice versa is not only a matter of five, seven or ten years of investment but feared to be one for life with a potential to tilt the delicate balancing towards prosperity and honour, the complexity increases far more than that in a prisoner's dilemma; and excessive individual calculation leads to moral and social crises. While dealing with the prisoner's dilemma in the above example the two prisoners were brought up for analysis as sovereign individuals in their own right. But why does this logic not hold well when it comes to female children in the present-day Indian society? Are all risks treated as equal to each other? What risks are acceptable and what are bad risks? The prisoner's inability to sort out the dilemma for mutual benefit is at variance with what parents in India are presumably resorting to for prestige maximization through sex-selective abortions. People do not wish to be prisoners of life and death situations as life comes to them. They seek to take charge of their lives through the use of NRTs. They have multiple compelling concerns and precious stakes to protect. They feel, think and act within the culturally significant values of raising and marrying of a daughter in the spirit of gifting a virgin to a suitable recipient. How does the utilitarian logic, by which a social order is produced automatically out of the self-interested actions of rational individuals, bring the most good to most people? There is little answer from utilitarianism about what to do in a situation when breaking a rule is personally gainful for a person and others cannot punish this. It is a serious ethical theoretical problem.

The wedding rupture in a woman's life is a signifier of another uncertainty period, owing largely to the principle of gender in her life. But one must hasten to return to the hypothetical example of 100 young mothers who are not trying to have no daughter at all. It is the larger considerations of having a better spread of risk-aversion and reward probabilities in relation with others in the community and society that takes priority. It is thus not that parents have a total disregard for establishing affinal links through their daughters and having a brother-in-law for their son. They strive to have a son and as a next priority have a brother-in-law for him through their daughter's marriage. It is not the woman's individual choice in all the above considerations. She is part and parcel of the household and the family. Family advancement is her responsibility as much as that of the other members. Also, she considers it her moral and social obligation to enhance the honour of the family. Political, moral, legal and economic decisions have essentially interrelated elements in terms of motives and purposes.

The utility theory deals with individuals' ranked preferences but not with objective rights and wrongs. The subject matter of economics is out of the political arena. The issue of acceptable risk lies with valuation itself. Gender and family values coexist with economic, moral and political circumstances from which sources of decisions are derived. The dialogue about risk and justice tends to be conducted in two languages: language based on freedom of individual choice and on regulation. Each individual may have a private risk budget. The household risk budget is a semi-individual risk budget. In interaction with others, couples reckon upon a common risk pool and assessment of social probabilities of risk aversion. In very familiar areas there is a tendency to minimize the probability of bad outcomes. Rational behaviour implies some ordering of alternatives in terms of relative desirability. It makes a lot of difference to a decision if the alternatives involve choosing between certainty and uncertainty. Douglas (1986) compares risk and uncertainty and states that risk is governed by known probabilities, but if not enough is known about probabilities, it is uncertainty that people are dealing with. While risk-takers prefer a small probability of a large gain, the risk-evaders prefer a certain small loss (insurance premium) to avert a small chance of a large loss. Clearly, there is less certainty in the gamble, that is, more than one daughter's birth than the certainty in a son's. Couples may not be certain of outcomes of raising daughters but they try to assess some rough and ready probabilities of taking or averting the risk of having to raise one or more than one daughters.

Notes

1. Reported by Bose 2003, workshop on *Missing Girls in India: Political Economy of Emotions*. Department of Sociology, Delhi University.
2. Dr Gabriele Alex (2003) reports the case of a low caste Mutturaja man marrying a yet lower caste Vagri woman in Thanjavur in 1998. He was not allowed to settle in his father's house and had to move to the Vagri street as an excommunicate would. Many reported to Alex that if a man marries a woman from a caste lower than his, he would be excommunicated. (unpublished Ph.D. thesis submitted at the University of Brunel, UK).
3. Several academic colleagues in Delhi and Punjab have mentioned this in personal communication and so have some of the parents whose children are settled in Europe and N. America.

References

Agnihotri, S.B. (2000). *Sex Ratio Patterns in the Indian Population: A Fresh Exploration*, Sage Publications, New Delhi.

Arnold, F., S. Kishor and T.K. Roy (2002). Sex-selective Abortions in India, *Population and Development Review*, 28(4), pp. 759–85.

Banerjee, N. and D. Jain (2001). "Indian Sex Ratio through Time and Space: Development from Women's Perspective", in V. Mazumdar and N. Krishnaji (eds.), *Enduring Conundrum: India's Sex Ratio*, Rainbow Publishers, Delhi, pp. 73–119.

Basu, Alaka Malwade (1989). Is Discrimination in Food Really Necessary for Explaining Sex Differentials in Childhood Mortality? *Population Studies*, 43, pp. 193–210.

Beck, U. (1992). *Risk Society: Towards a New Modernity*, Sage Publications, London.

Becker, G.S. (1981). *A Treatise on the Family*, Cambridge, MA: Belknap.

Bose, A. and M. Shiva (2003). *Darkness at Noon: Female Foeticide in India*, Voluntary Health Association of India, New Delhi.

Bujra, J. (2000). "Risk and Trust: Unsafe Sex, Gender and AIDS in Tanzania", in P. Caplan (ed.), *Risk Revisited*, Pluto Press, London, pp. 59–84.

Caplan, P. (2000). "Introduction", in P. Caplan (ed.), *Risk Revisited*, Pluto Press, London, pp.1–28.

Chen, Lincoln C., Emadadul Huq and Stan D'Souza (1981). Sex Bias in the Family Allocation of Food and Health Care in Rural Bangladesh, *Population and Development Review*, 7, pp. 55–70.

Das Gupta, M. (1987). Selective Discrimination against Female Children in Rural Punjab, India, *Population and Development Review*, 13, pp. 77–100.

Douglas, M. (1986). *Risk Acceptability according to the Social Sciences*, Routledge and Kegan Paul, London.

Douglas, M. (1992). *Risk and Blame*, Routledge, London.

Giddens, A. (1991). *Modernity and Self-Identity: Self and Society in the Late Modern Age*, Cambridge University Press, Cambridge.

Hatti, N., T.V. Sekher and M. Larsen (2004). Lives at Risk: Declining Child Sex Ratios in India, *Lund Papers in Economic History*, No. 93.

Jeffery, R., P. Jeffery and A. Lyon (1984). Female Infanticide and Amniocentesis, *Social Science and Medicine*, 19 (11), pp. 1207–12.

Jha, P. et al. (2006). Low Male-to-Female Sex Ratio of Children Born in India: National Survey on 1.1 mn Households, *The Lancet*, published on line January 9, DOI: 10.1016/S0141-6736 (06) 6930-0.

Kishor, Sunita (1993). May God give Sons to All: Gender and Child Mortality in India, *American Sociological Review*, Vol. 58, April, pp. 247–65.

Kishor, S. (1995). "Gender Differentials in Child Mortality: A Review of Evidence", in Monica Das Gupta, C. Lincoln Chen and T.N. Krishnan (eds.), *Women's Health in India: Risk and Vulnerability*, Oxford University Press, Bombay.

Levi-Strauss Claude (1969). *The Elementary Structures of Kinship*, Boston, MA: Beacon Press.

Luker, K. (1975). *Taking Chances: Abortion and the Decision Not to Contracept,* University of California Press, Berkeley.

Mandelbaum, D. (1970). *Society in India,* 2 Vols., University of California Press, Berkeley.

Miller, Barbara D. (1981). *The Endangered Sex: Neglect of Female Children in Rural North India,* Cornell University Press, Ithaca, NY.

Miller, B.D. (1989). Changing Patterns of Juvenile Sex Ratios in Rural India, 1961–1971, *Economic and Political Weekly,* 22 (2), pp. 1229–36.

Papps, Ivy (1980). *For Love or Money: A Preliminary Economic Analysis of Marriage and the Family,* The Institute of Economic Affairs, London.

Patel, T. (1994). *Fertility Behavior: Population and Society in a Rajasthan Village,* Oxford University Press, Delhi.

Patel, Tulsi (2003). Rise of Instrumental Reason: The Missing Girls in India, paper presented at the workshop on Missing Girls in India, Department of Sociology, Delhi University, October.

—— (2005). Difficult to find a Suitable Boy: Who cares for the Statistics! public lecture delivered at Punjab University, Chandigarh, March.

Premi, M.K. (2001). The Missing Girl Child, *Economic and Political Weekly,* 26, May 1875–1880.

Registrar General and Census Commissioner of India (2003). *Missing: Mapping the Adverse Child Sex Ratios in India,* Office of the Registrar General and Census Commissioner of India.

Sen, A. (1990). More than 100 Million Women are Missing, *New York Review of Books,* 20 December, pp. 61–65.

Sudha, S. and S.I. Rajan (1999). Female Demographic Disadvantage in India 1981–1991: Sex-selective Abortions and Female Infanticide, *Development and Change* 30, pp. 585–618.

Swaminathan, M., A. Mangai and Samuel S. Raja (1998). Confronting Discrimination: Some Approaches to the Issue of Female Infanticide, *Search Bulletin,* July–September 13 (3), pp. 64–74.

Visaria, P. (1971). The Sex Ratio of the Population of India, Census of India 1961, Monograph No.10, Office of the Registrar General of India, New Delhi.

Visaria, L. (2002). Deficit of Women in India: Magnitude, Trends, Regional Variations and Determinants, *The National Medical Journal of India* 15(1), pp. 19–25.

Vishwanath, L.S. (2000). *Social Structure and Female Infanticide in India,* Hindustan, Delhi.

Winch, R.F. (1964). *The Modern Family,* Holt, Rinehart and Winston, NY.

TWO

Inter-generational Interests, Uncertainty and Discrimination

Declining Child Sex Ratios in India

Mattias Larsen, Neelambar Hatti and Pernille Gooch

During the past 50 years India has achieved considerable social and economic progress. It is also generally assumed that the future progress will be even more rapid and that India will be an important player in the global market. Despite this unbridled optimism, the future for India's unborn female children looks increasingly bleak. In fact, the country is undergoing a social and demographic development of stunning proportion, which can only be expected to have far-reaching social and economic consequences.

The numerical relationship between males and females in the population, the sex ratio, is the most basic indicator of equality between men and women in a country at a specific point of time. Changes in this relationship reflect the underlying changes, for better or worse for women, in the country's socio-economic and cultural patterns. To date, much research has been done on the nature of India's declining sex ratios, in particular the rapidly declining sex ratio in the age group 0 to 6.[1] Though intuitively significant, the relationship between the processes of rapid social and economic changes and the worsening plight of girl children has so far received little attention. This paper is an attempt to develop a conceptualization of the process of declining child sex ratios (CSR) with particular attention to the dynamic aspect of the problem.

In India, the natural biological sex ratio of slightly more females than males in the population is reversed, particularly in the youngest age group. Although there has been a heightened consciousness of the problem, census figures clearly show that the sex ratio of the age group 0–6 has declined at a rather disturbing pace since 1981.[2] The CSR have continued to decline despite improvements in general welfare and female status and point to deeply rooted structures of gender inequality. Alongside the ongoing process of transformation and smaller families, it appears that a substantial number of younger couples are apprehensive about bringing up daughters and deliberately choose not to.

The 2001 Census of India results also show marked declines in areas and social groups that earlier showed more balanced sex ratios. This indicates that discrimination against daughters has spread to new regions and from higher social strata to lower, suggesting a necessity to analyse the structure and dynamics of the problem. In order to understand the economic, social and cultural realities behind the disturbing census figures comparative case studies from different regions of India are needed. Areas where declining CSR are a relatively recent phenomenon are of particular interest. In this paper we try to approach the problem from a more holistic perspective in order to capture the transient quality of the structure in which girls are disfavoured and their lives put at risk.

This paper builds upon the recognition that the declining CSR are a result of an ongoing process of societal change. Looking at areas which have shown significant declines in CSR between 1991 and 2001, the paper draws on results from recently conducted field studies in rural areas of Karnataka in the South and of Uttaranchal in the North. Uttaranchal has shown an alarming decline in the CSR from 948 in 1991 to 906 in 2001. Of special interest are results of case studies from Siddapur taluk,[3] Uttara Kannada district, in the Western Ghats of Karnataka and from Pithoragarh tehsil, Pithoragarh district, in the eastern part of Uttaranchal.[4] For both cases the outstanding feature is a very low child sex ratio. Two additional cases with high child sex ratios are used for comparative purposes.

To begin with, we need to consider the overall process of societal change making up the context in which the decision-making behind the discrimination of daughters takes place. At the centre of the factors concerning the problem of daughter discrimination stands the family. The problem of "missing girls" can be ascribed to social, economic and cultural factors, which together create incentives for son preference and disincentives for raising daughters. Nonetheless, it is within the family that the decision-making takes place. Hence, it is of importance to analyze the relationships between these factors with a focus on the family. Intra-household relations are related to development and changes in society, which shape and change the social structures and norms which condition relationships within the household. Changes such as rising levels of education, development of a wage economy, and in living arrangements are examples of such structural aspects that directly affect the institution of the family (Thornton and Fricke, 1987). We will argue that parents, as a reaction to the uncertainty that those very changes produce in terms of decision-making, 'fall back' on traditional norms regarding gender and domestic roles. This makes the criteria for the allocation of resources highly adversarial for girls, creating a structure in which there is little space for daughters.

Transformation, Uncertainty, Cooperation and Conflicts within the Household

India is in a transitional phase where traditional and modern coexist, where old norms and expectations clash with modern ideas; in other words, India is experiencing a process of transformation with considerable changes in its social and economic fabric. During the 1990s India underwent fundamental economic reforms and changed from being an economy characterized by an emphasis on centralized planning, to a liberalized and globalized economy, with great faith in the efficacy of the market mechanism (Nair, 2004). With its relatively sustained, high rate of growth during recent years, rapidly expanding private and service sectors, rising demand for well-educated professionals and a growing middle class, India is undergoing far-reaching changes. The Green Revolution has contributed to large productivity gains in agriculture. There has been a spread of cash economy, improvements in communications and transport. The media has grown in importance and there has been an increase of contract-based relationships replacing previous personalized patron-client ones. Fertility decline and the government's efforts in propagation of family planning have added a justification and rationalization of deliberate family planning strategies which have contributed to the spread of sex-selection techniques (Chatterjee and Riley, 2001; Patel, 2005). These changes have either directly or indirectly increased the value attached to the acquisition of basic levels of information and knowledge (Kabeer, 2000). It is against this background of a traditional society in transformation, a situation of fluidity, that the problem of daughter discrimination needs to be conceptualized.

As a point of departure, we suggest that parents' basic obligation is to make decisions concerning the future of their children as the children are not able to do so themselves. However, we also have to recognize that in the Indian context, where no institutional alternative to the family as a source of social insurance has emerged, parental decisions are likely to be powerfully motivated by their concerns about their own security in old age and the best ways to assure it (McNicoll and Cain, 1989; Kabeer, 2000).[5] Three aspects of family in India stand out in stark contrast to western patterns of family organization. These are the vital need to nurture personal bonds within the community in order to secure one's existence and to gain social status, to secure old age support through children, and to arrange suitable marriage alliances. These are also the three most important factors, which tie the interests and the decision-making of one generation to the next. Family has always been a foundation of Indian society and pride is still taken in the centrality of marriage and family life.[6] Children have a special place in the family and the nurturing of interdependency and support across generations is uniquely valued in the Indian family system (Carson and Chowdhury, 2000). Naturally, these connecting interests are stronger. The greater the 'generational depth', the more extended or joint the structure of the family is.[7]

The existence of such an understanding and commitment between parents and children, commonly called an inter-generational contract[8] (Greenhalgh, 1985; Kabeer, 2000, 1996; Croll, 2000; Collard, 2000), is one of the factors which appear to have become threatened through the overall social and economic changes (Sen, 1990). As society transforms and parents' investments in educational expenditures increase, the direction of inter-generational income transfers eventually becomes altered. Correspondingly, a rising market valuation of human capital gradually erodes the inter-generational contract and parental authority (Parsons, 1984; Fapohunda and Todaro, 1988). While economic changes may have left child to parent flows intact, they have altered the flow of resources from parent to child (Caldwell, 1982). This suggests how socio-economic changes may have put a strain on the conditions for an inter-generational contract, thus making the disincentives against raising daughters even stronger. In this context, it is possible to talk of a 'parental dilemma', in which parents are compelled to make a decision regarding the gender composition of the family.

Closely related to this is another important aspect to keep in mind, the "life course perspective" (Das Gupta, 1995; Caldwell, 1978; Kandiyoti, 1988), which has particular importance in a joint or extended family setting with closely connected interests of different generations of family members. If one manages to tolerate a presently oppressive situation, it can yield rewards later as sons become fathers and daughters-in-law become mothers-in-law. Naturally, this element is intimately linked with the interests of younger family members or future generations. Family members, who have subscribed to these social norms of the family, have opposing interests with young family members and even with their own children. With smaller preferred family sizes, a particularly unfortunate gendered consequence of this is how it expresses itself in a woman's position within the household increasing with the birth of a son (Kandiyoti, 1985, 1988; Dyson and Moore, 1983; Agarwal, 1994, 1997; Kabeer, 1996). Even though women can gain considerable power in the household in their old age, this depends on having sons who support their mother's voice at the expense of their own wives (Das Gupta et al., 2003). Within the family there thus appear to be two main factors causing daughters to be the first to be sacrificed: a gender dimension and a generational dimension (Croll, 2000; Greenhalgh, 1985). The inter-generational contract works to counter shifting dependency situations between generations as a way of insuring against vulnerability. In so doing, it also creates a hierarchical structure of the family based on resource flows. In other words, there is a gender hierarchy as well as a generational hierarchy and in both of them daughters come last. This means that, the inter-generational interests are gendered by nature. This would explain the apparent dichotomy between the value of a girl to her parents versus that of a woman to her in-laws.

Parents are compelled to include other interests than their children's, not least the parents' own, in their decisions. Once we have recognized that parents' obligations are to optimize these inter-generational interests, the obvious question that arises is why daughters come to be excluded from the results of these deliberations. The analytical concepts we will necessarily work with need to be clarified.

Societal transformation can be understood as a process of change with an increasing dependence on market mechanisms. From a rural perspective, this implies understanding transformation as a process of greater inclusion and integration of the village economy in the larger transformational direction of society where a "growing differentiation of needs" can be satisfied through impersonal exchange (Weber, 1978: 638). Important sources of structural change in India are increased penetration and, therefore, dependence on the market mechanisms along with government intervention particularly through land reform and technology in agriculture. Such a "Great Transformation" [Polanyi, 2001(1944)] is a process of 'disembedding' [Polanyi, 2001(1944); Beck, 1992; Giddens, 1990] of the economy from traditional social relations resulting in greater complexity in the period of transition, where "[i]nstead of economy being embedded in social relations, social relations are embedded in the economic system" [Polanyi, 2001(1944): 60].

The resulting uncertainty for actors generates a desire for a re-introduction of social devices to reduce the uncertainty faced [Polanyi, 2001(1944); Beckert, 1996].[9] It is a transformation away from pre-modern society in which economic relations are distinguished by a minimal need for trust (Giddens, 1990; Bourdieu, 1977[10]), a change from 'custom to contract'. We can distinguish four ways in which the integration of action in pre-modern society is organized. Kinship, geographical context, religion and tradition all structure interaction through their historicity, lending them stability (Weber, 1978; Giddens, 1990). As they are based on particularistic bonds they are 'taken for granted' and are not questioned. These are disembedded from the local community in the process of modernization.[11] In such a 'prestige economy' it is necessary to build and nurture personal bonds to not only secure one's existence but also to gain social status. This is dependent upon the community's acceptance and acknowledgment not only of one's personal actions but, more importantly, those of other family members as well. It is of course also in the interest of the community as a whole that individuals and families conform to the proscriptions of the community. Needless to say, this is a main reason why the arranged marriage has such a central importance in India. Such a "capital of rights and duties built up in the course of successive generations" provides "an additional source of strength which can be called upon when extraordinary situations break in upon the daily routine" (Bourdieu, 1977: 178). This "capital of honour and prestige" is "readily convertible" (Bourdieu, 1977: 179) into economic capital with the family name as the means. However, even though "social honour, or prestige, may be the basis of economic power, and very frequently has been", it becomes 'disembedded' during the process of transformation since the market is impersonal (Weber, 1978: 926). This 'disembedding' affects the family by transferring many of the family's functions to other institutions, something which is visible in the emergence of such laws as those regulating minimum age for marriage, or instituting legal rights for children in relation to their parents and for women's individual property rights in relation to their spouses. Through this process, the family "ceases to be a coercive institution and becomes a persuasive institution" [Commons, 1991(1900): 528]. Thus, the disembedding process intrinsic to societal transformation entails a shift from structured forms of life as the provider of meaning to that of the individual as an agent who chooses to give loyalty to structures and institutions (Beck, 1992).

Increased division of labour itself leads to higher complexity.[12] The process of transformation 'disembeds' social and economic exchange from traditional forms of trust as they prevent the spread of division of labour from which novel cooperation and exchange relations emerge (Weber, 1978). Cooperation and exchange become possible without having to rely on traditional mechanisms because disembedding mechanisms "remove social relations from the immediacies of context" (Giddens, 1990: 28). However, when the structuring influences of kinship, tradition, and religious cosmologies on actions are disembedded, the basis for cooperative relations is replaced by a situation in which their necessary stabilization can only be achieved through the active inter-subjective communication of actors. Trust is built up gradually through the process of exchange itself (Curtis, 1986). The trust achieved through such communicative processes of reproduction is thus distinguished from the traditional forms of trust by its contingency. The increasing contingency in expectations of what others will do gives rise to uncertainty and a growing need to shape stable contexts of trust (Beckert, 2002). The uncertainty we refer to here therefore concerns uncertainty in terms of decision-making, and should thus not be confused with a more general insecurity. The increased potential for socio-economic mobility and the uncertainty which it entails also increases the need to plan family size and gender composition more deliberately (Das Gupta, 1997). Thus, the direction of our analysis should be toward the reflexive interplay of parents' intentional rationality (Beckert, 1996, 2002) and the 'social devices'[13] they use to confront the uncertainty of the situation in which decisions have to be made regarding the future of their children.[14] The discussion thus leads to a focus on the relationship between change and the structures used to confront it.

The most basic tension in society is between the changing nature of the social world and the "frozen structures" or institutions needed to function socially, to interact, in the highly complex, continually changing, and thus uncertain world we live in.[15] The complexity of causal relations arises from the unintended consequences of our actions (Giddens, 1984). The relationship between structure and action is therefore reflected in how actors, through their actions, produce and reproduce the structures they experience as conditions of action without having the ability to control intentionally their concrete content (Giddens, 1984). Our perceptions of ourselves and of our interests as well as of our relations to others are conditioned by the institutional context; they are vital elements of our socialization. The complexity of the social world due to unintended consequences prevents the anticipation of outcomes; the resulting uncertainty complicates decision-making when actors have insufficient structure to base their decisions on. Correspondingly, institutions are the outcomes of individuals' need, or demand, for order and coherence in the face of change and uncertainty. They create reciprocal expectations which limit the choice set of actors, and thereby reduce uncertainty as they "secure expectations" (Commons, 1934: 705; Knight, 1992). Institutions and conventions emerge both as responses and as definitions of uncertainty (Heiner, 1983; Storper and Salais, 1997; Knight, 1992; Cornwall and King, 2003).

Institutions are representations of the basic understanding of the changing world around us. That understanding is fundamentally embedded in the "shared habits of thought and behaviour", i.e., cultural and religious beliefs of society (Hodgson, 2003; Harriss, 2003; North, 2005). However, institutions are dynamic manifestations of peoples' ongoing legitimizations of their own actions and the reproduction of the institutions themselves. Institutions are thus changing even though their function is to provide constancy. An institution is, after all, by definition constant during a period of time. Structures provide 'fixity', in the form of 'social devices', but there is a continuum of 'fixity' resulting from these devices just as there are absolute and relative values. However, 'sub-optimal' outcomes where one group is systematically disadvantaged are common and institutions that provide appropriate behavioural rules will not necessarily arise (Knight, 1992). It is thus not enough with a 'functionalist' understanding of institutions since they legitimize inequalities and discrimination. Institutions are also the media through which power relations are reproduced (Goehler, 2000) and this quality is central in understanding institutional change or rigidity (Knight, 1992; Harriss, 2003).

Situations where actors cannot anticipate outcomes of decisions and therefore also not assign probabilities to the outcomes are situations characterized by uncertainty (Knight, 1921; Alchian, 1950; Heiner, 1983; Knight, 1992; Beckert, 1996, 2003; Dequech, 2001; 2003; Harriss, 2003). There is thus an apparent link between uncertainty and the degree of complexity and change of the surrounding social context and the way decisions are made. Uncertainty in this sense concerns the problems actors have in assigning means to ends. But the goal ambiguity and the uncertainty stemming from not knowing the ends does not mean that parents do not make efforts to optimise outcomes with their choice of means.

The central obligation of parenthood is, after all, for parents to make decisions for their children as they may not be able to do so for themselves. The Indian situation with arranged marriages places particularly great responsibilities on parents. It is a question of optimizing in terms of the situational structure and therefore also a question of rationality. The fact that the child sex ratios are low exemplifies how parents optimize the utilization of means at hand.[16] When parents undertake a collective enterprise such as having and rearing children, they make plans for something far in the future and for that they need to establish a basis for trust not only in one another, but also in the wider family circle (Curtis, 1986). Therefore, the inter-generational interests include reproducing the social structure or institution of the family.

Nevertheless, it is not appropriate to think of rationality in terms of conventional use in economic theory where "rational does not refer either to means or to ends, but rather to the relating of means to ends" (Polanyi et al., 1957: 33). In the same sense it is important to point out the necessity of distinguishing between uncertainty and risk. While risk is quantifiable and perhaps even predictable, uncertainty, according to our definition, implies a fundamental inability to quantify and predict.[17] Instead, the uncertainty of the situation in this case relates to both ends and means as parents have increasing difficulties in formulating the ends since their children may have, in many ways, completely different ideas about how they want to live their lives. It is therefore a question of intentional rationality in which structural rigidities take on an important role (Beckert, 1996; 2002). It is in this context that institutions and social structures are central as they play the double role of both constituting the context and of enabling actors to make decisions based on that situational context, i.e., being both constraining and enabling (Commons, 1931; Giddens, 1984; Sewell, 1992; Hays, 1994; Ensminger and Knight, 1997).

A very useful way of conceptualizing the linkages between structure and agency in the micro foundations of the institution of the family is in terms of cooperative and conflicting aspects of intra-household relationships. Such a conceptualization focuses on the nexus of sociological and economic theories as it incorporates congruent (sociological) and conflicting (economic) interests (Swedberg, 2003). These are shaped and influenced quite differently depending upon the endogenous characteristics of the family and the exogenous material conditions.

Serious conflicts might be involved in decisions regarding household arrangements, concerning who does what and who gets which benefits, but the nature and form of the family organization require that these conflicts be shaped within the general frame of cooperation, in which conflicts are treated as deviant behaviour (Sen, 1987, 1989). A family should thus be seen not only as a space of harmony, but also of conflicting power relations where some member's interests are set aside for other's in order for the household to persist over time. The institutional set-up of social norms and rules built on active participation in cooperation and based on the obvious benefits from cooperation, is also the context within which everyday conflicts of interests are played out. It is through this structuring, normative, aspect that interaction becomes biased. It is, in other words, in the coexistence of congruent and conflicting interests that inequality exists.

This conceptual framework is thus intended to place parents' expected and deliberate optimizing in its structural context while at the same time allowing for a dynamic analysis of how that structure changes as society transforms.

Case Studies

The outcome of daughter discrimination is, in fact, not difficult to see quantitatively. It is, for example, possible to get a clear-cut picture of the ratio between sexes from attendance registers of how many girls and how many boys attend, or not attend, the local kindergartens. Likewise, it is possible to trace the inequalities in sex ratios to geographical area, to social groups and to economic groups. However, if one's intention is to analyze the underlying reasons for this anomaly, it is necessary to shift focus from the outcome, the ratio, to the social process, which results in skewed sex ratios.

Empirical evidence used in this paper consists of data collected in interviews, in focus group discussions (FGDs) and in participant observations. This information has been complemented by village level and taluk level data also collected during fieldwork.[18]

Karnataka

Situated on a tableland where the Western and Eastern Ghat ranges converge into the Nilgiri range, the South Indian state of Karnataka has a population of about 53 million. Karnataka is commonly divided into four regions according to their physical characteristics, namely, Coastal, Malnad, Maidan Plains and Southern Maidan. Each region also has its own distinct social, economic and cultural characteristics. According to the 2001 Census, the total literacy rate for the state is 66.6 per cent. Rural literacy is 70.4 per cent for males and 48 per cent for females. The overall sex ratio is 965 while the rural sex ratio is slightly higher at 977. The CSR has declined from 960 in 1991 to 949 in 2001.

Uttara Kannada district and Siddapur taluk are situated in the north-western Malnad part of the state. It is characterized by ecological features typical of the Western Ghats range. The deciduous forests and the elevation give it a relatively mild climate and access to natural irrigation from the many rivers that flow in the valleys. The rural literacy rate is 81.6 for males and 63.5 for females. The district CSR was 946 in 2001. The distinct physical features of the area have shaped the villages, which tend to be small and scattered; it also makes communications difficult and in the more remote villages communications are still sparse. Traditionally, a majority of the people derive their livelihood from the cultivation of paddy and areca.[19] The areca palm trees are grown in gardens or plantations and are normally situated down in the valleys. These are mostly inter-cropped with spices such as cardamom, pepper and to an increasing extent also with vanilla, together with coffee and various fruit trees. The case study was conducted on the plantation economy side in the border area between plantation and paddy economy.

The district, as well as the area of study, is characterized by two types of cultivation and its distinct economies.[20] (Joshi, 1997) Changes in structure have been fundamental in the paddy economy, whereas the plantation economy has remained largely unchanged (Pani, 1997; Joshi, 1997). The most notable changes came with the Karnataka Land Reforms (Amendment) Act of 1974, an important feature of which was the abolition of tenancy by conferring ownership on the erstwhile tenant (Joshi, 1997). This affected the paddy economy with its very high incidence of tenancy and high farm rents. In the plantation economy, where a labour shortage posed a major problem, where tenancy was rare and where the land rent was low, the agrarian structure has remained relatively intact. Today, farm wages for women in this area are the highest in the state while wages for men are the third highest (Government of Karnataka, 2004).

Instead of structural change, the plantation area has experienced a transformation from increased availability of education facilities and from the diffusion of 'modern values' through TV. Perhaps equally important has been the improvements in transport and communications. In other words, the area has become 'modernized' in the sense of access to certain aspects of modern life. It is a relatively well-off area as it enjoys fertile soils, natural irrigation and relatively lucrative cash-crop agriculture.

Siddapur taluk as a whole, where the study areas are located, has one of the lowest child sex ratios in the state. According to the 2001 Census, the overall sex ratio in the district is 970/1,000 and for the taluk it is 973. The child sex ratio of the taluk declined from 927 in 1991 to 896 in 2001. While Kalahalli[21] has a very high child sex ratio (1,217/1,000), Minnahalli is characterized by a low child sex ratio (868/1,000) in 2001. This significant decline has many implications.

The availability of diagnostic technologies were made clear in statements like these: "Nowadays doctors don't tell the sex of the child straight away. It wasn't banned earlier and then it was no problem finding out. Even now, if people ask, and many people ask, they will be told. Everybody is aware, people from all classes and castes. If you want to find out it is no problem to do it. It may cost Rs 500–1,000". Apparently, decisions concerning childbearing have become increasingly conditioned by economic factors. Indeed, the preliminary findings of our study substantiate that childbearing is closely linked to economic reasoning where many children are considered a financial burden. But it is important to remember that such a change in reasoning may not affect the way parents legitimize their son preference, but when such a preference is strong it would indeed have an effect in terms of lower CSR.[22] This in turn is reflected in comments like this: "The ideal family is of one son and one daughter. For us it will be difficult in the future since we already have two daughters". Differences in agrarian system appear to influence the child sex ratio. Problems of poor rains hit the paddy cultivators harder as they have no reserves, which the comment above clearly illustrates.

Practically in all respects Kalahalli is less developed. It was quite isolated until very recently and even today it only has limited communications to other areas. Although there have been considerable changes in agriculture after the tenancy reform, making it possible for people to cultivate their own land and subsequently earn more, there is still a big difference in income level when compared with Minnahalli. The low level of education is reflected in how the young people of Kalahalli do not look for possibilities outside their village. One respondent put it like this: "In our village most people have their fathers land and they find it sufficient. They feel that if they work there it is enough. This is the kind of attitude we have here". Their situation gives very little confidence to try to live a different life and their mobility is considerably lower than the one of young people of Minnahalli. The dilemma they face is that they feel: "Even if we go to school we will just fall back into agriculture, so because of that many people don't see the point of going to school".

This situation should be seen in contrast to the one in Minnahalli where the young use the opportunities and mobility given to them through education and look for different ways to live their lives than their parents do.

The mean age at marriage for women in Kalahalli is 17.5 and it is still so, as one woman explained: "To some extent and in some cases, education is discontinued once the marriage has been fixed". Nevertheless, this type of attitude seems to be changing; "Girls have more courage now to question the age at which their parents want them to marry", as explained by the women in one focus group discussion (FGD). Changes are taking place and women are gradually getting more say about their own life and their mobility is increasing. However, there is a long way to go and the villagers constantly return to how they feel backward, subordinate and cut off.

On the other hand, Minnahalli, with very low CSR, has had greater access to 'modern' aspects of life. Not only has fertility gone down with smaller family sizes, there has also been a rise in education level where at least a college degree is the minimum the better off families expect and provide for their children. The rise in education has lead to an increased mobility among the young. The young generation also marries considerably later. An effect of this development was explained in a male FGD in Minnahalli: "Now, there are equal opportunities for boys and girls particularly when it comes to education. With regards to education for girls, it is now becoming so that the girls themselves are not ready to marry a boy who lives in a village. They want to have a good groom who lives in town and has a good steady income".

Both study areas share a son preference expressed in such remarks as: "According to tradition one son and one daughter is the ideal. With one daughter we need a son. A son is needed for heading the household or for agriculture work. With only daughters the land will go to the daughter's husband's side", or "The ideal family is one son and one daughter. The son continues the bloodline and is old-age support. The daughter is important to expand the social network". However, while not one respondent in Minnahalli talked about attaining the preferred gender composition of their families through the traditional way of repeated births until a son is born, this is still the method parents use in Kalahalli. This was expressed in statements like: "A son is necessary to take care of us in old age and also to perform ceremonies when we have passed away. First, we had three daughters and then we finally had a son. Now, everybody shows more affection to him".

In Minnahalli this practice has given way to modern methods of determining the gender composition of the family. This was illustrated in comments like the one given by one woman: "I needed at least one son. He will stay close to me and take care of me. I first had one daughter, and then I wanted to have at least one son. If the second had been a daughter I would not have gone through with the birth. The daughters move out when they marry". Most likely she had undergone a sex determination test and as indicated by the statement was ready to abort the foetus had it been a girl. That foeticide is a widespread practice was expressed in remarks such as: "A doctor from [a nearby town] does the SDTs. For a higher price he brings patients to the town. He also performs abortions". Or in statements such as: "If somebody has a boy they don't try to have more children, people will only try to have one more child if the first child is a daughter and only to get a son. People want to have male children. Therefore, regardless of if it is against the law the female foetus will be aborted". Thus, there has been a shift from son preference to active daughter discrimination made possible by modern technology in Minnahalli but not in Kalahalli. When people reason as they do in Kalahalli: "With two children I will stop, even if it is two daughters", it indicates how a similar shift has not taken place there.

While both areas have a strong son preference in common, it has been increased by the changes brought along by modern 'values', particularly in an increased mobility for the young, in Minnahalli but not in Kalahalli. At the same time, there has been a change toward actively discriminating against girls, whether unborn or born, facilitated by modern techniques. This change appears to be what has contributed to the decline in child sex ratio.

These two patterns of change could be explained in terms of 'push' and 'pull' factors. In Kalahalli, agriculture has undergone such changes through tenancy reforms, what we consider a 'push' factor, that the economic reality for the rice cultivating families has been altered. At the same time, the families continue to use the traditional method of repeated births in order to achieve the desired gender composition. On the other hand, in Minnahalli, the increased availability of opportunities outside agriculture, what we would call 'pull' factors, has created strong incentives for investment in education and in individuals. This, in turn, has meant a diffusion of new values and greater socio-economic mobility, which has lead to a shift from the traditional method of achieving desired gender composition towards a method facilitated by modern techniques.

Uttaranchal

In 2000, after many years of agitation, the central part of the Indian Himalayas, formerly known as the U.P. Hills, severed its bands with Uttar Pradesh and was constituted as Uttaranchal (now Uttarakhand), the 27th state of the Republic of India. Women and environmental movements were an important part of the history leading up to the creation of the new state. This illustrates how sustainable use of the environment and better conditions for women are central issues for a majority of the people of the state.

Uttaranchal is situated north-west of Uttar Pradesh, India's most populous state. It borders Tibet, Nepal, Himachal Pradesh, and the UP plains districts. The state can be divided into three distinct geographical regions, viz., the high mountain region, the mid-mountain region and the Terai region. The economy of the state is predominantly agrarian and the rural scenario is still dominated by small-scale utilization of available environmental resources where women (and girls) do most of the work. This is complemented by a 'money order economy' due to large-scale migration of younger men to the plains for jobs in the armed forces, the government, or in the private sector.

Farooquee and Rawat (1997) lay down some of the main constraints to rural development in the hills such as physical isolation, poor infrastructure, high cost of transportation, absence of market, limited production possibilities, and absence of irrigation facilities. They further state that the environmental fragility of the hills set limits for intensive production systems. On the positive side are factors such as diversified activities, specialized and skilled handicraft, and maximum utilization of available resources. The backbone of economical activity in the hills has traditionally been small-scale agricultural ventures depending mainly on local input and production for subsistence rather than for the market. This scenario is now changing with, on one hand, commercialization of agriculture and, on the other, diversification of occupations where agriculture loses its importance to salaried employment outside the village. The development in the state appears to affect women—and especially the girl child—negatively. While the overall sex ratio in Uttaranchal rose from 936 to 964 between 1991 and 2001 the CSR fell from 948 to 906.

For Uttaranchal comparisons have been made between two areas positioned at opposite ends of the spectrum of high respectively low child sex ratios. At one end we find Pithoragarh tehsil, which has the lowest sex ratio in Uttaranchal in the 0–6 years age groups with an average of 855 girls to 1,000 boys.[23] Pithoragarh district, which was carved out of Almora district in 1960, stretches from the middle to the high mountains and it borders Nepal to the east and China (Tibet) to the north.

Pithoragarh tehsil is situated in the mid-hills in the southern part of the district. With a rural CSR of 867 and an urban CSR of only 819, it demonstrates the general trend, found in the last census, that one consequence of economic growth, education, and access to modern medical facilities could be fewer girls in the population. Pithoragarh tehsil resembles Siddapur taluk in Karnataka in so far as it has a very low child sex ratio. With greater exposure to 'modern' lifestyles new values have been accepted leading to lower fertility and smaller family size. One reason for this is new opportunities for employment in salaried occupations, especially for males. Many men from the hills join the army. This is particularly so for Pithoragarh where it is estimated that about half of the households have a male member in the army or an elder man receiving an army pension. This influx of cash from outside is contributing to a marginalization of agriculture. Just as in the cases from Karnataka also in Pithoragarh a preference for sons was expressed during interviews. This was articulated in statements from women such as: "We must have at least one boy" or "we cannot afford more than one daughter due to high marriage expenses", but they also said: "Our in-laws are the biggest problem, they are the ones who want the boys most". While all those interviewed denied that they themselves used ultrasound in order to abort female foetuses, which is illegal, they all knew that the method existed and said that they were sure that many families in the area made use of it. This was not difficult either as the town of Pithoragarh, with all its medical facilities, was within easy reach from the villages of our study.

Puraula tehsil in Uttarkashi district, used for comparison, stands at the opposite end of the child sex ratio with an equal number of girls and boys (1,000/1,000), the highest ratio at tehsil level in the state. The two tehsils also stand in contrast when it comes to female literacy, in this case with Pithoragarh at top with a female literacy rate of 72.5 (male literacy 94.5) and Puraula at the bottom with 38.5, only about half of that of male literacy which is 73.7. This further demonstrates that development in the form of education and shortening of the gender gap in literacy does not automatically lead to more equal conditions for women and girls in terms of sex ratios.[24] Uttarkashi is situated in the western part of Uttaranchal, bordering Himachal Pradesh to the west and China (Tibet) to the north. Puraula tehsil, which is exclusively rural, constitutes the north-western part of the district. This goes with a more 'traditional' lifestyle together with continued dependence on agricultural production based on female labour both for subsistence and for the market as well as a higher fertility and bigger families. Mori Block, from which the case study used here is fetched, is the most remote part of the tehsil and considered one of the most marginalized parts of Uttaranchal. Here people report that dowry is a new phenomenon evolved only during the last decade. Earlier, the groom's family had to give money to the bride's family. In discussions women said that a girl who was badly treated in her in-laws house could return to her native home and her parents would remarry her somewhere else. But they also said that this practice was declining, as somebody "who was educated would surely not marry such a girl".

In this remote part of the state new opportunities for salaried employment are few. Young men do migrate to jobs in the plains but these are mainly low paid menial jobs. Their sisters also might take jobs as maids in the towns in the lowlands of the state. Transformation is here expressed as an increasing dependence on market powers within agriculture; in other words, a 'push' transformation. Crops produced for the markets in the plains below are replacing traditional crops produced to sustain the household but it is still women doing most of the farm work.

Just as in Karnataka, our study from Uttaranchal also indicates that differences in agrarian production appear to influence the child sex ratio. In both cases from Uttaranchal we have agricultural systems dominated by household female labour,[25] the difference being that in Puraula farming is still essential for the economic survival of the household while in Pithoragarh its importance is declining, being substituted by incomes from salaried employment for men. Thus, Puraula is characterized by a 'push' transformation while Pithoragarh exhibits a 'pull' transformation. The fact that women's contribution to the household is no longer considered important was bluntly expressed by a male respondent from a rural household with two sons and no daughters: "We cannot afford girls because their contribution is not important". Growth in new job opportunities for men and consequent increasing remittances of money from outside also seem to have inflated demands for dowry, resulting in very high costs for marrying off daughters. New values as regards family size and the rise in marriage expenses result in smaller families and a decline in the number of female children. Thus, the economies of Pithoragarh and Puraula are undergoing structural changes with different gendered outcomes.

Table

Comparison of Case Study Areas

Cultivation	*Karnataka-Case study area Paddy+Areca*		*Uttaranchal- Case study area Paddy+Orchard*	
	Kalahalli	*Minnahalli*	*Pithoragarh*	*Puraula*
Child Sex Ratio	1217	868	867	1000
Mobility	Low	High	High	Low
Education	Low	High	High	Low
Transformation	'Push'	'Pull'	'Pull'	'Push'
	Structural change—tenancy reform	Transformed through increased access	Diversification of occupations	Commerciali-zation of agriculture

Source: Census of India, 2001.

Differences in Child Sex Ratios and Transformation

Our case studies show links between areas with low CSR but also between areas with high CSR which are not dependent upon region. Instead, similar features are common to high CSR areas in both our North and South Indian cases. These features illustrate the linkages between 'pull' transformation, the disembedding of the young whom it entails and low child sex ratios.

The areas with high CSR in Karnataka and in Uttaranchal are relatively isolated areas where the level of education is lower. In these areas there has been a transformation of agricultural economic conditions, a structural change, from within. In Karnataka, it has mainly been a combination of population pressure and land reform that has changed the agrarian structure and the conditions for agricultural production while in Uttaranchal it has been a change from subsistence cultivation to cultivation for the market.

In the areas where the child sex ratios are low and the education level relatively high, this has not been the case. Instead, the low CSR areas have experienced changes in economy from a diversification of occupations with increased possibilities for employment outside agriculture. Here, people are convinced that there are gains to be made, at least economic, by educating the younger generation and investing in individuals. This change has led to a process where the young are becoming increasingly disembedded from customary social relations and a gradual transformation of the inter-generational relationships is taking place.

Our cases illustrate how 'push' transformation first changes the economic and then the social conditions, as in the form of commercialization of agriculture with changing crop patterns or from land reforms. When structural change occurs through 'push' factors, where the economic changes are mainly related to livelihood insecurity and rather associated with downward economic mobility as in our high CSR cases, it appears to lead to a more penetrating and broad institutional change. As 'push' factors emerge from necessary changes in livelihoods, be they government induced in the form of land reforms or as necessary reactions to climatic and economic changes in the form of different agricultural strategies with different crops, they affect the economic basis of the whole family regardless of generation.

On the other hand, in the study areas with low CSR in both Uttaranchal and Karnataka, change has instead been induced through what can be described as 'pull' factors. The increased access to certain aspects of modern life such as possibilities for higher education, as opposed to structural change, has meant employment opportunities outside agriculture; for example, in the expanding private and service sector. 'Pull' transformation is thus foremost characterized by an existence of a market situation where a valuation of human capital is developing. This is paralleled by how education has become important for economic reasons as people are convinced that it gives economic benefits, something there are many examples of. However, no one is certain of these gains especially not in the case of each individual. Where downward economic mobility signifies 'push' transformation, possibilities of a positive and upward economic mobility characterizes 'pull' transformation.

When 'pull' factors such as wider economic opportunities and modern communication cause young people to migrate, it affects individual family members first and changes the family through those individuals. Individual incomes give rise to income differentials within the family. Perhaps the most well-substantiated consequence of this change is a decline in the extent to which family elders can influence and control younger family members, a central aspect of an extended family system (Goode, 1963; Thornton and Fricke, 1987; Mason, 1992). This is also an important contributing factor in the subsequent division of joint families into nuclear families. An essential part of the disembedding process of India is the 'nuclearization' of the Indian family, signifying a movement away from the traditional joint household toward a nuclear household situated in an extended family system.

Individual incomes pose a challenge to the existing criteria on which the allocation of resources is based. A direct result of 'pull' transformation thus appears to be that norms guiding allocation of resources within the household change from being tacit to becoming directly confrontational. When younger generation family members start earning individual incomes, these tacit criteria of intra-household resource allocation are confronted and the existing consensus comes to be questioned, whether intentionally or not. This also offers an explanation as to how 'pull' transformation and individual incomes produce uncertainty. The change it provokes, from tacit to explicit norms, introduces new contingencies in the relationships between family members. In other words, the changes are induced through the younger generation, causing tension between generations as the young are disembedded from traditional forms of social relationships and the older generation is only indirectly, albeit profoundly, affected by these changes. Work and family become separated and a growing number of relationships become contract based. It is in such a context that uncertainty comes to characterize the decision-making regarding inter-generational interests. The central point is thus that 'pull' transformation leads to a disembedding of the young.

Disembedding, Uncertainty and Falling back on Established Social Devices

The disembedding process the young in the low CSR areas are experiencing, and the effects it has on the inter-generational interests, is strongly illustrated by the countless statements parents in those case study areas give. However, a central thing standing out in the pull-transformation areas is how parents give two distinctly different kinds of statements regarding reasons for son preference. The most common statements reflect some of the most well-documented reasons such as: "A son will give us old-age support and carry the family line further, a daughter will move out after marriage and before that it requires more responsibility to raise daughters", or "without a son it is like a family being without electricity. There is no light in the family". Or perhaps more differentiated as one woman explained it: "For a family, one boy and one girl is the ideal. It is a blessing. A daughter is important for social networking and a son for carrying the family lineage further. The son performs all after death ceremonies. Without a son there is no salvation". Entwined with this cultural reasoning are economic reasons: "According to tradition one son and one daughter is the ideal. If we have a daughter we need a son. A son is needed for heading the household and for doing agriculture work. With only daughters the land will go to the daughter's husband's side".

On the other hand, there are many statements generally given later on in the same conversations as exceptions to the already mentioned conventional reasoning. They are therefore often along lines like these, this time more specifically concerning old-age support: "Sons are not as emotionally close to their parents as their daughters. Daughters will stay close. I am more confident about daughters, their behaviour and conduct", or "generally, sons will take care of us, otherwise daughters do it". Another respondent said: "My father now realizes that even though he gave preference to his son to study, who has not done it properly, it is his youngest daughter who has studied till 10th standard and who with her own effort has become a policewoman. She now takes care of the whole family".

Parents talk specifically about concerns over sons' future interests and behaviour, but they also recognize the influence on this process that the changing attitude in girls and young women has and how this is related to the higher level of awareness through education that they now have. This is illustrated in statements like: "Well-educated sons want to move out of agriculture. Educated girls don't have the same opportunities. Even if they want to it depends upon how far away the job is. Nowadays it even happens that girls will ask if boys live with their parents or not, since they prefer to live alone with their husbands. It is the time for women now. At least nowadays girls are asked if they want to marry the boy chosen for them or not".

Equally common are hints of uncertainties regarding the future and the way in which the young are likely to behave differently, as illustrated in statements such as: "To control a daughter's conduct is difficult. Before marriage she should not have contact with men. Sexual contact is completely forbidden. If she fails to control her conduct there will be big difficulties for her as well as for the whole family. But for sons there are no such restrictions. It is like having an iron ball in one hand and a banana in the other. If I drop the iron ball there is no harm to it, but if I drop the banana it is spoiled and cannot be used". In fact, such statements can be interpreted as direct descriptions of a disembedding process in which daughters' increased autonomy and expected behaviour is construed by the parents and the community to be negatively related to the family's social status as a means through which to function in society.

There are obvious contradictions between these statements. Indeed, these contradictions show, first of all, that the first group of standard statements is examples of conventions and of depictions of the social norms influencing the existence of son preference. Even more interesting are the accounts exemplifying breaks with convention and, instead, directly describe the disembedding process which the young are experiencing. This means that parents on the one hand give conventional statements which reflect all the well-documented reasons for son preference, but on the other hand, also give unconventional statements reflecting the actual present situation.

The contradiction between the conventional and the unconventional statements illustrates not only the uncertainty characterizing the conditions under which parents are obligated to make decisions, but also the relationship between that uncertainty and the social devices on which parents' fall-back, i.e., the conventional attitudes which legitimize and enable parents to rationalize their son preference. It is the break with those conventions itself that from an inter-generational perspective generates uncertainty. The conventional statements thus exemplify a legitimization and rationalization of parents' active son preference and as such what parents fall back on. The unconventional statements illustrate what generates uncertainty, and the contradiction itself illustrates the actual falling back. A near perfect example of the contradictory situation parents experience is reflected in this statement: "According to tradition and customs sons will stay close, but in the future we don't know. Through the influence of society sons want to live alone".

The disembedding thus has two sides: it entails changes for the individual in the form of greater possibilities and capabilities. However, those possibilities also challenge the cooperative frame of the family through the challenges to the existing criteria of resource allocation within the household. For young women these new possibilities are still restricted but they are now able to make demands on what kind of husband they want.[26] This highlights how the inter-generational interests are still intact in their structuring function but strained, partly by the increased autonomy of unmarried daughters but also by the greater social and economic mobility foremost for sons.[27]

It implies how the increased autonomy of the young generation, and the disembedding attached with it, involves uncertainty in the context of intergenerational interests. Indeed, it is these intertwined interests that make structuring norms and avoiding uncertainties important.

We have seen how the disembedding of the young changes the institution of the family in gendered terms. It has changed from being a coercive institution to being a persuasive institution when it comes to sons but *not* with regard to daughters. This is experienced by the family as directly related to its status within the community. The disembedding which generates uncertainty is thus only indirectly gendered as it in most cases appears to be sons who are the agents of the process. This is more evident in Uttaranchal than in Karnataka. At first, this may appear contradictory in relation to daughter discrimination. However, although the disembedding process is not directly gendered, the reactionary response indeed is. The social devices resorted to by the parents give guidance to decision-making in the form of conventions that constitute a legitimization of son preference and, in the end, imply a rationalization of active daughter discrimination. The disembedding of the young, particularly the emancipation of sons from their fathers and their earlier separation from the paternal household, but also the emancipation of young women through greater access to education and awareness, robs the older women of their power and respectability as mothers-in-law (Kandiyoti, 1988). This lends explanation to the falling-back as a reaction to the uncertainty this creates through consideration of this "life cycle element" (Caldwell, 1978: 563). It is not surprising that it often is the mother-in-law who applies the greatest pressure on the young daughter-in-law and her son to actively discriminate against daughters and produce a son. Thus, the outcome is highly gendered and the result is an intensified gender inequality illustrated by extremely low CSR.

The difference between high and low CSR areas is thus not only in the level and form of transformation but rather, and more importantly, in the uncertainty caused by it. It is against the background of this uncertainty that parents are compelled to fulfil their obligations as regards the future of their children. The parents find their way of facing this uncertainty by falling back on established conventions regarding domestic roles, which contradict the younger generation's understanding of those same roles. The anticipated increase in the autonomy of the younger generation of women comes to be perceived as a threat to the future of the older generation.

The young generation's needs are in many regards contrary to the traditional values that their parents still try to uphold. Increasing access to various aspects of 'modern' life has imputed new values in the form of lower fertility and smaller family sizes, higher education and mobility and higher mean ages at marriage. These factors have been the main components in the process of ongoing social change in India and have contributed to the declining trend in CSR (Rele and Alam, 1993; Caldwell et al., 1982; Hatti and Ohlsson, 1984, 1985). They have played an important role in the low CSR study areas but are yet to make their way into the social fabric of the study areas with high CSR. Indeed, this finding substantiates what earlier studies have concluded that increase in socio-economic development and welfare contributes to continuing, and often more pronounced, son preference (Das Gupta, 1987; Clark, 2000). Not only has it become more costly to raise children as education has become more important (Caldwell, 1982; Croll, 2000), but parents now feel vulnerable to the increased mobility and autonomy of their children (Croll, 2000). This development introduces uncertainty into the decision-making concerning inter-generational interests, in reaction to which parents fall back on conventional legitimizations of son preference thereby rationalizing the active discrimination of daughters.

Conclusion

We have seen how 'pull' transformation leads to a disembedding of the young from conventional or traditional forms of social relations. This appears to first of all lead to an introduction of new contingencies in the relationships between generations, as expressed by respondents concerns about the future. Our case studies show how 'pull' transformation has led to a greater gap between generations, thus increasing uncertainty for parents. Unfortunately, the uncertainty introduced through 'pull' transformation appears to result in even less flexibility in the translation of norms into allocation. The allocation of resources within the household constitutes one of the main factors upon which son preference and daughter discrimination are legitimized.

The context of inter-generational interests is central to understand uncertainty. The uncertainty experienced by the parents concerns partly apprehensions about future social obligations such as arranging marriages and partly the young gradually becoming disembedded from those intergenerational interests. These concerns are demonstrated in the contradictory statements respondents have given. It is also the contradiction in statements that gives an understanding of how parents react to the uncertainty which the disembedding of the young produces by falling back to conventional arguments for son preference. Falling back also offers an alternative to uncertainty and a basis for making decisions concerning the interests of the family that are intergenerationally tied through the socio-cultural obligations of parenthood.

While 'push' transformation changes the material conditions of the household in a way that influences all family members, pull modernization leaves existing power structures intact only to be challenged by the young generation. When uncertainties through 'pull' transformation results in a falling back on social devices, and hence to a limiting of the cooperative space, girls' life chances are affected negatively. Uncertainty becomes particularly detrimental for the situation of women and girls in the family as its intertwined interests of different family members impinge on the cooperative space. It is in this situation, this 'parental dilemma', of decision-making concerning intergenerational interests that the interests of women and girls are excluded and daughters lose out.

Falling back offers a situational structure for decision-making, which concurs with the obligations towards inter-generational interests. It is in terms of this situational structure that optimizing inter-generational interests leads to active daughter discrimination; something for which the necessary technological infrastructure is available. The obligated intentionality influencing parents to fall back on conventions and social devices is understandable from a perspective where considerations of inter-generational interest condition preferences and decision-making. It adds a context to the already prescribed intentionality in which it finds its rationality. It is in the face of uncertainty caused by the disembedding of the young that the situational context of social devices brought down through centuries of gendered cultural prescriptions is fallen back upon and receives its renewed importance. Unfortunately, this context is constituted by highly gendered norms. Nevertheless, it is in this context of intergenerational interests, changing economic conditions and social prerequisites, that the nature of the institutional change can be analyzed and the process of declining child sex ratios in India conceptualized. From a conceptualization which contextualizes the problem of declining child sex ratios in the overall process of societal change India is experiencing, we can both understand and explain the dynamic context in which daughter discrimination is legitimized and rationalized.

We began this paper with the stated intention of conceptualizing India's growing daughter discrimination and of analyzing declining child sex ratios in dynamic terms as inherently related to the transformation India is experiencing. We believe that we have succeeded in our intention. We have conceptualized daughter discrimination and shown how such a conceptualization can offer new possibilities for empirical work to understand and explain the process of declining child sex ratios in India.

Notes

1. See for example Das Gupta and Mari Bhat (1997), Sudha and Rajan (1999), Agnihotri (2000) and Hatti et al. (2004).
2. The child sex ratio (CSR) decreased from 945 to 927. Census of India measures the sex ratio as number of females per 1,000 males as opposed

to the standard international norm of number of males per 1,000 females.

3. Taluk and tehsil are different terms used in different regions for the same thing, namely, the major revenue, administrative and planning unit below the district.
4. We assume that some basic cultural differences between northern and southern India are reflected in demographic behaviour (Dyson and Moore, 1983), which is why a north-south comparison is of interest.
5. In fact, the right of parents without any means of their own to be supported by their children is recognized in section 125 (1) (d) of the Code of Criminal Procedure, 1973, and in section 20 (3) of the Hindu Adoption and Maintenance Act, 1956 (Bhat and Dhruvarajan, 2001).
6. Patel writes: "The family is an institution that simultaneously envelops and unfolds the ideal and normative on one hand and actual behaviour on the other. It works as a conduit, and sanctions and provides the potential for continuity as well as change in structures of kinship, marriage and reorganization of living arrangements in accordance with the times" (2005a: 31).
7. The joint family is a characteristic of traditional India (Patel, 2005), and in a joint family, the freedom of the individual member is subject to the interest of the group and the concept of duty is central (Cormack, 1953). A joint family consists of brothers and their respective wives and children as well as old parents living together. Family members share property, residence and kitchen (Ramu, 1988; Jeffrey and Jeffrey, 1997; Bhat and Dhruvarajan, 2001). Family matters are handled jointly and the household head, the oldest male member, has the final authority and responsibility. A joint family draws on the economic advantages of a collective undertaking. The benefits are in the form of cost efficiency from a collective ownership and use of necessities. A nuclear family, on the other hand, is composed of the husband, wife and their unmarried children.
8. In a rural, agricultural context there are distinct economic reasons for the existence of an intergenerational contract and a continuation of the farming enterprise within the family. A succeeding family receives an operating business plus land and dwelling together with the obligation to provide the parents with secured income for the rest of their lives. There is an economic advantage to the succeeding family in relation to alternative earnings from labour. This stems from the lower transaction costs of a family undertaking from intra-family cooperation and family labour ('self-exploitation') [Chayanov, 1986 (1925); Netting, 1993].
9. Polanyi's [2001(1944)] assertion of an inherent 'countermovement' necessary to create stability after movement toward a laissez-faire

economy has found resonance also in analysis of family development in Degler (1980), who argued that the 20th century American family was created an exact opposite of the market economy's concept of human relations. For Polanyi, the important point is that both processes are politically engineered and that the 'disembedding' is a necessarily abortive process. This is also something which Beckert reasserts, namely that; "on theoretical grounds, the claim of modernization theory that economic processes are increasingly removed from their social embeddedness with the development of market economies can be rejected" (Beckert, 2002: 293).

10. In Bourdieu's terms this would entail a shift in importance from symbolic capital to economic capital.
11. We deliberately use the term 'transformation' as opposed to 'modernization'. Our intention is to thereby avoid an understanding of change as a linear process as is often the case when the concepts 'traditional' and 'modern' are used in a polarizing fashion (Gusfield, 1967).
12. Ester Boserup [1970(1989): 5] writes in her seminal work: "[e]conomic and social development unavoidably entails the disintegration of the division of labour among the two sexes traditionally established in the village. With modernization of agriculture and migration to towns, a new sex pattern of productive work must emerge, for better or for worse".
13. Beckert exhaustively describes 'social devices' as "encompass[ing] all forms of rules, social norms, conventions, institutions, social structures, and power relations" (1996: 820).
14. Indeed, what Monica Das Gupta (1987) pointed out in her seminal article by emphasizing that the discrimination was "selective" and not general was that it implies an *intentionality,* or what she called "conscious and voluntary behaviour" (Das Gupta, 1987: 95) and her main intention was to provide more "understanding of the dynamics of sex discrimination at the household level and its relationship to family-building strategies" (Das Gupta, 1987: 77).
15. This argument presupposes a tension in society but it should be pointed out that this tension is not to be understood as a "state of nature" or as tension between people. Rather, it is a tension between change and the devices with which people confront it. It is therefore not to be understood in a deterministic sense as something which is inherent to and unalterable in human relations. What is implied is a meta-theoretical, ontological, understanding in which "agents cannot learn all the relevant future inter-temporal contingencies through time because the past does not provide a reliable guide to the future" and where"[h]uman institutions such as money and firms have evolved to cope with uncertainty but have unintendedly been a further source of uncertainty" (Dunn, 2000:

431; see also North, 2005). Thus, the underlying structures of society are also seen to change with the effect that cumulative learning does not necessarily diminish uncertainty.

16. One very clear example of how the choice of means is done in a disturbing, yet optimizing way is of course the extent and speed at which sex determination tests and subsequent abortions have gained popularity.
17. The classic definition of uncertainty comes from Frank H. Knight (1921) who made this same distinction between risk and uncertainty, where risk is a condition in which it is possible to assign probabilities to outcomes and where uncertainty is a condition under which no such probability distribution exists.
18. The factors behind the dynamic are highly relative in nature and to a large degree the outcome of the subjective interpretations made by the actors involved. Thus, the decision-making process, which leads to discrimination of girls, has to be understood in terms of the social context. That social context is conditioned by relationships of power between its actors, the norms under which they act and the social structure to which they contribute and act within, all of which is of a qualitative nature.
19. The Areca nut, or betel nut, is the main ingredient in the stimulant *paan*, widely popular in South Asia and parts of Southeast Asia.
20. Collins (1925) divided the area of study into two distinct tracts. A rice tract covering an area of 83.7 sq m, with 45 villages and a population density of 155 per sq m, and a garden/plantation tract of 248.2 sq m with as many as 157 villages and a density of population of only 77 per square mile (Joshi, 1997),
21. For reasons of discretion, we have chosen to use the fictitious names Kalahalli and Minnahalli.
22. This corresponds to what Das Gupta and Mari Bhat (1997) terms 'intensification effect'.
23. Laxar tehsil in Haridwar district also has a CSR of 855 but as Laxar is situated in the plains we have chosen Pithoragarh in order to compare two tehsils both situated in the hills.
24. See Jha et al. (2006) for a very recent account of this.
25. The general situation where north India is characterized by low female agricultural labour participation being supply constrained, and the South Indian situation characterized by female farming and participation (Harris-White, 2001) is in our cases reversed. In the study areas in Karnataka, participation of women in agricultural work is less intensive than in the study areas from Uttaranchal where they are the backbone of agriculture.

26. The preferences expressed during fieldwork were most often for a husband with an employment living in an urban setting.
27. In fact, the parents themselves often encourage their children in this regard.

References

Agarwal, Bina (1994). *A Field of One's Own: Gender and Land Rights in South Asia*, Oxford University Press, Delhi.

—— (1997). "Bargaining" and Gender Relations: Within and Beyond the Household, FCND Discussion Paper No. 27, International Food Policy Research Institute.

Agnihotri, S.B. (1995). Missing Females: A Disaggregated Analysis, *Economic and Political Weekly*, Vol. 30(19), pp. 2074–84.

—— (2000). *Sex Ratio Patterns in the Indian Population: A Fresh Exploration*, Sage Publications, New Delhi.

Alchian, Armen (1950). Uncertainty, Evolution and Economic Theory, *The Journal of Political Economy*, Vol. 58(3), pp. 211–221.

Bardhan, Pranab K. (1974). On Life and Death Questions, *Economic and Political Weekly* 9, Nos. 32–34 (August), pp. 1293–1974.

—— (1982). Little Girls and Death in India, *Economic and Political Weekly 17*, No. 36 (September), pp. 1448–50.

Beck, Ulrich (1992). *Risk Society: Towards a New Modernity*, Sage Publications, London.

Beckert, Jens (1996). What is Sociological about Economic Sociology? Uncertainty and the Embeddedness of Economic Action, *Theory and Society*, Vol. 25, No. 6, pp. 803–40.

—— (2002). *Beyond the Market: The Social Foundations of Economic Efficiency*, Princeton University Press, New Jersey.

—— (2003). Economic Sociology and Embeddedness: How shall we Conceptualize Economic Action? *Journal of Economic Issue*, Vol. 37, No. 3, pp. 769–87.

Bhat, Anitha Kumar and Raj Dhruvarajan (2001). Ageing in India: Drifting Intergenerational Relations, Challenges and Options, *Ageing and Society*, Vol. 21, pp. 621–40.

Boserup, Ester (1970). *Woman's Role in Economic Development*, Earthscan, London.

Bourdieu, Pierre (1977). *Outline of a Theory of Practice*, Cambridge University Press, Cambridge.

Caldwell, John C. (1978). A Theory of Fertility: From High Plateau to Destabilization, *Population and Development Review,* Vol. 4, No. 4, pp. 553–77.

—— (1982). *Theory of Fertility Decline,* Academic Press, New York.

Caldwell, John C., P.H. Reddy and Pat Caldwell (1982). The Causes of Demographic Change in Rural South India: A Micro Approach, *Population and Development Review,* Vol. 8, No. 4, pp. 689–727.

Carson, David K. and Aparajita Chowdhury (2000). Family Therapy in India: A New Profession in an Ancient Land, *Contemporary Family Therapy,* Vol. 22, No. 4, pp. 387–406.

Chatterjee, Nilanjana and Nancy E. Riley (2001). Planning an Indian Modernity: The Gendered Politics of Fertility Control, *Journal of Women in Culture and Society,* Vol. 26, No. 3, pp. 811–45.

Chayanov, A.V. (1986). *The Theory of Peasant Economy,* University of Wisconsin Press, Madison.

Child Development Project Office (CDPO), (1996–2003). *Anganwadi Attendance Records,* Siddapur Taluk.

Clark, Shelley (2000). Son Preference and Sex Composition of Children: Evidence from India, *Demography,* Vol. 37, No. 1, pp. 95–108.

Collard, David (2000). Generational Transfers and the Generational Bargain, *Journal of International Development,* Vol. 12, No. 4, pp. 453–62.

Commons, John R. (1931). Institutional Economics, *American Economic Review,* Vol. 21, pp. 648–57.

—— (1934). *Institutional Economics: Its Place in Political Economy,* MacMillan, NY.

—— (1991). "John R. Commons on the Family", *Population and Development Review,* Vol. 17, No. 3, pp. 525–30, previously published as "A Sociological View of Sovereignty, V", in *American Journal of Sociology,* Vol. 5, No. 5, pp. 683–95, 1900.

Cormack, Margaret (1953). *The Hindu Woman,* Greenwood Press, Connecticut.

Cornwall, Marie and Brayden King (2003). Gender and New Institutionalism: Theorizing about Durability and Potential for Change, Under Review, *Sociological Theory.*

Croll, Elisabeth (2000). *Endangered Daughters: Discrimination and Development in Asia,* CUP, Cambridge.

Curtis, Richard F. (1986). Household and Family in Theory on Inequality, *American Sociological Review,* Vol. 51, No. 2, pp. 168–83.

Das Gupta, Monica (1987). Selective Discrimination against Female Children in Rural Punjab, India, *Population and Development Review*, Vol. 13, No. 1, pp. 77–100.

—— (1995). Life Course Perspectives on Women's Autonomy and Health Outcomes, *American Anthropologist*, New Series, Vol. 97, No. 3, pp. 481–91.

—— (1997). Liberté, Egalité, Fraternité: Exploring the Role of Governance in Fertility Decline, *Harvard Working Paper Series*, No. 97.06.

Das Gupta, Monica and P.N. Mari Bhat (1997). Fertility Decline and Increased Manifestation of Sex Bias in India, *Population Studies*, Vol. 51, No. 3, pp. 307–15.

Das Gupta, Monica, Zhenghua, Jiang, Bohua, Li, Zhenming, Xie, Chung, Woojin and Hwa-Ok, Bae (2003). Why is Son Preference so Persistent in East and South Asia? A Cross-country Study of China, India and the Republic of Korea, *Journal of Development Studies*, Vol. 40, No. 2, pp. 153–87.

Degler, Karl N. (1980). *At Odds: Women and the Family in America from the Revolution to the Present*, Oxford University Press, NY.

Dequech, David (2001). Bounded Rationality, Institutions and Uncertainty, *Journal of Economic Issues*, Vol. 35, No. 4, pp. 911–29.

—— (2003). Uncertainty and Economic Sociology: A Preliminary Discussion, *American Journal of Economics and Sociology*, Vol. 62, No. 3, pp. 509–32.

Dunn, Stephen (2000). Fundamental Uncertainty and the Firm in the Long Run, *Review of Political Economy*, Vol. 12, No. 4, pp. 419–33.

Dyson, Tim and Mick Moore (1983). On Kinship Structure, Female Autonomy and Demographic Behaviour in India, *Population and Development Review*, Vol. 9, No. 1, pp. 35–60.

Ensminger, Jean and Jack Knight (1997). Changing Social Norms: Common Property, Bridewealth and Clan Exogamy, *Current Anthropology*, Vol. 38, No. 1, pp. 1–24.

Fapohunda, Eleonor R. and Michael P. Todaro (1988). Family Structure, Implicit Contracts and the Demand for Children in Southern Nigeria, *Population and Development Review*, Vol. 14, No. 4, pp. 571–94.

Farooquee, Nehal A. and D.S. Rawat (1997). *Development Dilemma, Indian Scenario and Rural Himalaya: A Central Himalayan Perspective*, Indus, New Delhi.

Giddens, Anthony (1984). *The Constitution of Society: Outline of the Theory of Structuration*, Polity Press, Cambridge.

Giddens, Anthony (1990). *The Consequences of Modernity*, Cambridge University Press, Cambridge.

Goehler, Gerhard (2000). "Constitution and Use of Power", in Henri Goverde, Philip G. Cerny, Mark Haugaard and Howard Lentner (eds.), *Power in Contemporary Politics: Theories, Practices, Globalizations,* Sage Publications, London.

Goode, William J. (1963). *World Revolution and Family Patterns,* Free Press, NY.

Government of Karnataka (2004). *Directorate of Economics and Statistics,* www.des.kar.nic.in, 2004–06–20.

Greenhalgh, Susan (1985). Sexual Stratification: The Other Side of "Growth with Equity" in East Asia, *Population and Development Review,* Vol. 11, No. 2, pp. 265–314.

Gusfield, Joseph R. (1967). Tradition and Modernity: Misplaced Polarities in the Study of Social Change, *The American Journal of Sociology,* Vol. 72, No. 4, pp. 351–62.

Harriss, John (2003). Institutions, Politics and Culture: A Polanyian Perspective on Economic Change, *International Review of Sociology: Revue Internationale de Sociologie,* Vol. 13, No. 2, pp. 343–55.

Harriss-White, Barbara (2001). Development and Productive Deprivation: Male Patriarchal Relations in Business Families and their Implications for Women in S. India, *QEH Working Paper Series–QEHWPS 65,* February.

Hatti, Neelambar, T.V. Sekher and Mattias Larsen (2004). Lives at Risk: Declining Child Sex Ratios in India, *Lund Papers in Economic History, Population Economics,* No. 93. (www.ekh.lu.se)

Hatti, Neelambar and Rolf Ohlsson (1984). Age at Marriage: A Quantitative Study of Sirsi Taluk, 1960–1979, *Demography India,* Vol.13, No. 1, pp. 36–41.

—— (1985). Impact of Education on Age at Marriage in India, 1960–1979, *Demography India,* Vol. 14, No. 2, pp. 159–73.

Hays, Sharon (1994). Structure and Agency and the Sticky Problem of Culture, *Sociological Theory,* Vol. 12, No. 1, pp. 57–72.

Heiner, Ronald A. (1983). The Origin of Predictable Behavior, *American Economic Review,* Vol. 73, No. 4, pp. 560–95.

Hodgson, Geoffrey M. (2003). The Hidden Persuaders: Institutions and Individuals in Economic Theory, *Cambridge Journal of Economics,* Vol. 27, pp. 159–75.

Jeffrey, Roger and Jeffrey Patricia (1997). *Population, Gender and Politics: Demographic Change in Rural North India,* Cambridge University Press, Cambridge.

Jha, Prabhat, Rajesh Kumar, Priya Vasa, Neeraj Dhingra, Deva Thiruchelvam and Rahim Moineddin (2006). Low Male to Female Sex

Ratios of Children Born in India: National Survey of 1.1 Million Households, *The Lancet,* published online, January 9, pp. 1–8.

Joshi, G.V. (1997). "Implementation of Tenancy Reforms: The Case of Uttara Kannada District", in Abdul Aziz and Sudhir Krishna (eds.), *Land Reforms in India, Karnataka, Promises Kept and Missed,* Sage, New Delhi.

Kabeer, Naila (1996). Gender, Demographic Transition and the Economics of the Family: Population Policy for a Human-centred Development, *Occasional Paper* 7, UNRISD.

—— (2000). Inter-generational Contracts, Demographic Transitions and the 'Quantity-Quality' Trade-off: Parents, Children and Investing in the Future, *Journal of International Development,* Vol. 12, No. 4, pp. 463–82.

Kandiyoti, Deniz (1985). *Women in Rural Production Systems; Problems and Policies,* UNESCO, Paris.

—— (1988). Bargaining with Patriarchy, *Gender and Society,* Vol. 2, No. 3, Special Issue to Honor Jessie Bernard, pp. 274–290.

Knight, Frank H. (1921). *Risk, Uncertainty, and Profit,* Houghton Mifflin and Co., NY.

Knight, Jack (1992). *Institutions and Social Conflict,* Cambridge University Press, Cambridge.

Larsen, Mattias, Neelambar Hatti and Pernille Gooch (2005). Uncertainty and Discrimination: Family Structure and Declining Child Sex Ratios in Rural India, Lund Papers in Economic History, *Population Economics,* No. 99.

Mari Bhat, P.N. (2002). On the Trail of 'Missing' Indian Females, I: Search for Clues, Special Articles, *Economic and Political Weekly,* Dec. 21, pp. 5105–18.

—— (2002). On the Trail of 'Missing' Indian Females, II: Illusion and Reality, *Economic and Political Weekly,* December 28, pp. 5244–63.

Mason, Karen Oppenheim (1992). Family Change and Support of the Elderly in Asia: What do we know? *Asia-Pacific Population Journal,* Vol. 7, No. 3, pp. 13–32.

McNicoll, Geoffrey and Mead Cain (1989). Institutional Effects on Rural Economic and Demographic Change, *Population and Development Review,* Vol. 15, Supplement: Rural Development and Population: Institutions and Policy, pp. 3–42.

Miller, Barbara D. (1978). Changing Patterns of Juvenile Sex Ratios in Rural India: 1961 to 1981, *Economic and Political Weekly,* 24, No. 22, pp. 1229–35.

—— (1981). *The Endangered Sex,* Cornell University Press, Ithaca, NY.

Mitra, A. (1978). *India's Population: Aspects of Quality and Control,* Abhinav Publications, New Delhi.

Moore, Henrietta L. (1994). *A Passion for Difference: Essays in Anthropology and Gender,* Cambridge University Press, Cambridge.

Nair, K.G.R. (2004). Economic Reforms and Regional Disparities in Economic and Social Development in India, Report of a Research Project funded by the SER division of the Planning Commission of the Government of India.

Netting, Robert McC. (1993). *Smallholders, Householders: Farm Families and the Ecology of Intensive, Sustainable Agriculture,* Stanford University Press, California.

North, Douglass C. (2005). *Understanding the Process of Economic Change,* Princeton University Press, New Jersey.

Pani, Narendar (1997). "Towards Decentralized Agrarian Reform: Lessons from Karnataka's 1974 Experience", in Abdul Aziz and Sudhir Krishna (eds.), *Land Reforms in India, Karnataka, Promises Kept and Missed,* Vedams Books, New Delhi.

Parsons, Donald O. (1984). On the Economics of Intergenerational Control, *Population and Development Review,* Vol. 10, No. 1, pp. 41–54.

Patel, Tulsi (2005b). The Indian Girl at Risk: Caught between Individual Rationality and Public Good, paper presented at the Workshop on "Lives at Risk: Vulnerable Daughters in a Modernising Society", 28th and 29th September, ISEC, Bangalore, India.

—— (ed.), (2005a). *The Family in India: Structure and Practice,* Sage, New Delhi.

—— (ed.), (2007) *Sex-Selective Abortion in India; Gender, Society and New Reproductive Technologies,* Sage Publications, New Delhi.

Polanyi, Karl (1944) 2001. *The Great Transformation: The Political and Economic Origins of Our Time,* Beacon Press, Boston.

Polanyi, Karl, Conrad M. Arensberg, and Harry W. Pearson (1968). "The Economy as Instituted Process, 1957", in George Dalton (ed.), *Primitive, Archaic and Modern Economies: Essays of Karl Polanyi,* Beacon Press, Boston.

Ramu, G.N. (1988). *Family Structure and Fertility: Emerging Patterns in an Indian City,* Sage Publications, New Delhi.

Rele, J.R. and Iqbal Alam (1993). "Fertility Transition in Asia: The Statistical Evidence", in Richard Leete and Iqbal Alam, *The Revolution in Asian Fertility: Dimensions, Causes and Implications,* Oxford University Press, USA.

Sekher, T.V. and Neelambar Hatti (2007). "Vulnerable Daughters in a Modernizing Society: From 'Son Preference' to 'Daughter

Discrimination' in Rural South India", in Isabelle Attane and Christophe Guilmoto (eds.), *Watering the Neighbour's Garden*, CICRED, Paris.

Sen, Amartya (1987). "Gender and cooperative conflicts", in Irene Tinker (ed.), 1990, *Persistent Inequalities: Women and World Development*, Oxford University Press, Oxford.

—— (1989). Cooperation, Inequality and the Family, *Population and Development Review*, Vol. 15, Supplement: Rural Development and Population: Institutions and Policy, pp. 61–76.

—— (1990). More than a 100 Million Women are Missing, *New York Review of Books*, 20th December, pp. 61–66.

Sewell, Jr. and H. William (1992). A Theory of Structure: Duality, Agency and Transformation, *American Journal of Sociology*, Vol. 98, No. 1, pp. 1–29.

Storper, Michael and Robert Salais (1997). *Worlds of Production: The Action Framework of the Economy*, Harvard University Press, Cambridge.

Sudha, S. and S.I. Rajan (1999). Female Demographic Disadvantage in India 1981–91: Sex-selective Abortions and Female Infanticide, *Development and Change*, Vol. 30, pp. 585–618.

Swedberg, Richard (2003). *Principles of Economic Sociology*, Princeton University Press, Princeton.

Thornton, Arland and Thomas E. Fricke (1987). Social Change and the Family: Comparative Perspectives from the West, China and South Asia, *Sociological Forum*, Vol. 2, No. 4, Special Issue: Demography as an Inter-discipline, pp. 746–79.

Visaria, Pravin (1971). *The Sex Ratio of the Population of India*, Monograph 10, Census of India, Office of the Registrar General, India, New Delhi.

Weber, Max (1978). *Economy and Society: An Outline of Interpretive Sociology*, Guenther Roth and Claus Wittich (eds.) University of California Press, Berkeley.

THREE

From 'Fertility Control' to 'Gender Control'?

Evidences of Daughter Discrimination in Rural South India

T.V. Sekher, Neelambar Hatti and Preethi Bhat

The high masculine sex ratios of the Indian population have been a matter of concern for some time. Considerable attention has been paid to different dimensions of female deficits in India and persisting regional variations (Sen, 1990; Agnihotri, 2000; Miller, 1981 and 1989; Bhat, 2002; Croll, 2000), since the numerical imbalances between the male and female sexes were pointed out in the seventies (Visaria, 1971; Natarajan, 1972). The 2001 Census has set off further debates on the issue and has narrowed the focus to the changes in the juvenile or child sex ratio.[1] Changes in the sex ratio of children aged 0–6 are better indicators of status of girl child in India, known to be more hostile to females in their early ages. It also reflects the sum total of intra-household gender relations. Why millions of girls do not appear to be surviving in contemporary India, despite an overall improvement in welfare and state measures to enhance the status of women? Why are female children still at risk? Why is daughter discrimination on the rise despite progress in female literacy and growing participation of women in economic and political activities? Is there a significant shift from perceived 'son preference' to deliberate 'daughter discrimination'? There is need to focus attention on daughter discrimination and other aspects related to children differentiated by their gendered value.

Human population exhibits definitive characteristics in terms of its sex composition. In most parts of the globe, fewer females are born, yet females, as compared to their male counterparts, typically survive longer to exceed the males numerically at any given point of time. However, this demographic attribute eludes India where males decisively outnumber the females and women constitute less than half of the total population. Sex ratio is a direct indicator of women's status and welfare. The sex ratio changes are usually analyzed in a framework that underlies (relatively) greater deprivation and discrimination of females as opposed to males.

The major determinants of numerical imbalances revolve around factors such as under-enumeration of women, fertility, mortality and migration. Under-enumeration of females, relative to their male counterparts, typically encountered in the Indian context due to lower status of women, also makes census sex composition more masculine. However, the accelerated fall in the child sex ratio after 1981 is largely due to the diffusion of prenatal sex-selection techniques in regions with well-entrenched gender bias (Bhat, 2002; Hatti et al., 2004).

While the 2001 Indian Census shows that the overall male-female sex ratio has marginally improved from 927 women per 1,000 men to 933 per 1,000 during the last decade, the number of girls to boys in the youngest age group fell from 945/1,000 to 927/1,000. The regional disparities also appear to have increased; the northern states generally exhibit a worsening trend in male-female sex ratio as compared to the southern states. The census evidence suggests a clear cultural preference for male children, particularly among some north Indian states. The census lists 'sex-selective female abortions', 'female infanticide', and 'female neglect'—typically through giving girls less food and medical care than boys—as "important reasons commonly put forward" for this shocking anomaly. The new figures point to the use of new technologies to determine the gender composition. Furthermore, as social norms are changing toward smaller families, the availability of and access to new reproductive technologies (NRTs) provide an easy way for parents to achieve such goals. Amartya Sen has called it a "technological revolution of a reactionary kind".

Fertility Trends and Son Preference in Contemporary Asia

One of the most remarkable changes in the last century has been the shift from high to low fertility. Indeed, this has been described as the greatest single demographic change in the second half of the century (Caldwell, 1993). The timing, onset, pace and magnitude of this decline varies between countries. In the 1990s, India had experienced a new fertility decline at the national level. The 2001 Census indicated that, after a large spell of unprecedented population growth, the country experienced a gradual decline in the fertility levels. However, there is also evidence that there is growing disparity between the north and the south, with the southern states having been more successful in controlling population growth.[2] In a vast country like India with considerable demographic diversity and heterogeneity and varying levels of socio-economic development among states, the levels and phases of fertility decline vary significantly from one state to another (Bhat, 1994; Guilmoto and Rajan, 2002; Sekher et al., 2001).

Several studies suggest that cultural factors have played an important role in determining fertility trends (Basu, 1992; Jeffery and Jeffery, 1997; Das Gupta, 1987). While attention has been drawn to the importance of cultural factors in studying demographic behaviour, few studies have examined in detail the relations between cultural and economic aspects. One important cultural (and economic) feature is the value attached to sons. It is important to further analyze the nexus of economic, social and cultural factors that underlie daughter discrimination, thus shifting the focus from son preference to daughter discrimination.

Fertility Decline and Adverse Sex Ratio

During the last two decades, considerable debate has taken place, particularly in India, on the imbalance in sex ratio and the question of 'missing women'. In a significant article titled as "More than 100 million women are missing", Amartya Sen (1990) brought to focus the increasing gender discrimination by analyzing the male-female ratio. He has argued rather convincingly that the problem of missing women is clearly one of the momentous and neglected problem facing world today. Miller (1981), in her anthropological study of neglect of female children in North India, has illustrated the strong relationship between culture and mortality. It is the cultural bias against females in North India, which brings into play neglect and mistreatment of unknown numbers of children. According to her, the solution to this problematic future lies "in giving high priority to achieving gender equality in economic entitlement and increased awareness of the social importance of equal health and survival of males and females" (214).

There have been a number of studies, which have attempted to illustrate how the decline in fertility will affect gender bias and greater imbalance in juvenile sex ratios (Clark, 2000; Das Gupta and Bhat, 1997; Bhat and Zavier, 2003; Vella, 2005; Nanda and Veron, 2005). A substantial decline in fertility presupposes a desire for fewer children as well as access to the means to limit the family size. Both these conditions can be achieved with increase in social and economic development. It is generally accepted that the pace of demographic transition is closely associated with the levels of socio-economic development. However, there are evidences to show that, even in the poorer regions, substantial decline in fertility has occurred through political interventions, in the form of family planning programme. However, the social and economic development and governmental interventions do not ensure any substantial change in the cultural ethos of the society. In South Asian societies, it is believed that a major barrier for decline in fertility was the prevalence of strong son preference, irrespective of social and economic development. It is also argued that with the increase in welfare and economic development, the influence of son preference would decline gradually. These assumptions are being questioned by some studies indicating that there has been an increase in son preference during the years of fertility decline. This occurs not only in poorer communities but also in populations where women have taken to education, employment and have achieved considerable social status. Das Gupta (1987) has found that excess female mortality for second and subsequent parity daughters was 32 per cent higher than their siblings for uneducated mothers and 136 per cent higher if the mothers were educated. Basu makes a similar observation: "although her capacity to increase the chances of survival of her children seems to increase with education, the typical Uttar Pradesh women's ability to treat her male and female offspring equally actually decreases" (1992: 196). The existence of strong son preference has resulted in the desire to prevent the birth of daughters by carefully balancing the desired family size and desired sex composition of the children. In other words, the decline in fertility partly explains the rising masculinity of many populations (Das Gupta and Bhat, 1997; Croll, 2002). It is hypothesized that as fertility declines, two opposing forces could affect the child sex ratio, what is called as 'parity effect', which leads to a reduction of sex bias and 'intensification effect', which increases it. Considering this dimension, there is a need to examine the influence of the mirror image of son preference, namely, the daughter discrimination. Does a strong son preference ultimately result in deliberate discrimination against daughters? Miller asserts that "the problem is that son preference is so strong in some areas of India and amongst some classes that daughters must logically suffer in order that family's personal and culturally mandated needs are fulfilled" (1981: 25). Logically, this would mean that stronger the son preference, more intense the daughter discrimination.

Rather than going through repeated pregnancies bearing daughters in an attempt to produce male progeny, the norm of small family size and reduced fertility seem to imply that unborn daughters are the first to be 'sacrificed'. Generally, both infanticide and fatal neglect of female children seem to be supplemented by sex identification and sex-selective abortion, to achieve the desired family size and desired gender composition. Better opportunities for women's education, increasing labour force participation and a greater exposure to urban life do not guarantee equal status for daughters. In many Indian communities, daughters are associated with a double loss. Firstly, a daughter leaves the natal family after her marriage and the benefits from investments made on her upbringing accrue to the new family, constituting a loss to her natal family. This is further compounded by the weight of expenses of her marriage, particularly dowry, which is a heavy burden for the bride's family.[3] Sons, on the other hand, are considered as assets, deserving short and long-term investment. In India, the birth of a boy is thus a time for celebration while a birth of a girl, especially second or subsequent one, is often viewed as a time of crisis (Bumiller, 1991). Besides economic considerations, there are cultural factors that support son preference. All these factors put together contribute to the firm belief that daughters cannot substitute sons. A general explanation for son preference and daughter discrimination is that sons can provide old age support. In India, a majority of the old parents live with married children, who are usually sons. The Indian context, characterized by high levels of uncertainty, where no institutional alternative to the family as a source of social insurance has emerged, parental decisions are likely to be powerfully motivated by their concerns about their own security in the old age. The existence of such an understanding and commitment between parents and sons, known as inter-generational contract, is one factor that appears to have remained unchanged through overall socio-economic changes. Sons are also important because they alone can perform the funeral rituals of the parents. Added to this, most women have very limited opportunities to contribute towards their parents' welfare. This creates an apparent dichotomy between the value of a girl to her parents and that of a woman to her parents-in-law. It has also become more expensive to raise children as education has become more important and a necessity in a transforming society. The increasing cost of education and marriage of girls is a major drain on the household resources, which acts as a strong disincentive to have daughters.

The underlying workings of female discrimination are undoubtedly highly complex. However, a number of broad factors have been identified which together create a situation where sons are preferred and daughters are neglected. The patterns of inheritance are typically patrilineal in India with property passing from father to son (Miller, 1981; Kabeer, 1996; Agarwal, 1994). Upon marriage the bride leaves her natal home to live with the family of her husband. In this exogamous lineage system women are left out. They become dispensable essentially because they count for very little as individuals.

In recent years, a major factor directly influencing the imbalance in child sex ratio is the widespread use of sex determination technologies and sex-selective abortion. Parents use these methods to achieve the desired sex composition of the children within the desired family size. Misuse of sex determination tests has been a subject of media attention for many years. Health activists and women's organizations voiced their concern forcing the government to act. In 1994, the Government of India banned the tests at the national level, with the Pre-natal Diagnostic Techniques (PNDT) (Regulation and Prevention of Misuse) Act. As per this legislation, only government-registered clinics and laboratories may employ prenatal diagnostic procedures that can be used to assess the sex of the foetus. The Act also specifies that no prenatal diagnostic procedures may be used unless there is a heightened possibility that the foetus suffers from a harmful condition or genetic disease. It also states that no person conducting prenatal diagnostic procedures shall communicate to the pregnant women concerned or her relatives the sex of the foetus by words, signs, or in any other manner. This Act was again amended in the light of the newer techniques of pre-conception tests and the amended rule came into effect from February 2003. Now, the Act is renamed as the Pre-conception and Pre-natal Diagnostic Techniques (Prohibition of Sex-Selection) Act, 1994.[4]

Female foetuses are liable to victimization on the basis of their sex alone even before they are born. Only far-reaching social changes that aim at increasing female autonomy, female economic power and the value of the girl child are likely to make a significant impact on the demand for sex-selective abortion. Interestingly, there is no reliable statistics available on sex-selective abortions at the state or national level in India. An indirect estimate using the data from two rounds of National Family Health Survey[5] (NFHS) indicates more than 1,00,000 sex-selective abortions in India every year (Arnold, Kishor and Roy, 2002). The evidence of substantial sex-selective abortions in states such as Punjab, Haryana, Delhi and Maharashtra is consistent with the high rates of use of ultrasound and amniocentesis (Retherford and Roy, 2003).

Using the NFHS data again, it was observed that at the national level, the sex ratio at birth for mothers who had either ultrasound or amniocentesis was 934 female births per 1,000 male births. The lower sex ratios for births to mothers who had either of these tests could be attributed to sex-selective abortions. NFHS survey has demonstrated that ultrasound and amniocentesis are often used for sex determination and sex-selective abortions of female foetuses have been rampant in many states of India. Though ultrasound and amniocentesis tests on pregnant women are legal in India, the divulgence of the sex of the child to the parents is illegal since 1996. The legislation has been a miserable failure in preventing the couples seeking sex determination tests and abortions and the medical practitioners performing them. Enforcement of legal procedures alone will not reduce these incidences unless there are significant changes in the attitudes and socio-economic environment.

Two Village Studies in South India

At the national and state levels, we have reasonably good idea about the levels of fertility decline, the extent of son preference and the relationship between the two, based on the analysis of large-scale data from various demographic and health surveys. But, how this really manifests at the village level, particularly in the context of widespread availability of sex-selection techniques at low cost? By studying two villages in the low-fertility regions of South India, we attempt to understand how these factors interplay at the micro level, with changing socio-economic conditions.

The main objective of these village studies was to study the precarious situation of female children before birth (their chances of being born at all), at birth and during the first six years of childhood. In order to gain an understanding of the dynamics, it is essential to look into household and individual behaviour. Here, the main concern is how reproduction strategies and specific gender discrimination practices vary among households belonging to different socio-economic groups. It is important to understand how the desire for sons, whether strong or weak, is directly related to daughter discrimination and neglect. The focus group discussions (FGDs) and in-depth interviews concentrated to a small group were done to elicit information about the value of boys and girls, reproductive preferences and strategies. The qualitative research methods employed in the two study villages provided very useful insights. A focus group, generally consisting of 8–10 persons with similar socio-economic and demographic background, encouraged lively discussions on specific issues, moderated and facilitated by the researchers. The entire discussion was tape-recorded which helped in the preparation of detailed transcripts later. FGDs provided not only experiences and opinions of the participants but also their perceptions on various issues. The information gathered through FGDs was supplemented with individual interviews. All these qualitative information was pooled together and synthesized to arrive at conclusions. The average time taken for an FGD was 90 minutes. FGDs were conducted in panchayat offices, temples, *anganwadi* centres[6] and in some cases, at the residences of some members. Retaining all the participants till the end of the FGD was a challenging task. In general, villagers were very forthcoming in expressing their views and revealing their perceptions.

Mandya District in a Low-Fertility Region of Karnataka State

Mandya district is located in the central belt of southern part of Karnataka, which has been geographically classified as southern *Maidan* (plains) region of the state. The district is compact with high population and village densities. More than 60 per cent of the total population of the district belongs to a single peasant community, the Vokkaligas (Gowdas). With the paucity of land for further expansion of area under cultivation, the long history of irrigation and its impact, and the Vokkaliga's love for land and cultivation have been documented by social scientists (Epstein, 1962 and 1973; Srinivas, 1976). There were fewer land transactions and the land values have increased considerably in recent decades. Predominant small holding is the characteristic feature of this district. Landholdings of less than 2 hectare form nearly 85 per cent of all holdings. The large holdings with more than 10 hectares accounted for only 0.33 per cent of the total holdings and about 4.54 per cent of the total land held. Thus, marginal and small farmers were predominant in the district. The fortunes of a man generally depended upon the size of landed property of his father and the number of siblings with whom he would have to share the property.

Canal irrigation is a characteristic feature of Mandya district. The major irrigation work, the Krishnarajasagar dam across river Cauvery was partly completed by 1921 and water was made available to the farmers of the district. Agricultural land, with assured canal irrigation, is the backbone of the economy of the district. The major crops are paddy, sugarcane, ragi and coconut. Sericulture and handloom weaving are the two other important economic activities, which provide work for thousands of families. The district recorded a population density of 355 per sq km in 2001. The male literacy rate was 72 per cent and female literacy 52 per cent in 2001.

Observations from the Study Village M

Village M is located about 8 km from Mandya town (district headquarters). Coconut gardens and fields of sugarcane and paddy along with canals and streams surround the village. As per 2001 Census, there were 637 households in this village with an average household size of five. The literacy rate was about 60 per cent. The general sex ratio was 926 (females per 1,000 males) and the child sex ratio (0–6) was 732 in 2001—a considerable decline from 825 in 1991.

With assured irrigation and the Visvesvaraya Canal passing through this village, many important changes have taken place in the agriculture of this village. The advent of irrigation brought overall changes in the pattern of cultivation and, consequently, improved the economic condition of landowning families. Ownership of land implies regular food availability and income for the families. Therefore, land is the most important economic resource for the villagers. Most farmers use high yielding varieties of seeds and apply fertilizers. The availability of irrigation pumpsets, tractors and power tillers in a way replaced significant part of agriculture labour. The easy availability of credit and marketing facilities also helped farmers. The easy access to the commercially vibrant Mandya town with many trade and industrial establishments also encouraged many villagers to take up employment in the town. However, fragmentation of land and unpredictability of agricultural production and prices made many of them sceptical, as narrated during FGDs.

> It was better before. Rainfall was sufficient and the crop yield was good. We used to get sufficient water from Krishnarajsagar (KRS) dam across river Cauvery and there was not much problem for our agriculture. We were getting good crops and, we were happy.

> Due to insufficient rainfall, canal water from KRS for our agriculture is becoming difficult. All the villages in the surrounding area have the same kind of problem.

> Because of the financial constraints everybody has been limiting the family size. Fragmentation of land has taken place due to partition of the families, and everybody having only smallholdings. So, parents don't want to have more children and again don't want to divide their land.

The population of the village has increased from 761 in 1951 to 2,921 in 2001. Nearly 70 per cent of the households were Vokkaligas—the dominant community in the village as well as in the district. Vokkaliga in local language means 'cultivator', and they are traditional agriculturists. They are the Gangadikar Vokkaligas enjoying higher rank within the Vokkaligas. Undoubtedly, Vokkaligas control the bulk of the cultivable land in the village. According to 2001 Census, 36 per cent of the total workers were cultivators and 24 per cent were agricultural labourers in this village.

Twenty-one per cent of the households belonged to Scheduled Castes (SCs, deprived communities).

We observed that dowry, wealth flow from bride's family to groom's family, has become a common practice in all castes and communities. The communities that did not practise dowry in the past have now started this in a big way. This has put a heavy burden on the girl's family in arranging for dowry demanded by the boy's family and also meeting the increasing marriage expenses. Having more children is a financial burden on the family in terms of sending them to school and in performing their marriages. Epstein, who studied two Mandya villages documents the emergence of dowry practice in the following words "In Wangala, it was Beregowda, one of the most enterprising peasants, who initiated change to dowry payments. He explained that three considerations had motivated him to take this step: first, he was keen to get an educated husband to his daughter. Second, his daughter had not been trained to work in the fields and far from being an economic asset she would be a liability as a wife; finally, he said, Brahmins had always given their daughters dowries" (1973: 197). Another study of South Karnataka village describes the changes in dowry practices: "The major change was the coming of dowry. In the early 1950s, the first dowries in Bangalore were paid by some Brahmin families. Not until the beginning of the 1960s did the first Brahmin landlord family in the study area provide a dowry and not until 1965 was this done by the first Vokkaliga (the major peasant caste) family. It is still not paid by Harijans (SCs), although in the largest village they ceased paying the *Tera* (brideprice) five years ago, and the payment is still small among some of the backward castes. Nevertheless, they all anticipate its arrival. In all castes, the bride's family now bears the major portion of the wedding costs, and it is they who seek loans and sell land" (Caldwell et al., 1982: 707). The observations from FGDs illustrate how dowry has emerged as essential part of marriage negotiations:

> In our colony, Kamala has two, sons. Her elder daughter-in-law has not brought anything, but the second daughter-in-law has brought a huge dowry. Therefore, the younger one receives more respect than the elder one. Including the husband and in-laws, threaten the elder one for not bringing dowry. I have seen them beating her also. Any time, she will be sent back to her natal home.

> Boy's parents consider that it is their right to collect dowry. They never think about the economic position of the girl's parents.
>
> They never realize it can happen to their daughter also.
>
> Even poor people have to give dowry. Even if the boy is an agricultural worker, he gets lot of gold and cash.
>
> Some parents are forced to give their land as dowry.
>
> No marriage in this village has taken place without giving gold and cash to the boy's family.
>
> I don't want daughters. Even if I spend Rs 5,000 for abortion, it is better than spending Rs 5,00,000 on dowry.
>
> People who are wealthy started giving huge money as dowry to maintain prestige. Slowly others also started following these people. A proverb says; ondu meke hallake bitthu antha yella meke hallake biluvdhe". (In a herd of sheep, if one fell into the well, should others also start jumping into it, without assessing the situation?)

Prosperous Gowda families are ready to pay even 0.5-million to 1 million rupees as dowry, besides giving gifts in the form of gold jewellery, car, furniture, etc. Usually, the girl's family has to bear the entire marriage expenses. The dowry paid and the gifts given depend upon the qualification and employment position of the boy and land owning status of the family (see Appendix 1). During our fieldwork we came across young Vokkaliga couples having only one child, mostly male, and deciding to accept family planning. According to them, if they had more than one child it would be extremely difficult to provide good education and meet the cost of upbringing. As narrated in our focus group discussions, since land was limited, it was difficult to maintain the standard of living:

> Earlier in this village, scheduled castes never used to give dowry. After seeing Gowdas, they also started. Some people believe that paying more dowry is a prestige issue for the family. They sell their land or borrow money to give dowry.
>
> Educated girls should insist that they are against dowry. I read in newspapers that, in cities, some girls refuse to marry when the

> boy's family demands dowry. Our village girls have neither the opportunity nor the courage to do like that.

> Even though girls with some education may try to oppose the payment of dowry in villages, they generally give in to the parental/family pressure as the marriage negotiations progress.

The discrimination in providing primary education to boys and girls was evident during the discussions with school teachers. Just to give a couple of examples:

> Some people send their sons to convent school (better quality education) and daughters to government school (poor quality education). Why does this difference exist?

> Why to spend on daughter? Son gets good education and will earn money for the parents. Daughter, one or another day, has to leave the house.

> What is the use of educating girls at all? If they get too much education they may start getting new ideas through magazines and films and oppose the parental wishes.

Generally, most of the Vokkaliga families are nuclear. After marriage, women have no right over the parental property including land. The sons inherit all family assets. During our interviews and FGDs, we found that there was a strong preference for small families, and interestingly, most of the couples had already accepted family planning. It was the Vokkaligas who by accepting birth control measures paved the way for other communities towards the acceptance in this village. A majority felt that it was a responsibility and sometimes a burden to have more children, particularly girls. The type of fertility transition experienced in this village and other parts of the district has been unique, and one can see a strong relationship between population pressure on land and rapid fertility decline (Sekher and Raju, 2004). Dependence on agriculture in Mandya district is far greater than anywhere else in the state. The paucity of cultivable land and availability of irrigation have resulted in increasing land values. The landowning Vokkaliga desires to have only one or two sons to avoid further fragmentation of land. As mentioned by Epstein (1998), "They now appreciate that large number of children creates economic problems of future generations. But most of them still have a strong son preference. They continue procreating until they have at least one son. For example, Shangowda had one son after his wife had given birth first to two daughters. He and his wife then decided that three children are enough for them. A large proportion of villagers pursue the same strategy. In this too, old beliefs and customs persist in a changed setting" (p. 196). Vokkaligas consider land as the source of old age security, along with the son. Beals, while studying social change in a Mysore village 50 years ago, has stated: "Namhalli's landowning group, while not threatened with starvation, has been faced, in recent years, with the problem of dividing a limited quantity of land among an ever increasing population. Within the village many solutions to this problem, ranging from abortion to the adoption of iron plows, have been tried. In almost every family in Namhalli, at least one child has been groomed for urban employment" (1955: 98).

The focus group discussions clearly illustrate the strong desire to limit the number of children:

> After having two daughters, my mother-in-law told me not to go for sterilization. Then I thought, if I continue like this, it will be very difficult for me, and I may die. Then I went to a doctor and decided to have operation.

> My husband wanted more children; he was very much against sterilization. But I went and had it. Now, he tells me that what I did was a correct thing.

> I got operated immediately after the birth of my second child. My husband gave me full support in this decision.

> I have a daughter; my husband wanted at least one boy. My mother-in-law became sad and cried when I gave birth to a girl child.

> When I became pregnant, my in-laws used to neglect me because my mother gave birth to only girl children and they believed that I will also give birth to a girl. Everyday I used to pray to god for a baby boy. When I delivered a boy I became a respectable person in the house. My in-laws became happy and my husband was also very happy. That day they distributed sweets to all our relatives and neighbours.

During our fieldwork we observed that a majority of the young couple underwent sex determination test, either in private clinic or nursing home. People from village M go to nearby Mandya town where two nursing homes are known for conducting abortions. During focus group discussions among Vokkaliga and SCs women, we found that almost all were aware of the facilities available to find out the sex of the foetus. We also came across cases where some public health workers, particularly Auxiliary Nurse Midwives (ANMs), were providing information and advising village women how to get rid of unwanted daughters. Many women openly admitted that several doctors in Mandya city conduct both the test and the abortion. In a few cases, people went to places like Bangalore and Mysore. This was expensive for the family, but rich Gowdas were ready to spend more money for, what they called as a 'good purpose'. For conducting sonography and disclosing the sex of the foetus, private nursing homes in Mandya charge between Rs 1,000 and Rs 2,000, and if a woman prefers to undergo an abortion she has to pay an additional Rs 5,000. During our focus group discussions many women justified persuading their daughters or daughters-in-law to opt for abortion saying that it is better to spend a few thousand rupees now than spending a million rupees later, thus avoiding all the future problems like education, marriage, dowry, etc. One woman belonging to the Vokkaliga community said that had this facility (ultrasound) been available 20 years ago, she would have gone for it to reduce the number of daughters. She said, "*Hecchu edi kere haal maadtu; Hecchu henninda mane haalaaitu*" (too many crabs destroy the lake and, similarly, too many daughters spoil the house). In her efforts to have a son 20 years ago, she gave birth to three daughters:

> In the neighbour's house they have done abortion secretly. Now, in our community one new thing has started. If one becomes pregnant, the family won't tell she is pregnant. She is taken to Mandya to find out the sex of the baby. If it is a girl, the foetus is aborted immediately. Everything is done in a secretive manner.
>
> When I went to the hospital last time, I saw Mahadeva and his wife, He has three girls and his wife is again pregnant. If it is a girl, he wants to abort. Then, the doctor shouted at him and said I am not ready to go jail for your sake. However, there are many other doctors who would do the abortion.

> Ram Gowda's wife died during abortion. Poor woman, she has left behind two daughters.
>
> When I took my sister to the hospital for delivery, next to her bed, there were two abortion cases which had been admitted. I came to know that they came for aborting female foetus.
>
> For my daughter-in-law, we did scanning to find out the sex of the baby. After taking 1,000 Rupees, the doctor did not reveal the sex of the baby. After that we went to another doctor who determined the sex of the foetus and terminated the pregnancy.

Another old woman explained the necessity for having a son: *"maga manege; magalu pararige"* (son is for our family and daughter is for other family). When asked about whether they depend on their sons for protection during old age, most men and women in village M said 'yes'. Some of them strongly felt the necessity to have at least two sons. Krishne Gowda quoting a local saying which substantiated his argument: *"ondu kannu kannalla; obba maga maganalla"* (one eye is not enough to see, one son is not enough for the family).

It is very evident that the incidence of dowry has gone up considerably in all the communities. The girl's family is under pressure to meet a series of payments for the marriage, beginning with engagement and concluding with the bride actually going to reside in the groom's house. In many communities, the practice of dowry was unheard of about thirty years ago but it has become an essential feature of the marriage today. The dowry payment includes cash, gold, silver and expensive consumer items like TV and refrigerator, and in many cases a vehicle, preferably a car or motorbike. A portion of the land and property is also transferred from the girl's family to the boy's family. Apart from all this, it is a well-established norm among all communities that all expenditures for conducting the marriage have to be borne by the girl's family. Considering all these expenses and practically no return, many feel that having a daughter is a 'real burden' for the family. A village woman appropriately summarized the situation: *"Yavaga Honnina bele Eruthade, avaga Hennina bele iliyuthade"* (whenever the value of gold goes up, the value of the girl comes down).

The findings from the sample household survey carried out in village M clearly indicate the changing attitude towards the perceived value of sons and that of daughters. The tables presented below are based on a survey of 96 young male or female parents (those having at least one child in the age group 0–6). Out of 96, 66 belong to Vokkaligas and the remaining from SCs. The son preference is strong among Vokkaligas, nearly 77 per cent of them want either one son or two sons (and no daughters!). Only 18 per cent of them consider that their ideal family comprised of one son and one daughter. More than four-fifths of them felt that daughters were more expensive to bring up than sons and 71 per cent were apprehensive of the problems/difficulties associated with suitably marrying off their daughters.

Table 1

Household Survey in Village M

A. Ideal family size according to the respondents

Ideal family size	*Communities (in percentages)*	
	Vokkaligas	*Scheduled Castes*
1 son	30.3	17.4
2 sons	46.9	47.8
1 daughter	4.6	4.3
1 son and 1daughter	18.2	30.4
2 daughters	—	—
Total	100.0	100.0

B. Value attached to the children by parents

	Communities (in percentages)	
	Vokkaligas	*Scheduled Castes*
Sons are more expensive to bring up than daughters.	21	24
Daughters are more expensive to bring up than sons.	87	72
Will you face difficulty in arranging marriage of your son?	18	42
Will you face difficulty in marrying off your daughter?	71	89
Son will take care of you when you are old.	63	74
Daughter will take care of you when you are old.	9	12

Cont'd...

Cont'd...

C. Parental perception about the future of their children

		Vokkaligas (in percentages)	
		Men	*Women*
How do you think life will be for your daughter(s)?	Better	NA	11
	Worse		49
	Like your own		40
How do you think life will be for your son(s)?	Better	39	NA
	Worse	12	
	Like your own	49	
Total		100	100

NA: not applicable.

Salem District of Tamil Nadu

Salem district recorded the lowest child sex ratio in South India in 2001. This district attracted considerable attention in the nineties for the prevalence of female infanticide (George et al., 1992). There were certain taluks in the district, which reported shocking anomalies in child sex ratio in 2001. A study carried out based on available PHC records confirms the incidence of female infanticide in the districts of Salem, Dharmapuri and Madurai (Chunkath and Athreya, 1997). The 2001 Census has amply substantiated the still existing and rampant practice of female infanticide in parts of Tamil Nadu, despite overall socio-economic changes.

In Salem district, the average household size was 4, with literacy rate 65 in 2001. Two major communities are Vanniyars and Kongu Vellala Gounders. Vanniyar originally formed fighting force of the Pallavas and hence, came to be called as 'Padayachi'. Their community cohesiveness is remarkable. Some of them practise agriculture as their main occupation. The traditional occupation of Vanniyar is oil pressing and oil selling. The nuclear family is the most common form. Sons inherit property and the eldest son gets a greater share. Daughter does not have any right to the property unless they have no brothers. Vanniyars are locally categorized as most backward caste and the state government has reservation policy for them. Kongu Vellala Gounder is an inhabitant of the Kongu region of the Tamil Nadu. Agriculture is the traditional occupation of this community. The other economic activities are animal husbandry, trade, industrial labour etc. They are hardworking agriculturists and specialized in garden cultivation.

Observations from the Study Village K in Mettur Taluk

This village has 1,341 households according to the 2001 Census with a total population of 4,983 (2,676 males 2,307 females). The average household size was 4. The overall literacy rate was 47 per cent. The general sex ratio is 862 (females per 1,000 males) and the child sex ratio was 616 in 2001—a decline from 673 as recorded in 1991. Besides SCs, two major communities in this village are Vanniyar and Kongu Vellala Gounder.

During our filedwork, we came across incidences of female infanticide from this village. Though some families, including women, were hesitant to talk about it, there were a few who openly justified the practice. Though the practice was more prominent among Vanniyars, other communities also occasionally practise infanticide (see Appendix 2). On many occasions, though the mother of the child was not directly involved, the elder members ensured the elimination of female infant within a week after birth. The methods used for this purpose included feeding the child with poison, loosening the knot of umbilical cord, suffocating baby to death, feeding with paddy husk, and starving the baby to death. A more 'modern' method recently observed was the use of pesticides or sleeping pills. Some elders use the prediction of local astrologers ('fortune tellers') as a strong justification to get rid of the daughter who would "cause destruction to the family". As one old woman, narrating the plight of her family said: "it is better they die than live like me". *Penn shisu kolai,* female infanticide in local language, is justified for various reasons. Though many families tolerate the first girl, the subsequent daughters are really at high risk. The general observation that the female infanticide was confined to certain backward communities like Kallars has been proved erroneous. It has spread to communities like Gounder, Vanniyar and Pallars. Our discussions in village K indicated that it was not only the poor who practised infanticide, but the rich and powerful in the village also practised the *penn shisu kolai.* There were few police cases registered recently against parents for committing the infanticide. But, the arrival of sex determination tests, even in villages, has given a new method for those who can afford to pay. Many economically better off families admitted that they avoided the birth of another girl "with the help of doctor". However, poor women in the SC colony said, "We cannot afford to pay for test and abortion. So, we still practise infanticide, which is much cheaper" (see Appendix 2). Our study in this village clearly shows the practice of female infanticide was being substituted by female foeticide, particularly among Gounder community. The combined efforts of the state, NGOs and some panchayat leaders have had some impact on reducing the incidence of female infanticide. Pregnant women already having a girl child used to be classified into high-risk category and were monitored closely by local NGOs. The girl child protection scheme of the state government is being used to motivate parents to care for female infants. Surprisingly, similar effort from the government and the public is absent in combating female foeticide.

Among the Kongu Vellala Gounders, dowry was reported as the major reason to avoid having daughters. A few observations are cited below:

> Parents of the bride borrow money from others; sometimes they sell their land to cover the marriage expenses.
>
> After paying so much dowry, they continue to demand more. If she fails to bring dowry, the husband and in-laws start harassing her. That is why many people don't want daughters.
>
> I have one daughter and one son. My in-laws wanted one more son but my husband was very particular about sterilization. One day he took me in his scooter to Mettur for the operation without informing at home. First, my in-laws were very angry with us. But now, they appreciate my husband's decision.

There was a phenomenal increase in the amount of dowry transacted from girl's family to boy's family. The landowning Gounder had to pay atleast 80 soverigns of gold, Rs 2 lakh cash and a car, as well as to meet all the lavish expenditure to conduct marriage. The manifold increase in dowry among all communities repeatedly came up for discussions in the FGDs. The landowning Vanniars are not far behind, the rates ranging between 40 to 60 sovereigns of gold, car or motorbike and marriage expenses. Even the landless Dalits (the poorest in the village and depending upon agricultural work for their livelihood) are forced to pay gold (5 to 10 sovereigns) and meet the marriage costs, which can easily exceed Rs 25,000. Borrowing money to meet these 'unavoidable' expenses has pushed many families into the trap of indebtedness on the one hand and social obligations on the other. According to one Dalit women, "having a daughter is a punishment for the sins committed in a previous life". In most of the marriage negotiations, the first criterion was how much dowry would be given. "Modernization ushered in the importance of material status, driving the need to be extravagant and to show off as a way of asserting one's social standing. For well-off Gounders performing *seeru* (dowry) at and the conduct of marriages of daughters became an important forum to display new found prosperity and to assert their status within their community (caste group)" (Srinivasan, 2005: 602). This factor clearly shows why many daughters were unwelcome resulting in a deliberate intensification of non-preference of daughters and consequent son preference. Even the affluent families who can 'afford' daughters and can provide them with good education are sceptical because, as a local leader put it, "the higher the education of the girls, the higher the dowry". It is also true that "an increase in the prevalence of dowry, which has raised the costs of bringing up children, and created a situation of financial distress, have also contributed to the fertility decline in some segments of population" (Krishnamoorthy et al., 2005: 245). Marrying off a daughter without giving a decent dowry can have serious consequences for the natal family as well as for the daughter. One respondent expressed this as follows:

> The in-laws may humiliate our daughter, demand more dowry, ill treat her and finally she may be forced to return to our home in shame. How can we allow this to happen to our daughter?

Apart from the demand at the time of marriage, the demand after marriage for more dowry, resulting in the fear of ill-treatment of their daughter if the demands are not met, is a perennial worry for many parents. The inability to pay the amount of dowry demanded could also lead to a delay in the marriage itself and an unmarried daughter would pose many a problem for the parents.

Concluding Observations

In both the study villages the observations clearly indicate that in the eyes of parents, even after improvement in girl's education and employment, daughters are rarely able to substitute for sons. Though the will for limiting the family size is quite evident across communities, 'smart couples' are able to achieve the desired family size and the desired sex composition of children together. The new reproductive strategies to attain desired number of sons are employed by parents across communities; notwithstanding the extent of use, it is also an indication of the easy availability and affordability of sonography and abortion facilities despite the legal hinders such as PNDT Act of 1994. As narrated by a literate woman in Village M: "Had these clinics were available 30 years ago, many of us would never have seen this world!" According to the NGO activist in our Tamil Nadu study village, "the real culprits here are the medical doctors who misuse the technology to increase their profits". Though the 'technological effect' may mainly be responsible for the elimination of female foetuses, the powerlessness of village women in our patriarchal societies is an equally important factor to be considered. Personal interviews with young women in the study areas reveal that many a time, they were forced to undergo sonography and abortion, much against their own wishes.

The FGDs in both the study areas clearly illustrate the people's tendency to identify having a daughter with dowry payments. The continuing trend of increasing dowry demands, in cash and in kind, across communities, both as a crucial factor in marriage negotiations as well as a 'status enhancer' within the community, has had significant impact on how the parents value the worth of boys and girls.

Interestingly, the two peasant communities (Vokkaligas and Kongu Vellala Gounders) in the study villages have become increasingly affluent as major beneficiaries of the access to irrigation and other inputs of modern agriculture. This affluence has meant a continuing rise in living standards, aspirations and consumption. Besides acquisition of various trappings of modern life, another way of demonstrating their economic affluence, according to the FGDs, was to catch a 'well-qualified son-in-law' since this would enhance their status and standing within the community and the village. This desire of course would gradually inflate the dowry demands of the boy's family and also increase the wedding expenditure of the girl's family. Hence, over time, the increasing costs of education and marriage and a conviction that dowry rates can only move upwards compel the parents to seriously consider the investment in and return from a daughter as against the benefits that can accrue to the parents from investing in a son. Both the landed and the landless in our FGDs cite this as the most important reason for preferring sons at the expense of daughters. Since both study areas have completed the fertility transition and small family is the accepted norm, the parents seem to make the deliberate choice between a son and a daughter since a son would mean inflow of wealth while a daughter implies a drain. The affluent communities, which not too long ago considered payment of large dowries as a symbol of their capability and status, now realize that such payments constitute a threat to their affluence, lifestyles and aspirations and, consequently, prefer not to have a daughter.

As a result of the growing affluence of the landowning communities, the cash flow among the landless agricultural labourers has also increased due to higher wages, most of which is now being paid in cash than in kind. This fact, coupled with the desire to imitate the customs of the higher castes in the village, a kind of sanskritization process, has meant that the practice of dowry payment has permeated to the landless lower castes, thus increasing the expenses of marriages. Consequently, these communities also exhibit similar preferences albeit to a lesser extent.

The field-level observations from the two low-fertility regions of South India and the data analyses clearly indicate a strong preference for sons, particularly among the peasant communities. However, with the substantial decline in fertility, the son preference appears to have resulted in an increased as well as intensified manifestation of deliberate discrimination towards daughters. The widespread use of sex-selection techniques has provided an opportunity for couples to choose a son rather than a daughter. Along with this, the increasing pressure on limited availability of land on the one hand and the spiralling costs of bringing up children, particularly girls, due to increasing demands for dowry to be paid, parents prefer to avoid having daughters. The medical technology has come in handy for many couples for achieving the desired sex composition and the desired small family size. The rapid fertility decline, not accompanied by changes in the cultural values and gender inequality, is in a way responsible for the intensification of gender bias and the deliberate attempt to deny the girls from being 'born at all'. In other words, female foetuses are increasingly being 'victimized' on the basis of their sex alone even before they are born.

Appendix 1

A. Range of Dowry in a Village in Mandya District (1970)

Community	*Occupation/education of the son-in-law*	*Dowry paid*	
		Cash (Rs)	*Items*
Rich Vokkaligas	Educated, with a job in the city	3,000–4,000	1–2 acres irrigated land. Jewelry (for Rs 6,000) Cloth (for Rs 3,000)
Middle Class Vokkaligas	Educated	1,000–2,000	Jewelry, cloth (for Rs 3,000)
Poor Vokkaligas		Up to 1,000	Cloth and jewelry (for Rs 1,500)

Source: Epstein, 1973.

B. Range of Dowry in Village M (2005)

Community/Caste	*Occupation/education of the son-in-law*	*Dowry (cost) in 2004*	
		Cash (Rs)	*Items*
Rich (Vokkaligas)	Groom is employed in government/private job and settled in the city.	3–5 lakh	Land, car, 100–130 grams gold, clothes, all other expenses towards marriage
	Groom is employed in government/private job and settled in the village.	2–3 lakh	Scooter, 80–100 grams gold, clothes and all other expenses towards marriage
Middle class (Vokkaligas and other castes)	Groom is in government/private job and settled in the City.	1–2 lakh	Land, scooter, 60–70 grams gold, clothes and all other expenses towards marriage
	Groom is in government/private job and settled in the village.	Less than 1 lakh	Land, scooter, 60–70 grams gold, clothes and all other expenses towards marriage
	Groom is an agriculturist, settled in the village.	50,000	60–70 grams gold, clothes and all other expenses towards marriage
Poor labourers (SC's and other castes)	Landless agricultural labour (groom).	10–20 thousands	10–20 grams gold, and clothes and all other expenses towards marriage
Vodda* households	Landless labour (groom).	5–10 thousands	10–20 grams gold, and all other expenses towards marriage, 101 articles like vessels etc.

*Vodda is a SC community, which migrated from Tamil Nadu and settled in the village in the 1960s.

Source: Focus Group Discussions carried out by the study team during 2004–05.

Appendix 2

Characteristics of three Communities in Tamil Nadu Village

Characteristics	*Vanniyars*	*KV Gounders*	*Dalits*
Joint/Nuclear family	Both joint and nuclear families exist among them.	Prefers mostly the nuclear family.	Since housing facility is not enough they (parents and married couples) live under the same roof, but cook separately.
Dowry	Depending on the economic status, dowry differs.	Dowry is common.	Demanding dowry is becoming common.
Preference of the size of the family	Prefers to have more than one child. Irrespective of economic status, they want at least one male child.	Prefers to have only one child that too a male child.	Maximum preferences of children are three and at least one to be a male child.
Practice of family planning	Women go for family planning without the consent of men.	Women consult men to undergo family planning with one child.	Both men and women discuss and undergo family planning.
Preference for choosing bridegroom	Employment is the main consideration, but in the past they gave importance to property.	Land holding and property were given more importance at the time of marriage.	Employment is the only consideration.
Practice of foeticide	Quite often.	Very rampant.	Not very common.
Practice of infanticide	Very rampant.	Rarely.	Quite often
Landholding	They have land holdings but less than gounders.	They have more land than other communities.	No landholdings.
Finding match/availability of girls	Due to female infanticide there may by shortage of girls after ten years.	Finding a bride is very difficult. (Impact of infanticide in the past).	The present trend in infanticide may lead to lack of girls in future.
Property sharing	After marriage no share is given to the daughters.	Some share of property to the girl is common. It is usually done after the death of parents.	No share is given to daughters.
Abortion	Abortion is common.	Fortune-tellers facilitating the abortion of female foetus.	Traditional practice of abortion still exists.

Source: Focus Group Discussions carried out by the study team during 2004-05.

Notes

1. The Census of India measures the sex ratio as number of females per 1,000 males as opposed to the standard international norm of number of males per 100 females. Defining the sex ratio by covering children in age group 0–6 may seem arbitrary but the census uses it for the purpose of literacy status, categorizing (from 1991 onwards) the entire population into two groups, those aged 0–6 years and those 7 years and above.
2. For a detailed review of fertility transition in South India, see, Guilmoto and Rajan (2005). Quantitative and qualitative analysis of fertility changes in four southern states that have been made available under the South India Fertility Project (www.demographie.net/sifp).
3. In the era of globalization and increase in consumerism, dowry payment is more a rule than an exception. Many communities in south India where the practice of dowry was totally absent have started making huge payments in recent decades at the time of marriage. In many families, even after the payment of dowry there is continuing uni-directional flow of resources from a woman's parental household to her in-laws. Dowry has emerged as a strategy to acquire higher standards of material life with adverse consequences to women's status, including their survival. For a detailed description of the changing nature of dowry practices in South India, see Srinivasan (2005).
4. However, the first court case and conviction under this Act did not happen until very recently when a doctor and his assistant in the state of Haryana were sentenced to two years in jail (*The Hindu*, Wednesday, March 30, 2006).
5. NFHS, similar to Demographic Health Survey (DHS) in other countries, comprises of a nationally representative sample of about 1,00,000 households, covering ever married women in the age group of 15–49 years. This survey has been conducted since 1992–93. For details on NFHS–1 (IIPS, 1995), NFHS–2 (IIPS and ORC Macro, 2000) and NFHS–3 (IIPS and Macro International, 2007).
6. The Anganwadi centres are nursery schools for children aged 3–6 years, which provide nutritious food under the Integrated Child Development Scheme (ICDS) of the government. Almost every village has Anganwadi centre which also provides a meeting place for pregnant and lactating mothers.

References

Agarwal, Bina (1994). *A Field of One's Own: Gender and Land Rights in South Asia*, Oxford University Press, Delhi.

Agnihotri, S.B. (2000). *Sex Ratio Patterns in the Indian Population: A Fresh Exploration,* Sage Publications, New Delhi.

Arnold, Fred, Sunita Kishor and T.K. Roy (2002). Sex-selective Abortions in India, *Population and Development Review,* 28(4), pp. 759–85.

Basu, Alaka (1992). *Culture, the Status of Women and Demographic Behaviour,* Clarendon Press, Oxford.

Beals, Alan R. (1955). "Interplay among Factors of Change in a Mysore Village", in McKim Marriott (ed.), *Village India: Studies in the Little Community,* The University of Chicago Press, Chicago, pp. 78–101.

Bhat, Mari P.N. (1994). Levels and Trends in Indian Fertility, *Economic and Political Weekly,* XXIX (51–2), pp. 273–80.

—— (2002). On the Trail of 'Missing' Indian Females (I and II), *Economic and Political Weekly,* 37 (51 and 52), pp. 5105–18 and 5244–63.

Bhat, Mari P.N. and Francis Zavier (2003). Fertility Decline and Gender Bias in Northern India, *Demography,* 40(4), pp. 637–57.

Bumiller, E. (1991). *May you be the Mother of a Hundred Sons: A Journey among the Women of India,* Penguin Books, New Delhi.

Caldwell, John, P.H. Reddy and Pat Caldwell (1982). The Causes of Demographic Change in Rural South India: A Micro Approach, *Population and Development Review,* 8(4), pp. 689–727.

Caldwell, J. (1993). "The Asian Fertility Revolution: Its Implications for Transition Theories", in R. Leete and I. Alam (eds.), *The Revolution in Asian Fertility,* Clarendon Press, Oxford, pp. 299–316.

Chunkath, S.R. and V.B. Athreya (1997). Female Infanticide in Tamil Nadu: Some Evidence, *Economic and Political Weekly,* 32(17), WS 21–28.

Clark, Shelley (2000). Son Preference and Sex Composition of Children: Evidence from India, *Demography,* 37(1), pp. 95–108.

Croll, Elisabeth J. (2000). *Endangered Daughters: Discrimination and Development in Asia,* Routledge, NY.

—— (2002). Fertility Decline, Family Size and Female Discrimination: A Study of Reproductive Management in East and South Asia, *Asia-Pacific Population Journal,* 17 (2), pp. 11–38.

Das Gupta, M. (1987). Selective Discrimination against Female Children in Rural Punjab, India, *Population and Development Review,* 13(1), pp. 77–100.

Das Gupta, M. and P.N. Mari Bhat (1997). Fertility Decline and Increased Manifestation of Sex Bias in India, *Population Studies,* 51(3), pp. 307–15.

Epstein, Scarlet T. (1962). *Economic Development and Social Change in South India,* Media Promoters and Publishers, Bombay.

—— (1973). *South India: Yesterday, Today and Tomorrow, Mysore Villages Revisited,* ELBS and Macmillan, London.

—— (1998). "Researcher's View", in S.T. Epstein, A.P. Suryanarayana and T. Thimmegowda (eds.), *Village Voices: Forty Years of Rural Transformation in South India,* Sage Publications, New Delhi, pp. 89–205.

George, Sabu, Rajaratnam Abel and B.D. Miller (1992). Female Infanticide in Rural South India, *Economic and Political Weekly,* XXVII, pp. 1153–56.

Guilmoto, C.Z. and S. Irudaya Rajan (2002). Spatial Patterns of Fertility Transition in Indian Districts, *Population and Development Review,* XXVII (4), pp. 713–38.

—— (eds.), (2005). *Fertility Transition in South India,* Sage Publications, New Delhi.

Hatti, Neelambar, T.V. Sekher and Mattias Larsen (2004). Lives at Risk: Declining Child Sex Ratios in India, *Lund Papers in Economic History,* No. 93, Lund University, Lund, Sweden. (www.ekh.lu.se).

IIPS (1995). *National Family Health Survey 1992–1993, India,* International Institute for Population Sciences, Bombay.

IIPS and ORC Macro (2000). *National Family Health Survey (NFHS–2) India 1998–99,* International Institute for Population Sciences, Mumbai.

IIPS and Macro International (2007). National Family Health Survey (NFHS–3), 2005–06: India, International Institute for Population Sciences, Mumbai.

Jeffery, Patricia and Roger Jeffery (1997). *Population, Gender and Politics: Demographic Change in Rural North India,* Cambridge University Press, Cambridge.

Kabeer, Naila (1996). Gender, Demographic Transitions and the Economics of the Family: Population Policy for a Human-centred Development, Occasional Paper 7, UNRISD.

Krishnamoorthy, S., P.M. Kulkarni and N. Audinarayana (2005). "Causes of Fertility Transition in Tamil Nadu", in C.Z. Guilmoto and S.I. Rajan (eds.), *Fertility Transition in South India,* Sage Publications, New Delhi, pp. 227–47.

Larsen, Mattias, Neelambar Hatti and Pernille Gooch (2005). Uncertainty and Discrimination: Family Structure and Declining Child Sex Ratios in Rural India, *Lund Papers in Economic History,* No. 99, Lund University, Lund, Sweden.

Miller, B.D. (1981). *The Endangered Sex,* Cornell University Press, Ithaca, NY.

—— (1989). Changing Patterns of Juvenile Sex Ratios in Rural India: 1961 to 1971, *Economic and Political Weekly,* 24(22), pp. 1229–35.

Nanda, A.K. and J. Veron (2005). "Child Sex Ratio Imbalance, Fertility Behaviour and Development in India: Recent Evidence from Haryana and Punjab", in I. Attane and J. Veron (eds.), *Gender Discrimination among Young Children in Asia,* French Institute of Pondicherry and CEPED, Pondicherry, pp. 91–131.

Natarajan, D. (1972). *Changes in Sex Ratio,* Census Centenary Monograph, (6), India, Office of the Registrar General, New Delhi.

Retherford, R.D. and T.K. Roy (2003). *Factors affecting Sex-selective Abortion in India and 17 Major States,* National Family Health Survey Series, No. 21, IIPS and Hawaii: East-West Centre, Mumbai.

Sekher, T.V., K.N.M. Raju and M.N. Sivakumar (2001). Fertility Transition in Karnataka: Levels, Trends and Implications, *Economic and Political Weekly,* XXXVI (51), pp. 4742–52.

Sekher, T.V. and K.N.M. Raju (2004). *Fertility Transition in Karnataka,* Monograph (5), Institute for Social and Economic Change, Bangalore.

Sen, A. (1990). More than 100 Million Women are Missing, *New York Review of Books,* 20, pp. 61–66.

Srinivas, M.N. (1976). *The Remembered Village,* Oxford University Press, Delhi.

Srinivasan, Sharada (2005). Daughters or Dowries? The Changing Nature of Dowry Practices in South India, *World Development,* 33(4), pp. 593–615.

Vella, Stephanie (2005). "Low Fertility and Female Discrimination in South India: The Puzzle of Salem District, Tamil Nadu", in C.Z. Guilmoto and S.I. Rajan (eds.), *Fertility Transition in South India,* Sage Publications, New Delhi, pp. 248–81.

Visaria, P. (1971). *The Sex Ratio of the Population of India,,* Monograph (10), Census of India, Office of the Registrar General, New Delhi.

FOUR

Factors Influencing the Use of Prenatal Diagnostic Techniques and the Sex Ratio at Birth in India

P.N. Mari Bhat and A.J. Francis Zavier

The Indian subcontinent is one of the few regions in the world where there are more males than females in the population. Before the landmark study of Pravin Visaria on the sex ratio of India's population, several hypotheses were in vogue to account for this unusual occurrence. Visaria (1971) persuasively argued that excess female mortality is the main reason for this anomaly. But India's sex ratio (males per females) has shown a more or less steady increase since 1901, even though the data from the sample registration system suggest narrowing of the sex differentials in mortality in recent years. The latest census in 2001 has recorded a significant increase in the sex ratio of children age 0–6 while registering a decline in the overall male-female ratio from the previous census in 1991. Many attribute the increase in the child sex ratio to a possible rise in the sex ratio at birth (SRB) owing to the increasing incidence of sex-selective abortions in regions where son preference remains strong (e.g., Das Gupta and Bhat 1997; Sudha and Rajan 1999; Arnold et al., 2002). But it has also been pointed out that there could be other factors at work such as changing pattern of age misreportings by sex, and increase in the SRB because of improvements in health status and midwifery practices and from the decline in the proportion of higher-order births (Bhat, 2002).

Although it is well established that under normal circumstances, more males than females are born among all human populations, the SRB cannot be regarded as a universal constant. But often the observed variations are due to smallness of the sample of births from which the ratio is calculated or incomplete coverage of births of particular sex. From an analysis of data for countries with relatively complete registration, Visaria (1971) concluded that the SRB varies generally between 103 and 106. There is also some evidence of secular trends in the SRB, predating the invention of modern technologies of sex selection. Some western countries with reliable and long-standing registration data, such as Sweden and England, have recorded increase in the SRB of the order of 2–3 per cent over a period of one or two centuries (Klasen, 1994). The data for British India complied by Visaria (1971) from the civil registration system showed that male-female ratio at birth increased from 107 in 1901–10 to 110 in 1940–46. The decline was seen in all the major provinces of British India except Bombay and Assam. However, Visaria was of the view that the observed trend was a spurious result of deterioration in the completeness of the registration system in British India. But fairly complete vital registration data available for four districts of Maharashtra (known as Berar during British rule) also showed a similar upward trend in the SRB during the first half of the 20th century (Dyson, 1989; Bhat, 2002).

The spatial and temporal variations in the SRB arise from social, demographic and biological factors affecting the SRB. Literature on the issue is replete with many speculations regarding the factors affecting the SRB. While a large number of factors are considered to be important, there are only a few studies that analyzed the relationship in the multivariate context (Teitelbaum, 1972; Chahnazarian, 1988). One of the main reasons for the paucity of such studies is because, national vital statistic systems, which provide data on large sample of births required for such an analysis, have information only for limited set of associated factors. The data from India's National Family Health Surveys (NFHS) provide an opportunity to analyze the effect of a larger set of factors from a fairly sizeable sample of births using multivariate techniques. Also, as the second round of the survey (NFHS–2) had collected data on the use of ultrasound and amniocentesis during pregnancies of live births born during the three-year period preceding the survey, they additionally make it possible to analyze how socio-economic and demographic factors affect the SRB through the 'misuse' of such techniques. Although some attempts have already been made to analyze this data set for this purpose (Arnold et al., 2002; Retherford and Roy, 2003), its potential is yet to be fully exploited. An attempt in this direction is made in this paper. We also take advantage of recently released data from the 2001 Census on fertility and age-sex distribution of the population in single years to study the influence of some key factors on the SRB in India.

Evidence from Census of 2001

Information on the sex ratio of children of age 0–6 years was one of the first data to be released from the 2001 Census. It caused widespread anguish as it showed significant fall in the proportion of females in this age group, indicating dramatic increase in the incidence of pre-birth elimination of females (Registrar General, India, 2003). But data on child sex ratios are also affected by sex differentials in child mortality, under-enumeration and age misreporting (Bhat, 2002). Recently, census data on population by single years of age have been released. This information can provide further clues to the nature of changes in the child sex ratio and its causes. In analyzing this information, before computing sex ratios, we applied a three-point moving average formula to smooth the single-year age data. In Figure 1, for all-India and the state of Punjab, we have plotted the difference in the sex ratio (males per 100 females) at the same single-year of age between 1991 and 1981, and between 2001 and 1981. However, instead of age, the graph shows the year of birth of children implied by their reported age in the census. For both Punjab and India, the increase in the sex ratio is more pronounced for more recently born children (i.e., at younger ages). As per the 1991 Census, the sex ratio steadily increased between 1985 and 1990 by 3 percentage points for India as a whole, and by 9 percentage points for Punjab. As per the 2001 Census, the sex ratio steadily increased between 1995 and 2000 by another 3 percentage points at the all-India level, and by another 11 percentage points in Punjab.

The pattern of change observed in the census data discounts the possibility of this change arising from a rise in excess female child mortality in recent times. If it were the cause, owing to the

Figure 1

Increase in child sex ratios between 1981 and 1991 and between 1981 and 2001 by single year of age, for India and Punjab

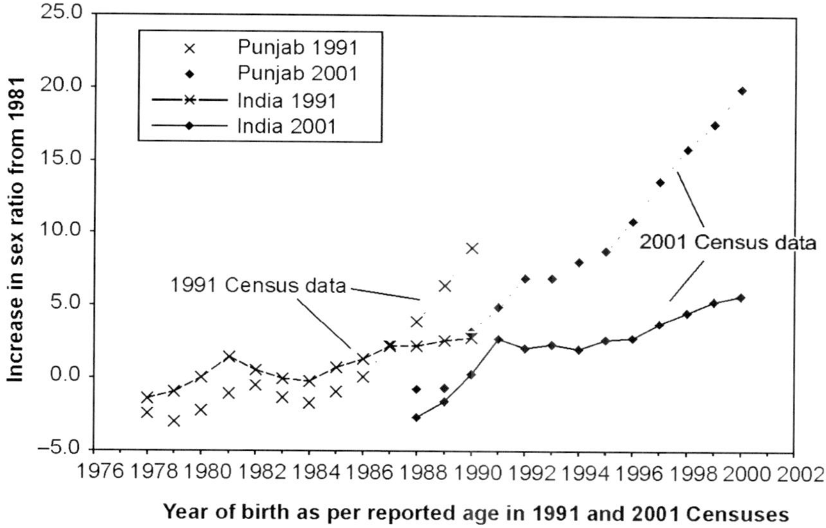

Source: Census of India, 1981, 1991 and 2001.

cumulated impact of the mortality differential, sex ratios at ages three-four years would have shown greater change than at ages one-two years. The systematic age (or time) pattern in the sex ratio increase raises doubts whether it could be explained by more accurate reporting of children's age. However, the role of age misreporting in distorting the trend in sex ratios cannot be completely ruled out since for the overlapping period of 1988–90, the rise in the sex ratios indicated by the censuses of 1991 and 2001 is not identical—while the former census indicates significant increase, the latter indicates no change or a even a decline (in comparison to the sex ratios of 1981 Census at corresponding ages).

To a large extent, the systematic rise in the sex ratio in the years preceding the census must have been due to the rising trend in the SRB. If it were the only cause, the implication is that between 1985 and 2000 the sex ratio at birth increased by 6 percentage points at the all-India level, and by as much as 20 percentage points in Punjab. Table 1 shows the sex ratio for the age group 0–2 years from the censuses of 1981, 1991 and 2001 for the states of India. Between

Table 1

Sex ratio for the age group 0–2 years in 1981, 1991 and 2001 censuses

State	Sex ratio, 0–2 age group			Change
	1981	1991	2001	1981–2001
All-India	102.7	105.4	108.3	5.6*
North-West				
Jammu & Kashmir	104.2	N.A.	109.0	4.8*
Himachal Pradesh	103.2	107.1	113.9	10.7*
Punjab	107.3	116.2	127.2	20.0*
Haryana	107.8	114.7	124.2	16.3*
Delhi	106.1	109.1	116.5	10.4*
North-Central				
Rajasthan	103.0	108.1	111.4	8.4*
Uttar Pradesh	103.1	105.9	108.8	5.6*
Bihar	100.5	103.5	105.3	4.8*
Madhya Pradesh	101.5	103.6	106.1	4.6*
East				
Assam	N.A.	103.4	103.8	0.4
North-east**	101.6	101.8	103.3	1.7
West Bengal	101.9	103.4	104.3	2.5
Orissa	101.0	103.3	105.8	4.8
West				
Gujarat	104.6	107.4	114.3	9.7*
Maharashtra	105.1	107.0	111.3	6.2*
Goa	104.5	103.7	108.1	3.6
South				
Andhra Pradesh	100.5	102.5	103.6	3.2
Karnataka	102.3	104.4	106.0	3.7*
Kerala	102.7	104.8	104.1	1.4
Tamil Nadu	102.9	105.2	106.0	3.1

Note: N.A.: Not available.

*Linear change with age statistically significant.

**Arunachal Pradesh, Manipur, Meghalaya, Mizoram, Nagaland, Sikkim and Tripura.

Source: Census of India, 1981, 1991 and 2001.

1981 and 2001 the sex ratio in this age group has increased in all the states. The increase is particularly large in states in north and western India. To check whether the 2001 Census implies a steady increase in the sex ratio in the years before the census, the single-year sex ratios for the period 1995–2000 (i.e., for ages one to five) were regressed on time (or age). In all states, in north and western India, except Goa, the observed rise in the sex ratio during this period was statistically significant. But, in the states in southern and eastern parts of India, except Karnataka, the recorded rise during this period was not statistically significant. Thus, in at least north and western parts of India, there have been sharp increases in the SRB.

The data on fertility from the 2001 Census provide more direct information on the SRB. They also make it possible to study factors influencing the SRB in greater detail as they have been cross-tabulated by more variables than the child sex ratios. Two types of data on fertility were collected in the census of 2001: (i) live births during the one-year period preceding the census for all currently married women (i.e., current fertility), and (ii) number of children ever born for all ever-married women (i.e., lifetime fertility). In both cases, data have been collected on the sex of the child. These data have been tabulated by mother's age, religion, and educational level for rural and urban areas of all states. Table 2 shows the SRB by mother's background characteristics for the entire country.

In all, nearly 20 million live births were reported during the year preceding the census. They imply an SRB of 110 males for 100 females. This sex ratio is higher than the sex ratio of 108 for children of age 0–6 years at the time of the census. As child mortality is higher for girls than boys in India, the child sex ratio should have been higher than the SRB. The discrepancy could be indicating either a rise in the SRB during the years preceding the census, or underreporting of female births that occurred during the year preceding the census, or greater exaggeration of age for boys than girls in the census. The foregoing analysis of child sex ratios by single year of age strongly supports the first possibility.

The census data on children ever born show a steady rise in the SRB from 105 for women aged 15–19 to 113 for women aged 45–49 in 2001. This is probably due to the failure of older women to report female children who died many years ago or who are married and living with their husbands. To minimize the effect of such recall

Table 2

India: Child sex ratio and sex ratio at birth by selected background characteristics in 2001 Census

Background characteristics	*Sex ratio of children of age 0–6 years*	*Sex ratio at birth*	
		Births during the preceding year	*Children ever born to women aged 20–34*
All	107.8	110.4	106.7
Residence			
Rural	107.1	110.4	106.3
Urban	110.3	110.6	108.3
Religion			
Hindu	108.2	110.9	106.9
Muslim	105.3	107.4	105.3
Christian	103.7	103.8	103.0
Sikh	127.3	129.8	119.1
Buddhist	106.2	108.4	105.2
Jain	115.0	118.0	110.5
Other religious communities	102.5	106.5	102.3
Caste/Tribe			
Scheduled tribe	102.8	106.4	103.1
Scheduled caste	106.6	108.6	105.8
Others	108.8	111.5	107.4
Mother's age			
< 15	N.A.	105.9	N.A.
15–19	N.A.	108.2	N.A.
20–24	N.A.	111.4	N.A.
25–29	N.A.	113.2	N.A.
30–34	N.A.	112.1	N.A.
35–39	N.A.	109.1	N.A.
40–44	N.A.	103.7	N.A.
45–49	N.A.	99.7	N.A.
50+	N.A.	75.7	N.A.
Mother's educational level			
Illiterate	N.A.	108.7	106.0
Literate but below primary	N.A.	110.0	106.3

Cont'd...

Cont'd...

Primary but below middle	N.A.	111.8	107.1
Middle but below matric or secondary	N.A.	113.0	107.5
Matric or secondary but below graduate	N.A.	115.3	109.4
Graduate and above	N.A.	114.1	109.7
Total births/children (in thousands)	1,63,820	19,887	2,37,622

N.A.: Not available/applicable.

Source: Census of India, 2001.

errors, Table 2 shows the SRB implied by the data on children ever born to women aged 20–34 years. In all, these women reported 238 million live births in their lifetime, with an SRB of 107. As these children were born on average 5–10 years before the survey, they would be indicating an SRB lower than that for the year preceding the census if the SRB has been rising.

Interestingly, the data on births for the year preceding the census show negligible rural-urban difference in the SRB, whereas data on children ever born shows, as expected, higher SRB in urban areas (108) than in rural areas (106). This may be indicating either that the rural-urban difference has disappeared in more recent years or that rural women have underreported more female births that occurred during the last year than urban women. But, the analysis of child sex ratios by single year of age did not indicate a convergence of sex ratios in rural and urban areas. For example, the child sex ratio for the age group 0–2 years in 2001 was 111 in urban areas compared with 108 in rural areas. The analysis of the increase in child sex ratios since 1981 by single year of age (similar to the one shown in Figure 1) showed that the SRB may have increased by 8 percentage points in urban areas compared with 5 percentage points in rural areas. It is therefore likely that in the census data on current fertility, the underreporting of female births was more in rural areas than in urban areas.

However, data on current as well as lifetime fertility show that the SRB increases with the mother's educational level. The data on births for the year preceding the census show that the SRB increases from 109 for illiterate women to 115 for women who have completed matriculation. But those graduated from college have reported an SRB of 114. The data on children ever born show that the SRB increases steadily from 106 for illiterate women to 110 for women with a college degree.

Religion is another variable that shows a systematic relationship with the SRB. As per both types of data, the SRB is 103–104 for Christians, depicting a little practice of sex-selective abortions. But, the SRB is much higher than the normal range among Sikhs and Jains. As per the data on births in the year preceding the census, it is 129 for Sikhs and 118 for Jains while as per the data on children ever born it is 119 and 111, respectively. Hindus, the main community, have an SRB of 111 and 107 respectively, as per the two types of data. The data on scheduled tribes (STs) indicate no evidence of sex-selective abortions (sex ratio being 106 and 103, respectively). As per both types of data, the SRB for SCs is 2 percentage points higher than that for STs.

The data on births for the year preceding the census have been tabulated by the mother's age at the time of the census. As in this case the time lapsed since the birth is less than a year, the mother's age is essentially her age at the time of birth. The SRB calculated from these data shows a curvilinear relationship with her age. It increases from 106 for mothers aged less than 15 to 113 for mothers aged 20–29 and then decreases steadily to 75 for mothers aged more than 50 years. Many studies have reported such a curvilinear relationship (e.g., James, 1987; Chahnazarian, 1988), which could be due to the relationship of maternal age with stillbirth rate and coital frequency. Such a pattern may be accentuated in a situation where sex-selective abortion is practised because this practice packs around the third birth order.

Table 3 shows the SRB computed from the two types of census fertility data for the states of India. None of the states in the southern and eastern parts of India show any evidence of sex-selective abortions, as the computed SRB from both types of data are well within the normal range. In these states, births occurred even to women who completed matriculation show no evidence of female foeticide. But there is a strong evidence of sex-selective abortions in northern and western parts of the country, especially in the states of Punjab, Haryana and Gujarat. For the year preceding the census, the SRB is 127 for Punjab and Haryana and 120 for Gujarat. The SRB computed from the data on children ever born to women

Table 3

Sex ratio at birth by residence and mother's educational level, 2001 Census

Region & State	From data on births during the year preceding the census					From data on children-ever born to women age 20-34 years				
				Mother's education					Mother's education	
	All areas	Rural	Urban	Illiterate	Matriculation or higher	All areas	Rural	Urban	Illiterate	Matriculation or higher
All-India	110	110	111	109	115	107	106	108	106	109
North-West										
J&K	105	105	103	102	114	109	108	113	107	116
Himachal Pradesh	118	119	117	112	127	109	109	114	105	115
Punjab	127	127	126	118	139	118	118	119	114	125
Haryana	127	127	127	120	141	116	115	117	113	122
Delhi	117	121	117	110	125	112	114	112	109	116
North-Central										
Rajasthan	116	115	119	113	124	109	108	111	108	113
Uttaranchal	117	117	117	114	124	107	106	110	105	112
Uttar Pradesh	111	111	109	110	119	107	107	110	107	111
Bihar	109	109	109	107	118	107	107	109	107	110
Jharkhand	110	110	114	109	116	104	104	107	104	107

Cont'd...

Cont'd…

Chattisgarh	108	107	109	107	112	102	102	104	101	107
Madhya Pradesh	111	110	113	109	116	106	106	109	105	109
East										
Assam	106	106	102	105	106	104	104	106	104	104
North-East	103	103	101	102	101	102	103	102	103	103
West Bengal	103	103	99	102	102	104	104	105	104	104
Orissa	108	108	105	106	111	104	103	105	103	105
West										
Gujarat	120	118	125	114	134	112	110	115	109	119
Maharashtra	114	115	112	110	118	108	107	108	106	111
Goa	109	106	112	105	109	105	104	106	105	105
South										
Andhra Pradesh	105	106	103	105	106	104	104	104	104	104
Karnataka	103	103	104	102	104	105	105	105	105	105
Kerala	103	103	104	102	104	104	104	104	105	104
Tamil Nadu	107	109	104	108	106	105	105	104	106	104

Source: Census of India, 2001.

aged 20–34 is 118 for Punjab, 116 for Haryana and 112 for Gujarat. In all the states of northern and western India (except Goa), the SRB reported by women who had passed matriculation is higher than 106. In Punjab and Haryana, the SRB for this group of women is as high as 139–141 as per the data on births during last year, and 122–125 as per the data on children ever born.

The existence of strong regional pattern in the SRB becomes even more evident when it is mapped for the districts of India. Figure 2 shows a map drawn using the data on lifetime births for women aged 20–34, while Figure 3 shows the map drawn using the data on births during the year before the census. As the former map is based on more number of births per district, it may be more reliable than

Figure 2

District-wise sex ratio at birth among children ever born to women aged 20-34 years in 2001 Census

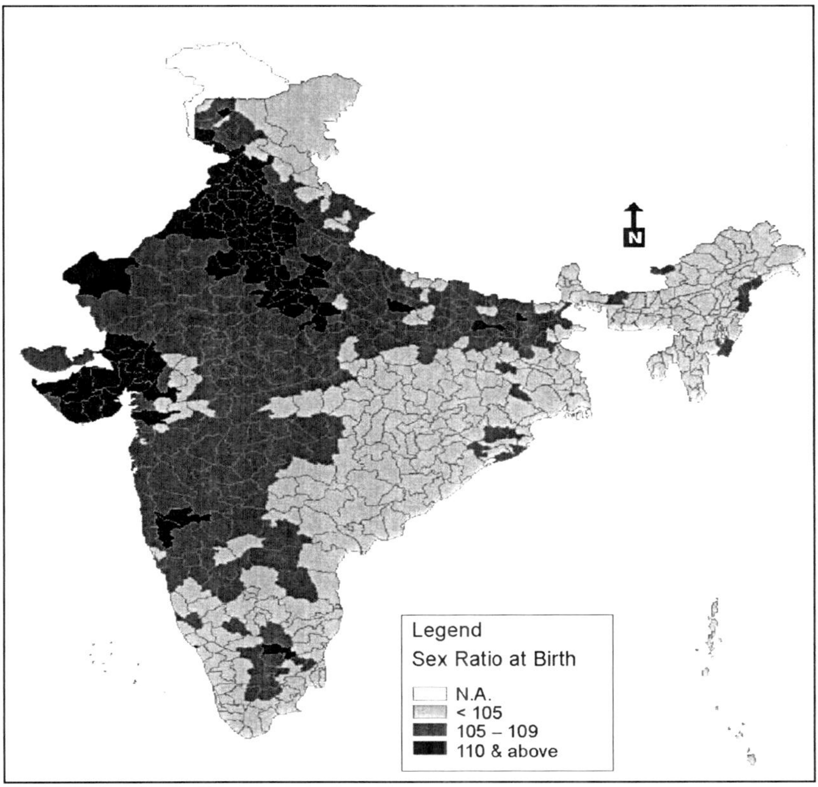

Figure 3

District-wise sex ratio at birth among those born during the year preceding 2001 Census

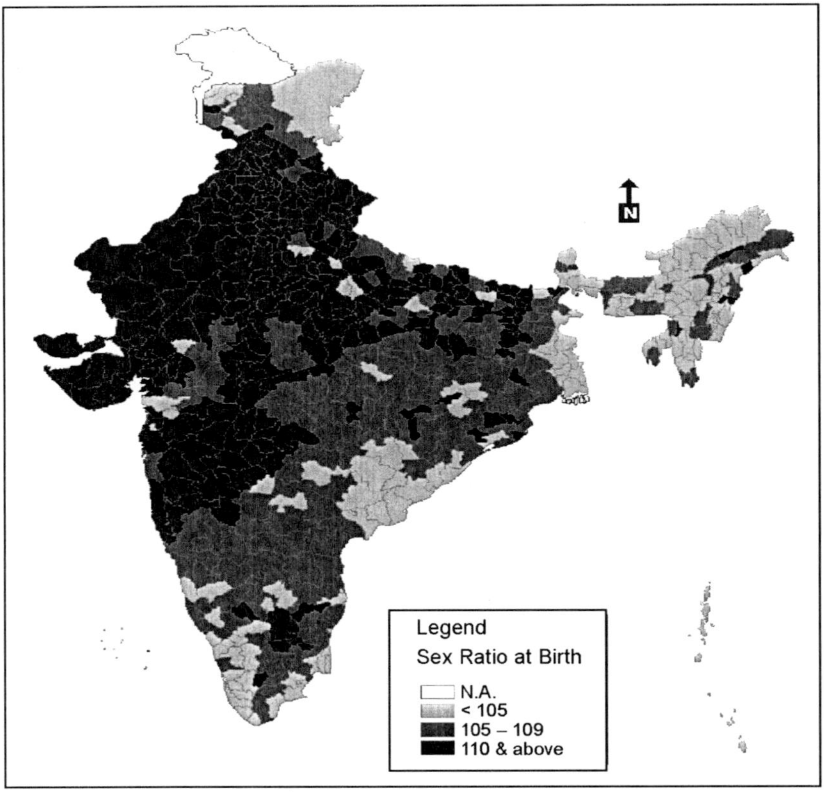

the latter but refers to an earlier period than the map in Figure 3. In Figure 2, a line drawn diagonally separating south and eastern India from north and western India would neatly demark the two regions of low and high SRB. Except for some isolated pockets (such as around Salem district in Tamil Nadu), the SRB was less than 105 in east and south India. In much of north and western India, the SRB was more than 105, and was in excess of 110 in Punjab, Haryana and Gujarat. The map drawn using the data on births during the year preceding the census (Figure 3) shows that the region with the SRB in excess of 110 has expanded considerably to cover virtually the entire area above the diagonal line that had SRB higher than 105. Also, the area with SRB less than 105 has shrunk considerably in south India, as many districts in Karnataka, Andhra Pradesh and Tamil Nadu have crossed the threshold. But north-east India has remained relatively untouched by this change.

Evidence from National Family Health Surveys

The NFHS conducted in 1992–93 (NFHS–1) and 1998–99 (NFHS–2) were designed on the lines of Demographic and Health Surveys (DHS) carried out in many developing countries with the financial assistance of USAID. They provide valuable information on birth histories of women, their background characteristics, including antenatal and delivery care during the pregnancy of most recently born children (during the four-year period preceding the survey in NFHS–1 and three-year period preceding the survey in NFHS–2). From NFHS–2, data on anthropometrical indicators and anaemia for all women, and the use of ultrasound and amniocentesis during the pregnancy of the recently born children, are also available. As the micro data from the surveys are available in electronic form, they provide greater scope than the census data for the analysis of determinants of the SRB as well as the use of prenatal diagnostic techniques (PNDT). But, as the data on number of births available from the NFHS are relatively small compared to that from the census, the results tend to be more suggestive than confirmatory.

Use and Misuse of Prenatal Diagnostic Techniques

A factor that has recently emerged and has a strong influence on the SRB is the use of sex determination tests during pregnancy followed by abortion of foetuses of the unwanted sex. Although conducting abortions became legal in India in 1971, it is only recently that prenatal diagnostic techniques became widely available. Because of its relative rarity, information on the use of these techniques was not collected in NFHS–1. But, in NFHS–2, this information was collected from the mothers who gave birth during the three-year period before the survey. In this survey, the use of PNDT (mainly ultrasound) was reported by mothers in 13 per cent of 32,000 live births that occurred during the three-year period before the survey. The SRB in the reported cases of PNDT was 112 compared with 107 among live births to women who did not report the use of PNDT. Clearly, in a significant percentage of cases, PNDT was misused to abort female foetuses, since if sex-selective abortions were not practised, the SRB would have been close to 105. Even the reported SRB for non-PNDT cases is relatively high indicating that some women may not have disclosed its use.

From the survey data, it is possible to arrive at rough estimates of the misuse of PNDT for sex selection as well as the true extent of its use. To do this, we assume that abortion after PNDT is done only when the foetus is detected to be female. Although some couples may abort male foetuses when all previous births are male, we shall later show that this tendency is pretty weak in India. Also, male foetuses may get aborted because of wrong diagnosis; we shall assume that such failures of PNDT are rare.

Let M_U and F_U be the number of male and female live births to reported users of PNDT during the pregnancy of these births. Also, let M_N and F_N be the number of male and female live births to reported non-users of PNDT. Let S be the ratio of male-to-female live births when no sex-selective abortion is practised. Using these notations, the SRB among reported users of PNDT can be written as:

$$S_U = \frac{M_U}{F_U}$$

Similarly, the SRB among reported non-users of PNDT can be written as:

$$S_N = \frac{M_N}{F_N}$$

If it is assumed that only female foetuses are aborted after PNDT, the number of abortion of female foetuses after PNDT can be computed as:

$$A_U = \frac{M_U}{S} - F_U = \left(\frac{1-1}{S\ S_U}\right) M_U$$

It may be noted that for A_U to be positive, $S_U > S$. If it is not the case, it will be assumed that $A_U = 0$

We define the index of the misuse of PNDT as the proportion of female foetuses aborted after the use of PNDT. If all women correctly reported the use of PNDT, then this index is given by:

$$\frac{A_U + A_U}{F_U + A_U} = 1 - F_U \frac{S}{M_U} = 1 - \frac{S}{S_U}$$

However, not all users may disclose the use of PNDT. This is indicated by S_N being significantly higher than S. The number of abortion of female foetuses done by reported non-users of PNDT can be computed as:

$$A_N = \frac{M_N}{S} - F_N = M_N \left\{ \frac{1}{S} - \frac{1}{S_N} \right\}$$

As before, for A_N to be positive $S_N > S$. If it is not the case, it will be assumed that $A_N = 0$

Thus, the adjusted proportion of female foetuses aborted after PNDT can be computed as:

$$\frac{A_U + A_N}{F_U + A_U + A_N}$$

We can also estimate the proportion of foetuses subjected to PNDT as:

$$\frac{M_U + F_U + A_U + A_N}{M_U + F_U + M_N + F_N + A_U + A_N}$$

In making actual computations, there is the practical problem of assuming a value for S, the SRB in the absence of sex-selective abortions. Although it is thought to be close to 105 males for 100 females, as the census data reviewed earlier show, it could be as low as 103 in India. In order to study the sensitivity of the estimates to the assumed value of S, Table 4 shows estimates of the misuse of PNDT and corrected estimates of PNDT use obtained from the NFHS data using the values of S ranging from 103 to 106. As can be

Table 4

Effect of assumed value of normal sex ratio at birth on estimates of use and misuse of prenatal diagnostic techniques

Assumed normal sex ratio at birth	*Estimated percent of female foetuses aborted after PNDT*		*Adjusted per cent of births subjected to PNDT*
	Est. 1	*Est. 2*	
103	7.9	26.6	14.7
104	7.0	22.0	14.3
105	6.1	16.9	13.9
106	5.2	11.3	13.5

Source: NFHS–2 micro data.

seen from the table, the corrected estimate of PNDT use for all-India is not sensitive to the assumed value of the sex ratio. It varies from 13.5 per cent to 14.7 per cent (against the uncorrected value of 12.8%) when the normal SRB is varied from 106 to 103. The estimate of misuse of the technology by those who reported the use of PNDT is also not very sensitive to the assumption on the normal SRB. It varies from 5 to 8 per cent when the normal SRB is varied from 106 to 103. However, if the observed higher SRB (107) among those who did not report the PNDT use is because of undisclosed use, the estimated misuse of the technology increases from 11 to 27 per cent when the normal SRB is varied from 106 to 103. Nonetheless, these results amply show that majority of the users of PNDT in India do not misuse it to abort female foetuses.

It is useful to investigate whether the use of PNDT and its misuse vary according to background characteristics of women. Table 5 presents information on them. The estimates presented in this table are computed assuming a normal SRB of 105. For India, as whole, the SRB of 112 among those who used PNDT indicates that 6 per cent of female foetuses were aborted after PNDT. But, if it is assumed that some of those who did not use PNDT may have actually used it, the estimated percentage of female foetuses aborted rises to 17 per cent, and the adjusted use of PNDT is 14 per cent instead of 13 per cent. Those who did not avail antenatal care (ANC) services clearly could not have used PNDT and resorted to female foeticide. Their SRB of 102 also testifies to this. But, the SRB among those who availed ANC from a doctor is 112. Twenty-five per cent of them had reported PNDT, which rises to 27 per cent if adjustment is made for the suspected non-disclosure of its use. If the normal sex ratio is 105, the SRB of 111 among PNDT users indicates that 6 per cent of the users may have used the technology to abort female foetuses. But this estimate rises to 23 per cent if an adjustment is made for the possibility that some of the reported non-users of PNDT users did not disclose its use (since the SRB among this group is 113). Among women who availed PNDT from providers other than the doctor, 5 per cent had reported the use of PNDT, and it is estimated that 24 per cent of them had misused it. In this group, among those who did not report the use of PNDT, the SRB is 104, indicating no misreporting of the PNDT status.

Table 5

Reported and adjusted use of prenatal diagnostic technologies and estimated percentage of females foetuses aborted after the use of these technologies by selected background characteristics: NFHS-2, 1998-99

Variables	*Total births in the sample*	*Per cent of births subjected to PNDT*		*Sex ratio at birth*			*Per cent of female foetuses aborted after PNDT*	
		Reported	*Adjusted*	*All births*	*PNDT not reported*	*PNDT reported*	*Est. 1*	*Est. 2*
Total	32,228	12.8	13.9	107.7	107.1	111.8	6.1	16.9
ANC status at pregnancy								
No ANC	10,987	0.0	0.0	102.4	102.4	0.0	0.0	0.0
ANC by doctor	15,745	24.5	27.0	112.6	113.1	111.1	5.5	22.8
ANC by others	5,395	5.0	5.3	104.7	104.0	119.5	12.1	12.1
Residence								
Rural	25,064	7.7	8.8	107.6	107.4	109.8	4.4	24.4
Urban	7,164	30.8	31.8	108.1	105.7	113.6	7.5	8.9
Region								
East	4,421	5.0	8.7	114.2	114.6	106.5	1.4	62.8
South	6,132	27.9	27.9	102.0	102.7	100.2	0.0	0.0
West	4,421	26.0	27.3	108.8	107.1	113.9	7.8	12.6
North-west	2,047	17.2	22.0	119.2	114.6	144.4	27.3	46.7
North-central	15,211	4.6	5.2	106.4	105.5	126.4	16.9	24.3

Cont'd…

Cont'd...

Birth order								
1	9,299	20.8	21.8	106.9	108.3	101.8	0.0	10.3
2	8,333	15.5	16.9	108.9	108.8	109.3	3.9	19.4
3	5,708	9.3	10.5	108.0	106.3	126.1	16.7	25.2
4+	8,892	4.3	5.3	107.3	105.3	166.9	37.1	40.0
Sex composition of sibling								
All sisters, no brother	7,874	13.9	18.9	119.1	116.2	138.7	24.3	51.2
All brothers, no sister	7,176	11.7	11.7	100.5	100.3	102.2	0.0	0.0
Other combinations	17,182	12.8	13.2	105.9	106.2	104.0	0.0	7.2
Religion								
Hindus	25,534	12.2	13.5	108.3	107.4	114.7	8.5	21.1
Muslims	5,042	12.0	12.0	101.4	101.8	98.0	0.0	0.0
Others	1,570	26.1	28.3	111.9	112.5	110.2	4.8	19.9
Caste								
Scheduled caste/tribe	9,491	6.3	7.8	108.7	108.8	107.7	2.5	35.8
Other backward caste	10,358	14.0	14.1	105.4	105.3	106.6	1.5	2.9
Others	12,000	17.4	19.2	110.0	108.7	116.5	9.9	22.0
Parents' educational level								
Both parents illiterate	8,922	2.7	2.8	105.1	105.3	96.7	0.0	10.2
Only father literate	9,890	5.3	5.7	104.3	103.4	121.5	13.6	13.6

Cont'd...

Cont'd...

Mother less than middle	5,821	14.2	14.2	103.2	103.3	102.5	0.0	0.0
Mother middle or more	7,510	33.8	37.6	119.0	121.4	114.2	8.1	27.8
Standard of living								
Low SLI	11,638	3.8	4.5	105.9	106.5	93.9	0.0	24.6
Medium SLI	15,068	11.8	12.2	106.1	106.0	107.4	2.2	8.4
High SLI	5,125	35.8	38.8	116.2	114.2	120.0	12.5	23.3
Mother's media exposure								
No exposure	15,314	2.7	2.9	105.2	104.9	115.9	9.4	9.4
Regular exposure	16,885	22.0	23.7	110.0	109.7	111.3	5.7	18.0
Mother's work status								
Not working	22,282	14.9	16.7	109.8	108.6	116.3	9.7	23.9
Working, not for wage	5,135	9.1	9.1	104.1	104.7	97.9	0.0	0.0
Working for wage	4,804	7.4	7.4	102.4	103.2	91.9	0.0	0.0
Mother's ideal family size								
1-2	15,480	21.5	24.4	113.8	114.3	112.1	6.4	28.0
3	8,675	5.8	7.7	109.5	108.8	120.7	13.0	43.8
4+ or non-numeric	8,073	3.9	3.9	95.1	95.1	96.2	0.0	0.0

Source: NFHS-2 micro data.

In urban areas, 31 per cent of live births were reportedly subjected to PNDT compared with only 8 per cent in rural areas. On the assumption that reported PNDT use is correct, 8 per cent of those who used PNDT misused it in urban areas while 4 per cent did so in rural areas. But, the sex ratio of those who did not report the use of PNDT shows that 32 per cent in urban areas and 9 per cent in rural areas may actually have used it and among them 9 per cent in urban areas and 24 per cent in rural areas may have misused it. Thus, the use of PNDT is certainly much higher in urban areas than in rural areas, but it is not altogether clear as to where the misuse is higher.

The use of PNDT is relatively higher in south and western regions of India where the reported use is 27–28 per cent. The

Figure 4

Reported use of prenatal diagnostic techniques in 77 natural regions of India: NFHS-2, 1998-99

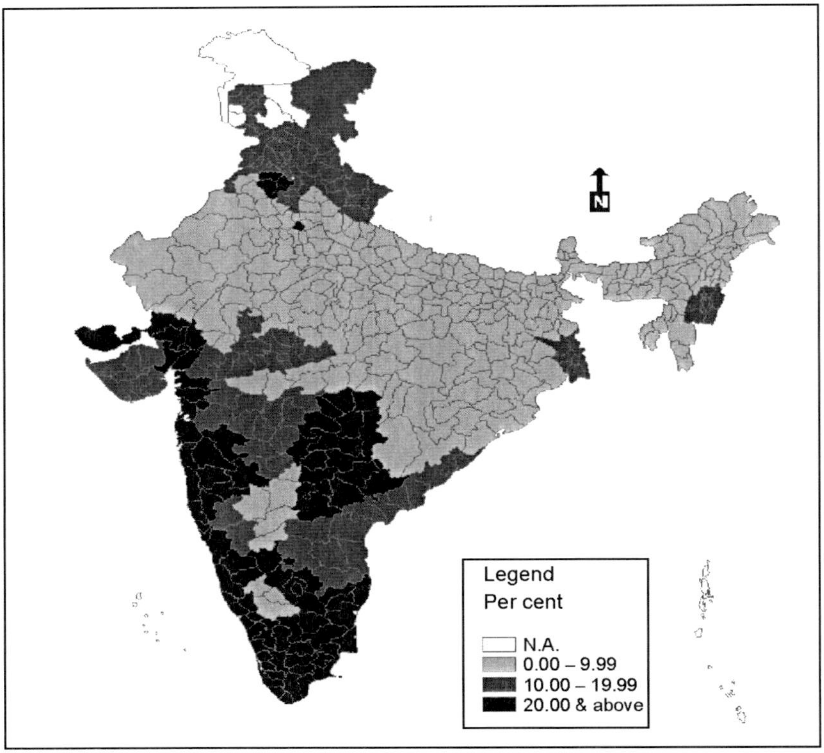

Source: NFHS-2 micro data.

reported use is less than 5 per cent in east and north-central regions of the country. In north-western parts, where the child sex ratios are high, the reported use is clearly seen in Figure 4 where we have mapped the use rate for 77 for natural regions of the country. One reason for the relatively higher use of PNDT in south and western parts of the country could be the maximum use of ANC services, especially from a doctor. However, as the Figure 5 shows, even when only cases with ANC by a doctor are considered, the regional pattern in the use of PNDT does not disappear. Reported use of ultrasound or amniocentesis is rare in east and north-central India, even when ANC is availed from a doctor.

Figure 5

Reported use of prenatal diagnostic techniques when doctor is the ANC provider in 77 natural regions of India: NFHS–2, 1998–99

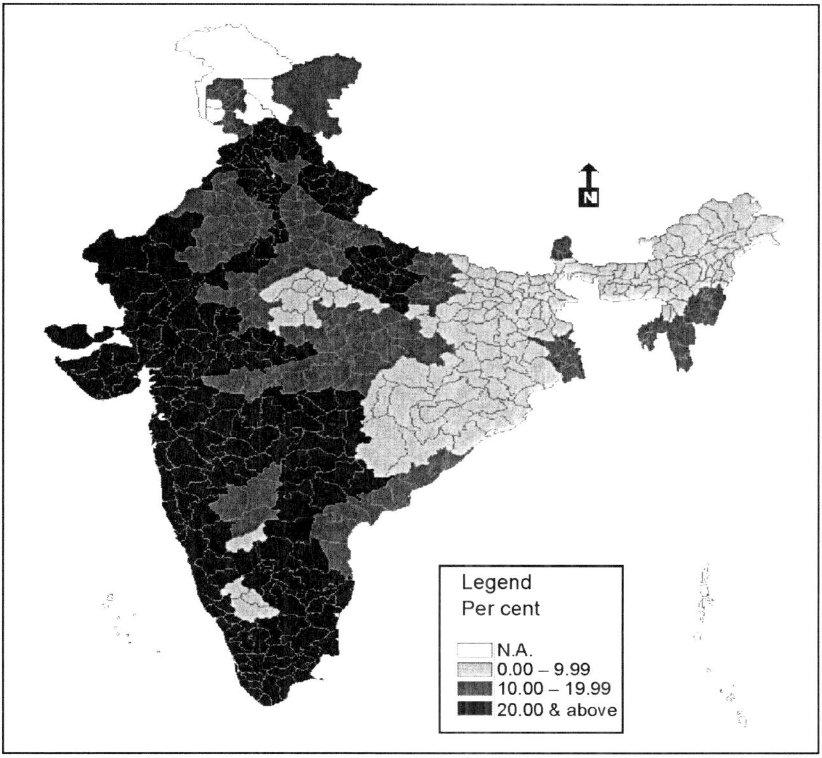

Source: NFHS-2 micro data.

Although south India shows the highest rate of PNDT use, its misuse is rare; as a consequence, the SRB is less than 105 in this region among both users and non-users (see Table 5). In the north-central region, though the use of PNDT is not often, misuse among those who use it is high (17–24%). But it is in the north-western region, where the misuse of PNDT is most frequent (27–47%). For north-western India, when the reported use is adjusted for its possible underreporting, the implied use rate increases from 17 per cent to 22 per cent. In other regions, the implied corrections for underreporting are small. Although east India shows the highest percentage of misuse if the high SRB for non-users is taken into account, it is most probably due to sampling errors in the data than the actual misreporting of PNDT status.

The reported use of PNDT declines as the order of birth increases. But, the misuse of the technology increases with the birth order. The reported use is 21 per cent for the first birth order but the estimated misuse, at the maximum, is only 10 per cent. On the other hand, when the birth order is four or more, only 4 per cent report the use of PNDT but nearly 40 per cent resort to abortion if the foetus is female. Thus, in the case of first birth, the predominant reason for the use of PNDT is to detect abnormalities of the foetus, while at higher orders the main reason for the use is to detect the sex of the child. The reported use of PNDT does not show significant variations with sex composition of previous children born to a woman. But, the misuse of the technology is highest when the woman had no son, but had one or more daughters. Among such women, the misuse is estimated to be 24–51 per cent. When women had no daughter but had one or more sons, the SRB is 101, and 102 for women reporting PNDT use. While this may be suggesting abortion of male foetuses by such women, the difference from the normal sex ratio can also be due to sampling errors. On the other hand, the SRB for women who had no sons but had two or more daughters is substantially high to be attributed to sampling errors (119 for all births and 139 for births with reported use of PNDT).

The reported use of PNDT is 12 per cent among Hindus and Muslims, and 26 per cent among other religions (mainly Christians and Sikhs). While those who misuse the technology are negligible among Muslims, it is 8–21 per cent among Hindus and 5–20 per cent among other religions. As would be expected, the reported use of PNDT increases from 6 per cent among SCs/STs to 14 per cent among other backward classes (OBCs) and 17 per cent among others. But, the misuse of the technology is least among OBCs (2–3%) while it is relatively high among other castes (10–22%).

The use of the technology increases with the level of education of parents. When both the mother and father are illiterate, only 2 per cent use PNDT. When only the father is literate, this increases to 5 per cent. When the mother has completed high school or gone to college, the reported use comes to 42 per cent. The misuse however does not show a consistent relationship with education. It is low when both the mother and father are illiterate (0–10%), but relatively high when the father is literate but the mother is not (14%) and when the mother has completed high school or gone to college (9–28%). Interestingly, misuse is almost negligible among mothers who are literate but have not completed middle school. To study the relationship of use and misuse of PNDT with the prosperity of households, we used an index of standard of living (SLI) computed from household amenities and assets (IIPS and ORC Macro, 2000). The reported use of PNDT increases from 3 per cent in low SLI households to 38 per cent in high SLI households. The estimated misuse among reported PNDT users also increases from zero per cent in the low SLI group to 2 per cent in the medium SLI group and 13 per cent in the high SLI group. But when adjusted for the possible misreporting of PNDT status, the estimated misuse of PNDT in the low SLI group (24%) turns out to be as high as in the high SLI group (23%) and substantially higher than the medium SLI group (8%).

The reported uses of PNDT increases with the mother's exposure to media. But it does not show a clear relationship with misuse. When only the reported use of PNDT is considered, misuse is marginally lower among women regularly exposed to media. But, when adjusted for possible underreporting of PNDT, the estimated misuse is higher among women regularly exposed to media. Women's work status however has a clear relationship with both use and misuse of PNDT. Both use and misuse are higher among non-working women compared with women working for wage or those who are self-employed or working in the family farm or business. Reported as well as the adjusted use rates increase with mother's ideal family size. When the ideal family size is one or two, 22–24 per cent had PNDT. When the ideal family size is four or more, only 4 per cent use PNDT. The misuse is highest when the ideal family size is three (13–44%), moderate when it is one or two (6–28%) and negligible when it is four or more.

The foregoing analysis shows that the use of PNDT tends to be systematically related to socio-economic factors, and the adjustments needed for possible underreporting of its use are relatively minor. Therefore, without significantly biasing the results, one can apply the multivariate techniques to the reported data on PNDT use to study the independent effects of key socio-economic variables on the use of PNDT. Table 6 shows the results of logistic regression of the determinants of PNDT use. Accordingly, most of the variables used in the regression have significant, independent effects on the use of PNDT. The use of PNDT increases with maternal as well as parental age. But, the use of this technology is lower if the order of birth is three or more. It is particularly low if the mother has already given birth to a son.

Urban residence, educational level, exposure to media and standard of living show strong, independent and positive effects on the use of PNDT. Its use is higher among Christians, and if the religion is other than Hindu, Muslim or Sikh. The use is lower among members of SCs/STs, even after controlling for standard of living and educational level. When compared with non-workers, the use is lower among mothers who work but not for wage. The use of PNDT is lower among mothers having larger ideal family sizes and among those who gave non-numeric answer to the question on ideal family size. Women who were visited by health workers during the pregnancy report lower use of PNDT. This finding is directly in contradiction with the claim of some activists that public health workers act as conduits of this technology in rural areas. Even after controlling these variables, eastern, north-central and north-western parts of India show lower use of PNDT than southern parts. In other words, the geographical pattern seen in the PNDT use cannot fully be explained by the observed socio-economic variations. This indicates the influence of neighbourhood on the use of technology.

Determinants of Sex Ratio at Birth

In recent years the use of PNDT has emerged as the key intervening variable through which other factors influence the SRB in India. There are, however, a number of factors that independently affect the SRB. Teitelbaum (1972) provides an early review of the literature on this subject. James (1987) and Waldren (1998) provide a more

Table 6

Results of logit analysis of determinants of the use of prenatal diagnostic technologies: NFHS–2, 1998–99

Explanatory variables	*Coefficient*
Maternal age	0.105**
Maternal age squared	–0.0008
Paternal age	0.134***
Paternal age squared	–0.0017***
Order of birth 3+ (no = 0)	–0.260***
No surviving male sibling and order 2 or higher (yes = 0)	0.082
No surviving female sibling and order 2 or higher (yes = 0)	–0.206***
Urban residence (rural = 0)	0.743***
Educational level (mother & father illiterate =0)	
Mother illiterate, father literate	0.360***
Mother less than primary	0.683***
Mother middle school	0.819***
Mother high school +	1.189***
Regular exposure to mass media (no = 0)	0.661***
Standard of living (low = 0)	
Moderate	0.415***
High	1.107***
Religion (Hindu = 0)	
Muslim	0.101
Christian	0.485***
Sikh	0.094
Others	0.374**
Caste/tribe (others = 0)	
Scheduled tribe	–0.589***
Scheduled caste	–0.308***
Other backward castes	–0.086
Female work status (Not working=0)	
Working for wages	–0.015
Others	–0.199**
Ideal number of children reported by mother	–0.449***
Ideal number of children squared	0.0278***
Non-numeric ideal children (numeric = 0)	–1.000***

Cont'd...

Cont'd...

Health worker visit during pregnancy (no = 0)	–0.275***
Region (south=0)	
East	–1.755***
West	0.060
North-west	–1.225***
North-central	–1.529***
Constant	–5.697***
Number of births	31,481
–2 Log-likelihood	16,671
Pseudo R2	0.231

*p<0.05, ** p<0.01, *** p<0.001

Source: NFHS–2 micro data.

recent review of the literature. Chahnazarian (1988) has applied multivariate techniques to test the independent effects of some of these variables using vital statistics data for several countries. For India, Retherford and Roy (2003) have used the NFHS data to test the significance of a limited set of factors. Here, using the same data set, an attempt is made to test the significance of far more variables on the SRB.

Accordingly, Table 7 shows the results of the logit analysis of determinants of the SRB using the data from NFHS–1 and NFHS–2. The results presented are with respect to the probability of having a male birth. Two sets of regression results are presented for each of the surveys, one using data on births that occurred during the 0–14 years before the survey, and another using data on births that occurred 0–4 years (for NFHS–1) and 0–3 years (for NFHS–2) before the survey. While the first set of regressions is based on larger sample of births, the latter set takes advantage of having information on more variables for the more recent births. Nonetheless, none of the regressions is able to account for more than 1 per cent of the variation in the probability of male birth (as indicated by values of pseudo R^2), which underscores the random nature of sex determination at birth. Since in such a situation statistically significant effects could be detected only in large samples, we have checked whether some additional variables become significant when 10 per cent probability level is employed for rejection of null hypothesis.

Table 7

Results of logit analysis of determinates of probability of having a male birth: NFHS–1, 1992–93 and NFHS–2, 1998–99

Explanatory variables	*Births during 0–14 years before survey*		*Births during*	
			1989–92	*1996–98*
	NFHS–1	*NFHS–2*	*NFHS–1*	*NFHS–2*
Maternal age	0.015**	–0.004	0.013	0.012
Maternal age squared	–0.0003**	0.0002	–0.0003	–0.0002
Paternal age	–0.009*	–0.006	–0.005	–0.030**
Paternal age squared	0.0001*	0.0001	0.0001	0.0005***
Paternal age not reported (reported = 0)	0.027	–0.070	N.A.	N.A.
Order of birth	0.002	0.000	0.011	0.011
No surviving male sibling and order 2 or higher (yes = 0)	–0.002	0.043***	0.004	0.110***
No surviving female sibling and order 2 or higher (yes = 0)	–0.025*	–0.022*	–0.035*	–0.041
Urban residence (rural = 0)	0.024**	–0.017	0.016	–0.039
Educational level (mother & father illiterate =0)				
Mother illiterate, father literate	–0.014	–0.007	–0.010	–0.025
Mother less than primary	–0.016	0.011	–0.073**	–0.017
Mother middle school	0.005	0.020	0.009	0.090*
Mother high school +	–0.064***	0.038*	–0.127***	0.068
Regular exposure to mass media (no = 0)	0.000	0.020	–0.020	–0.009
Standard of living (low = 0)				
Moderate	–0.018	–0.026**	–0.014	–0.005
High	0.007	–0.020	0.029	0.044
Religion (Hindu = 0)				
Muslim	–0.028*	0.013	–0.035	0.020
Christian	0.013	0.045*	0.012	0.031
Sikh	0.043	0.033	–0.014	–0.092
Buddhist	0.028	0.055	0.197*	–0.107

Cont'd...

Cont'd...

Others	0.040	0.057	–0.001	0.064
Caste/tribe (others = 0)				
Scheduled tribe	0.015	0.016	0.027	0.006
Scheduled caste	0.020	0.010	0.025	0.060*
Other backward class		0.011		–0.006
Female work status (Not working=0)				
Working for wages	–0.013	–0.010	–0.059**	–0.051
Others	0.004	–0.002	0.014	–0.014
Ideal number of children reported by mother	–0.043***	–0.070***	–0.043**	–0.064*
Ideal number of children squared	0.0018**	0.0046***	0.0016	0.0003
Non-numeric ideal children (numeric = 0)	–0.134***	–0.156***	–0.076	–0.232***
Consanguinity (no = 0)	–0.016	N.A.	0.012	N.A.
Health worker visited during pregnancy (no = 0)	N.A.	N.A.	0.032	–0.017
Birth attendance (untrained birth attendant=0)	N.A.	N.A.		
Trained birth attendant at home	N.A.	N.A.	0.085***	0.076*
Trained birth attendant at institution	N.A.	N.A.	0.040	0.070**
Iron and folic acid supplementation (no = 0)				
Received tablets/syrup	N.A.	N.A.	0.016	0.022
Fully consumed	N.A.	N.A.	N.A.	–0.041
Number of antenatal check-ups	N.A.	N.A.	0.008*	0.000
Maternal anaemia at survey				
Mild	N.A.	–0.015	N.A.	0.002
Moderate/severe	N.A.	–0.044***	N.A.	0.002
Not tested	N.A.	–0.025	N.A.	–0.113**
Mother's body-mazss index at survey (normal = 0)				
Low (below 18.5 kg/m2)	N.A.	0.005	N.A.	0.032
High (25 kg/m2 or more)	N.A.	–0.048**	N.A.	–0.109*
Not measured	N.A.	–0.202***	N.A.	–0.119***

Cont'd...

Cont'd...

Mother's height at survey	N.A.	0.007	N.A.	–0.001
	N.A.	–0.029	N.A.	0.029
Use of PNDT (no=0)	N.A.	N.A.	N.A.	–0.056
Interaction with PNDT use				
No surviving male sibling and order 2 or higher	N.A.	N.A.	N.A.	0.228***
No surviving female sibling and order 2 or higher	N.A.	N.A.	N.A.	0.015
Altitude more than 1,000 meters (lower = 0)	N.A.	–0.035*	N.A.	0.029
Region (south = 0)				
East	0.023	0.043**	0.079**	0.078*
West	–0.002	0.041*	0.040	0.060
North-west	0.043**	0.090***	0.129***	0.147***
North-central	0.051***	0.082***	0.090***	0.090**
Constant	0.110	0.317***	–0.051	0.550
Number of live births	175,815	158,840	53,591	31,353
–2 Log-likelihood	243,431	219,726	74,163	43,234
Pseudo R2	0.001	0.002	0.002	0.005

* p<0.10, ** p<0.05, *** p<0.01
N.A.: Not available/applicable.
Source: NFHS–2 micro data.

The most notable results from these regressions are with respect to the effects of sex composition of previously born children and the use of PNDT on the probability of male birth. Although order of birth does not show statistically significant relationship in any of the regressions, regressions using the NFHS–2 data set show that if the mother had at least one previous birth but had no son at the time of current birth, the probability of the birth being a male is higher and this effect is strongly significant. This suggests that such women were not resorting to sex-selective abortion in the 1980s but had begun to do so in the 1990s. The female-selection situation, characterized by women who had at least one previous child but had no daughter, reduces the probability of male birth, but its effect in the regressions is only mildly significant at 10 per cent level.

Information on the use of PNDT is available only for the recent births from NFHS–2. The regression using this data shows that PNDT use does not have a direct effect on the SRB. To test whether its effect depends on the sex-selection situation, we have interacted its use with dummy variables for male- and female-selection situations. As the results show, when women in male-selection situation (at least one previous birth and no sons) use PNDT, it has strong positive effect on the probability of male birth. Its effect in the case of women with female-selection situation is not in the expected direction (i.e., negative), and also not statistically significant. It may be noted that male-selection situation shows positive effect on the probability of having a male birth even in the absence of PNDT use, indicating that some women must have suppressed its use.

Another important result is with respect to the effects of antenatal and delivery care. In both NFHS–1 and NFHS–2, data on antenatal and natal care are available only for the recent births (for the last four years in NFHS–1 and last three years in NFHS–2). Both data sets show that the SRB is higher when trained personnel attend the birth. This could be due to the reduction in stillbirths when they attend the birth. But, the number of antenatal care check-ups and consumption of iron and folic acid tablets or syrup during pregnancy appears to have no effect on the SRB.

Urban residence, educational level, standard of living, exposure to mass media, religion and caste generally do not show statistically significant or consistent relationship in all the regressions. Mothers with high school education or higher have reported lower proportion of males in their births in NFHS–1. But, in NFHS–2, they have reported more males in their births, and the effect is mildly significant in the regression using data for births during 0–14 years before the survey. Mothers working for wage report lower probability of male births in all the regressions but the effect is statistically significant only in data on births during 0–14 years before NFHS–2. The regression results show that the SRB increases as the mother's ideal number of children decreases, though in a non-linear fashion. This effect is strongly significant in all the regressions. Also, those who gave non-numeric response to the question on ideal family size had fewer sons. This would seem consistent with the contention of some female activists that incidence of sex-selective abortions increases with the decrease in family size. However, the fact that this effect is also found in NFHS–1 data for the period when the incidence of female foeticides were rare (as indicated by the insignificance of the variable representing the male-selection situation) suggests that the observed relationship is spurious. Those who had sons tend to use contraception more than those who had daughters; in order to justify their non-use of contraception, the latter group has the tendency to report higher ideal family size.

Maternal and paternal ages show statistically significant relationship with the SRB in some of the regressions. In births that occurred during 0–14 years before NFHS–1, maternal age shows statistically significant non-linear relationship, indicating initially a rise in the SRB with maternal age and then a fall at older ages. This may be attributed to a similar relationship of maternal age with still-birth rate. But this relationship is not seen in the data from NFHS–2. As the role of men in sex determination of the foetus is well established, their age could have a bearing on the SRB. Some researchers have found that the SRB decreases with paternal age and speculated that it is due to the decrease in coital frequency with age (e.g., Chahnazarian, 1988). All of our regressions indicate that the SRB initially decreases with paternal age and then rises at advanced ages. This effect is strongly significant in births that occurred 0–3 years before NFHS–2 and mildly significant in the regression that used births during 0–14 years before NFHS–1. While the initial decrease is as expected, the suggested rise after age 30 or so needs further investigation. The significance of the quadratic term in the regressions may simply be indicating that the rate of decrement diminishes with age.

The possibility of maternal malnutrition influencing the SRB has been discussed in the literature on this subject. Anderson and Bergstrom (1998) had found that short maternal stature and obesity were independently related to low SRB in Africa. Data on mother's nutritional status and anaemia are available only from NFHS–2. When data on births during 0–14 years are used (i.e., larger sample of births), moderate and severe anaemia show strong negative effects on the SRB. Mother's height does not show any effect on the SRB, but the results strongly suggest that obese women tend to have fewer sons. But it should be noted that NFHS data on maternal anaemia and body-mass index refer to the time of the survey rather than to the time of the birth. Also to be noted is that women for whom data on body-mass index were not available had significantly lower SRB. This index was not calculated for pregnant women and those who had given birth during the two months before the survey. Such women were likely to have had more female births in the past because in societies with strong son preference, those who had sons are more likely to use contraception and stop childbearing.

Data on altitude are available only from NFHS–2. When births during the 0–14 years before the survey are considered, there is a weak indication that higher altitudes reduce the chance of male birth. This may be because of lower temperature and higher male fetal mortality at higher altitudes. It is also possible that people living at higher altitudes are genetically different from those living in low-lying areas. The information on consanguinity was collected only in NFHS–1. It shows no statistically significant relationship with the SRB. But, owing to the limitations of the information on consanguinity collected in NFHS–1, it served as a poor proxy for the level of inbreeding. In all the regressions, even after controlling for the foregoing factors, the SRB is significantly higher in north-western and north-central regions. This could be because of greater misuse of PNDT in these parts. However, as these regional differences are also significant (but smaller) in the regressions that use NFHS–1 data, they may be indicating the presence of some genetic factors such as levels of circulating gonadotrophin, or a tendency to underreport female births in northern India.

Summary and Conclusions

In recent years the use of PNDT, followed by sex-selective abortion, has emerged as a powerful determinant of SRB in India. In this paper, we have analyzed the factors influencing the use of PNDT as well as SRB. We presented evidence from the recently released data on fertility from the 2001 Census as well as from the NFHS. The census fertility data suggest that SRB in India may have increased to 110, and in some areas, to as high as 130. But this data may have been affected by underreporting of female births. However, even this data show that the SRB in southern and eastern parts of India is well within the range observed under normal circumstances, and thus discount the possibility of widespread use of sex-selective abortions in these areas. The census data also show that though there may be little rural-urban difference in the SRB, among the educated class the SRB is abnormally high.

The data collected in NFHS–2 (1998–99) show that 13 per cent of live births were subjected to PNDT, and 6 per cent of female foetuses may have been aborted after PNDT. But, if possible underreporting is taken into account, PNDT may have been used in 14 per cent of the cases, and in 17 per cent of such cases female foetuses may have been aborted. The use of PNDT is higher in southern and western regions of India while its misuse for selectively aborting female foetuses is higher in the north, especially in the north-western parts of the country. Also, the use of these techniques is higher at lower parities but their misuse is more at higher parities, especially if women had only daughters.

As would be expected, the use of PNDT is much higher in urban areas, among educated women, those with higher levels of standard of living, non-working women and those regularly exposed to media. The multivariate analysis applied to the data shows that these factors have independent effects on the use of PNDT. But they do not show a clear-cut relationship with its misuse. This may be because users of PNDT in the NFHS sample are not large enough to infer the patterns unambiguously. Interestingly, the analysis shows that those who reported the visit of health workers during pregnancy of the index birth have used the PNDT less than others. This contradicts the allegation of some activists who claim that government health workers are often used as conduits by private agencies to promote the use of this technology in rural India.

The analysis of determinants of SRB shows that PNDT use does not have a direct effect on the SRB because it is not generally misused. But, the analysis shows that when women in male-selection situation (i.e., with at least one previous birth but had no sons) use PNDT, it has a strong positive effect on the probability of male birth. It was found that women in male-selection situation have higher SRB even in the absence of PNDT use, indicating that some women must have suppressed its use in the survey.

Beyond the use of PNDT and sex composition of previously born children, several other factors are also found to influence the SRB. The SRB was higher when a skilled person attended the delivery. There was evidence suggesting that the SRB initially increases and then decreases with maternal age. On the other hand, there was even stronger evidence indicating that the SRB decreases with paternal age initially and then increases with it. Maternal anaemia and obesity are found to decrease the SRB. There was evidence, albeit weak, that SRB is lower at higher altitudes. Urban residence, educational level, standard of living, religion and caste/tribe failed to show significant or consistent relationship with the SRB. However, regressions suggested that probability of male birth was lower for wage-earning women. In spite of controlling for many socio-economic and demographic factors, the SRB was higher in north India, especially in north-western parts, indicating that women in these regions misused the technology more than others. But, the role of some genetic factors or underreporting of female births in explaining a part of the remaining regional variations cannot be completely ruled out.

Although, the study focused on the characteristics of women in analyzing the determinants of use and misuse of PNDT, we do not mean to suggest that their husbands had no part to play. Indeed, it is likely that women went for PNDT on the coaxing of their husbands and other family members. But, the differentials in the use and misuse are likely to be governed more by women's characteristics because in a culture of silence, the woman's involvement in decision-making would be more to do with her own characteristics (education, occupation, income, etc.) than that of her husband's. Also, as the NFHS had collected data from women, it was more appropriate to study the determinants in terms of their own characteristics or those they share with their husbands (religion, caste, standard of living, parity, etc.).

In conclusion, although the use of PNDT is now fairly common in many parts of India, only a minority of couples who use these techniques misuses it for aborting female foetuses. While income and education do increase the use of PNDT, their misuse is governed more by cultural factors and sex composition of children already born. The higher SRB observed among more educated and higher income groups is mainly because of their better access to these techniques rather than from their greater misuse.

Acknowledgement

We wish to acknowledge with gratitude the assistance of K.C. Das in drawing the maps included in the paper. Comments of Fred Arnold, Marcus Feldman and participants of the seminar on "Female Deficit in Asia: Trends and Perspectives" held at Singapore during December 5–7, 2005 were helpful in revising the paper.

This paper was published in *Economic and Political Weekly*, Vol. XLII, No. 24, 2007.

References

Anderson, R. and S. Bergstorm (1998). Is Maternal Malnutrition Associated with a Low Sex Ratio at Birth? *Human Biology*, 70(1), pp. 101–06.

Arnold, Fred, Sunita Kishor and T.K. Roy (2002). Sex-selective Abortions in India, *Population and Development Review*, 28(4), pp. 759–85.

Bhat, P.N. Mari (2002). On the Trail of Missing Indian Females, I: Search for Clues, II: Illusion and Reality, *Economic and Political Weekly*, 38(51 and 58), pp. 5105–18 and 5244–63.

Chahnazarian, A. (1988). Determinants of the Sex Ratio at Birth: Review of Recent Literature, *Social Biology*, 35(3–4), pp. 214–35.

Das Gupta, Monica and P.N. Mari Bhat (1997). Fertility Decline and Increased Manifestation of Sex Bias in India, *Population Studies*, 51(3), pp. 307–15.

Dyson, Tim (1989). The Historical Demography of Berar, 1881–1980, in Tim Dyson (ed.), *India's Historical Demography: Studies in Famine, Disease and Society*, Curzon Press, London, pp. 150–96.

International Institute for Population Sciences (IIPS) and ORC Macro (2000). *National Family Health Survey (NFHS-2)*, 1998–99, India, IIPS Mumbai.

James, William H. (1987). The Human Sex Ratio, Part 1: A Review of the Literature, *Human Biology*, 59(5), pp. 721–52.

Klasen, Stephen (1994). Missing Women Reconsidered, *World Development*, 22(7), pp. 1061–71.

Registrar General, India (2003). *Missing Mapping the Adverse Child Sex Ratios in India*, UNFPA, New Delhi.

Retherford, Robert D. and T.K. Roy (2003). *Factors affecting Sex-selective Abortion in India and 17 Major States*, National Family Health Survey Subject Report No. 21, International Institute for Population Sciences, Mumbai.

Sudha, S. and S. Irudaya Rajan (1999). Female Demographic Disadvantage in India 1981–1991: Sex-selective Abortions and Female Infanticide, *Development and Change*, 30, pp. 585–618.

Teitelbaum, Michael S. (1972). Factors Associated with the Sex Ratio in Human Populations, in G.A. Harrisson and A.J. Boyce (eds.), *The Structure of Human Populations*, Clarendon Press, Oxford, pp. 90–109.

Visaria, Pravin (1971). *The Sex Ratio of the Population of India*, Monograph No. 10, Census of India, 1961, Manager of Publications, Delhi.

Waldren, Ingrid (1998). Factors Determining the Sex Ratio at Birth in United Nations, *Too Young to Die: Genes or Gender?* Population Division, Department of Economic and Social Affairs, United Nations, NY.

FIVE

Imbalance in Sex Ratio in Rural Tamil Nadu

A Case Study of Salem District

C.P. Prakasam

Sex ratio at birth is a biological constraint with a value that lies in between 943 to 954 females per 1,000 males in India. As the male infant mortality is higher than female in normal populations, the child sex ratio would tend to increase and improve over male in the age group 0–6 years in developed countries. In India and in some developing countries, sex ratio at birth and in the age group 0–6 years favours male. A recent phenomenon in the developing countries, viz., China, Korea and India (especially Haryana and Tamil Nadu) shows a strong son preference contributed to the decline in sex ratio brought out by sex-selective abortion, foeticide and neglect of female babies. Studies carried out in India by Das Gupta and Bhat (1997), Sudha and Rajan (1999), Booth, Verma and Bari (1994) and Sachar et al. (1990) have discussed that prenatal sex determination perpetuated the discrimination against female foetus leading to imbalance in sex ratio. By using NFHS–2 data, Arnold, Kishor and Roy (2002) examined the evidence for the sex-selective abortions in Indian states and found the use of modern technologies to avert the birth of daughters, which impact on sex ratio at birth. Similarly, Retherford and Roy (2003), analyzing the NFHS–1 and NFHS–2 data of major states, concluded that imbalances in sex ratio at birth may be attributed to sex-selective abortions. The above studies also revealed indirect evidences of sex-selective abortion on sex ratio. But, there exist very limited studies (e.g., Chunkath and Athreya, 1997; George and Dahiya, 1998; Unisa, Prakasam, Sinha and Bhagat, 2003) which focus on the practices of female foeticide through induced abortion and infanticide in Haryana and Tamil Nadu influencing sex ratio.

Abortion or the procedure of extracting foetus within three months of pregnancy under medical supervision is considered safe and appropriate for the health of mother. Safe abortion practice has been considered one of the methods of delaying the pregnancy and used as a family planning method as well. However, in India and mostly in rural areas where a strong son preferences predominant, the practice of abortion for different reasons has been observed.

In the early 1970s, India was one of the first countries in the world to enact the Medical Termination of Pregnancy (MTP) Act. The passage of the Act implied that a woman who decided to terminate her pregnancy would no longer be hindered by the law in making this choice, nor would she be forced to risk her life doing so. Although the provision of MTP services has increased, restrictions have been provided by the Act and are said to be counterproductive to the availability of abortion services. It was noted that the stigma associated with induced abortion, limited access to authorized abortion providers, the financial costs associated with legal abortion, and low levels or awareness regarding the legality of the procedure has kept women away from availing safe abortion services (Nanda, 2000). The NFHS–1 data analysis by Das et al. (2000) covering 24 states in India revealed that about 4 per cent of the ever-married women had opted for induced abortion in their lifetime. The rate of induced abortion found among such women was about 1.3 per cent. The state-level analysis of the incidences of induced abortions showed the highest incidence being reported at Delhi (4.6%), followed by Tamil Nadu (4.3%). A community-based study, undertaken in rural South India (Varkey et al., 2000), revealed a high prevalence of induced abortion (28%) among the study population, mainly among the women who were not using contraceptives. Most abortions were carried out in the first trimester of pregnancy and unqualified practitioners performed 65 per cent of terminations.

Research studies also showed that the higher proportion of women who had undergone abortion belongs to the age group 20–34 years (Rao and Kanbargi, 1980; Khan et al., 1996; Chhabra and Nuna, 1993). The average number of children living at the time of acceptance of induced abortion varies between two to four (Rao and Kanbargi,1980; Jamshedji and Kokate, 1990). These research reviews confirm that women seek abortion for various reasons such as socio-economic, medical, failure of contraception, physical conditions, etc. But, the study carried out by Chunkath and Athreya (1997) revealed that women seek abortion for sex selection only and the practice of female infanticide exists in few blocks of Madurai and Salem districts influencing sex ratio. It is against this background the present study aims to find out the prevalence of abortion in the districts of Tamil Nadu and to explore the possible reasons for abortion in rural set-up and its influence on sex ratio.

Why Salem?

Sex ratio, which represents number of females for 1,000 males, was 974 in Tamil Nadu in 1991 and increased to 986 in 2001. During the 2001 Census period, of the 30 districts in the state, 15 districts have exhibited sex ratio less than 1,000. Among these the lowest sex ratio was reported in Salem district (929). It also observed to be lowest in 1991. Dharmapuri district has the second lowest sex ratio of 938 in 2001 Census. Figure 1 shows lowest sex ratio districts (Salem, Dharmapuri) in comparison with the state for the period 1961–2001. Sex ratio of Dharmapuri and Salem was found to be equal during

Figure 1

Lowest Sex Ratio Districts in Tamil Nadu 1961–2001

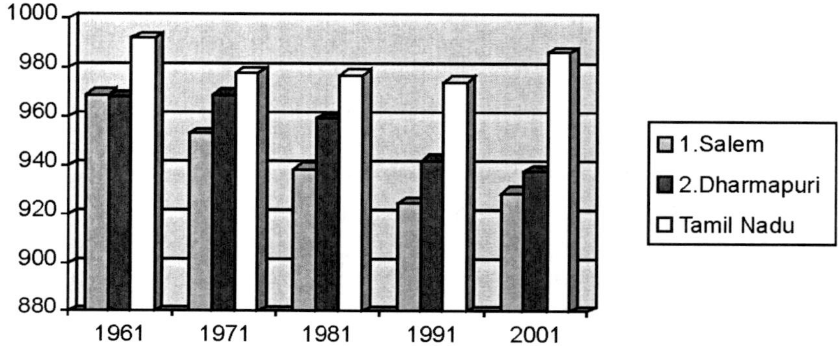

1961. In later period the sex ratio declined in Salem. From the census data the lowest sex ratio in Tamil Nadu was observed in Salem and this trend has been seen for the past three-four decades. Further, it has been observed that (Table 1) the overall sex ratio is found to be lowest in Edappadi taluka (868), followed by Omalur (878) and Sankari (889) talukas. Likewise, Edappadi (714) and Sankari (774) talukas exhibit lowest sex ratio in 0–6 population among nine talukas of Salem district. The 2001 Census data for the villages in Salem district have been analyzed in Table 2, which shows that there are only 10 villages having less than 800 sex ratio whereas in 0–6 population the number of such villages is 248. There are 12 villages in Sankari/Edappadi talukas where sex ratio in 0–6 population is found to be less than 500.

Table 1

Overall Sex Ratio and Sex Ratio of 0–6 Population in Talukas of Salem District, 2001

Talukas	*Overall sex ratio**	*Sex ratio of 0–6 population*
Mettur	885	776
Omalur	878	795
Edappadi	868	714
Sankari	889	774
Salem	954	905
Yercaud	970	942
Vazhapadi	968	912
Attur	976	911
Gangavalli	979	895
Salem district	929	851

*Females per 1,000 males.

Materials and Methods

This study is based on the data collected from a survey carried out in rural areas of Salem district, Tamil Nadu, during the third quarter of 2002.[1] As discussed, Salem district was selected because the overall sex ratio and sex ratio of 0–6 population found to be low and the number of abortions found to be high. From this district, at random, two tehsils are selected. At the second stage *eight villages* from these two tehsils have been identified as sample villages (Table 2).

Table 2

Number of Villages by Overall Sex Ratio and Sex Ratio of 0–6 Population in Salem District in Tamil Nadu, 2001

Sex Ratio	*Number of Villages (Overall Sex Ratio)*	*Number of Villages (Sex Ratio 0–6)*
Less than 500	—	12
501–550	—	4
551–600	—	19
601–650	—	25
651–700	—	59
701–750	2	62
751–800	8	67
801–850	71	55
851–900	134	68
901–950	112	52
951–1000	156	54
1001 and above	74	80
Total villages	557	557

A complete enumeration of the selected eight villages was done. The present study was confined to 1,565 currently married women in the age group 15–49 and experienced at least one pregnancy. The list of sample villages and the hamlets studied is given in Table 3.

Table 3

Number of Villages/Hamlets Selected from Salem District, Tamil Nadu

Villages/Hamlets	*Villages/Hamlets*	*Villages/Hamlets*	*Villages/Hamlets*
1. *Samudram*	2. *Koranampatty*	5. *Kattoor*	8. *Andipalyam*
(a) Narimedu	(a) Erikadu	(a) Kattuvulve	(a) Muniappan kovil
(b) Erangadu	(b) Ottatheru	(b) Vembadithalam	(b) Theerthangadu
(c) Karatukadu	(c) Kuthagaikadu	6. *N-Mettukadu*	(c) Pandarangadu
(d) Koolidasan vulvae	3. *Kalinganoor*	7. *N.Kattoor*	(d) Kombaikadu
(e) Kallampatti Vulvae	4. *Poochireddiyur*		(e) Kattukadu
(f) Mayilandi Vulvae			(f) Samiar Thottam
			(g) Thottakadu

Table 4 shows the currently married women by background characteristics. It has been observed that majority of women (72.1%) married less than 18 years. Around 61 per cent of currently married women were illiterate. Among the women 20 per cent experienced at least one abortion during their reproductive life. The prevalence of abortion (spontaneous and induced) has been studied by duration of marriage, previous delivery outcome, birth order, surviving children, and use of family planning method. The data collected from the currently married women reveals that nearly 11 per cent of women with marital duration of less than five years and 20 per cent with 5–10 years had experienced abortion. However, 25 per cent of women with more than 20 years of marital duration had experienced abortion (Table 5). Prevalence of abortion by outcome of pregnancy shows that around 5 to 7 per cent of women experienced spontaneous abortion during their reproductive life (Table 6). It has been observed that induced abortion increases with the order of pregnancy. Nearly 8 per cent of women with third order pregnancy seek induced abortion and this increases to 31 per cent at sixth and above order (Table 6). The higher percentage of women seeking induced abortion may depend upon previous outcome of pregnancy, hence the present outcome with the previous outcome by order of pregnancy has been analyzed. The results revealed that if the previous birth was live birth, the percentage of women seeking present pregnancy terminating as induced abortion increases with the birth order. It increases from 2 to 16.1 between first birth to fourth birth (Table 7). Further, women experiencing abortion (spontaneous and induced) by surviving children has been examined. With the increase in surviving children, the number of women experiencing abortion increases. It has been observed that 14.4 per cent of women experienced abortion with one surviving child, increases to 22.1 for women with two or more surviving children (Table 8).

Experience of spontaneous and induced abortions among women who are current users of family planning method has been analyzed. Out of 1,565 women, 35.7 per cent are current users of family planning. Table 9 shows women experienced spontaneous or induced abortion among the users and non-users of family planning. Among the users of family planning method (Table 9), it has been observed that induced abortion found to be high (16.3) than spontaneous abortion (8.6). Among the non-users of family planning method, the percentage of women experiencing spontaneous abortion found to be more (12.6%) than induced abortion (5.4%).

Table 4

Background Characteristics of Currently Married Women in Salem District

Background Characteristics	*Currently Married Women*	*Percentage*
Age at Marriage		
Less than 18 years	1128	72.1
19–25 years	399	25.5
26 years and above	38	2.4
Education Level		
Illiterate	960	61.3
Primary	217	13.9
Middle	310	19.8
Secondary	58	3.7
Graduate	20	1.3
Number of Abortions		
No abortion	1252	80.0
Only one abortion	212	13.5
Two abortions	69	4.4
More than two	32	2.0
Total Number of Women	1565	100.0

Table 5

Prevalence of Abortion by Duration of Married Life in the Study Area

Duration of Marital Life	*Experienced Abortion*		*Number of women*
	Yes	*No*	
Less than 5 years	10.5	89.5	325
5–10 years	20.3	79.7	370
11–19 years	21.6	78.4	388
20 years and above	24.9	75.1	482
Total	20.0	80.0	1565

Table 6

Spontaneous and Induced Abortions by Order of Pregnancy in the Study Area

Pregnancy Order	*Spontaneous Abortion*	*Induced Abortion*	*Total number of women*
First	5.7	0.1	1433
Second	6.4	1.8	1272
Third	5.8	7.8	833
Fourth	7.0	10.6	445
Fifth	5.5	20.6	199
Sixth and above	4.2	31.0	141

Table 7

Prevalence of Abortion by Present and Previous Pregnancy Outcomes

Previous Outcome	*Present Pregnancy Outcome*		*Total Number of Women*
	Prevalence of Spontaneous Abortion	*Prevalence of Induced Abortion*	
First			1272
Live birth	3.8	2.0	1152
Still birth	2.7	—	37
Abortion: Spontaneous	45.1	—	82
Induced	—	—	1
Second			833
Live birth	3.8	8.4	728
Still birth	7.1	—	28
Abortion: Spontaneous	29.0	1.6	62
Induced	—	20.0	15
Third			445
Live birth	4.6	9.2	371
Still birth	29.4	5.9	17
Abortion: Spontaneous	28.1	—	32
Induced	—	48.0	25
Fourth			199
Live birth	2.5	16.1	161
Still birth	—	25.0	4
Abortion: Spontaneous	43.8	—	16
Induced	—	77.8	18

Table 8

Prevalence of Abortion by Surviving Children in Study Area

Surviving Children	*Abortion*		*Total*
	No	*Yes*	
No	150(82.4)	32(17.6)	182(100.0)
One	255(85.6)	43(14.4)	298(100.0)
Two	442(78.2)	123(21.8)	565(100.0)
More than two	405(77.9)	115(22.1)	520(100.0)
Total	1252(80.0)	313(20.0)	1565(100.0)

χ–Square = 0.1973, not significant (N.S.).

Table 9

Experience of Abortion by Current Users and Non-users of Family Planning Method in Study Area

Experienced Abortion	*Current-users of Family Planning method*	*Non-users of Family Planning method*	*Total*
Spontaneous abortion			
Yes	48 (8.6)	127 (12.6)	175 (11.2)
No	510 (91.4)	880 (87.4)	1390 (88.8)
Total	558 (100.0)	1007 (100.0)	1565 (100.0)
χ-square = 0.0159 N.S.			
Induced Abortion			
Yes	91 (16.3)	59 (5.9)	150 (9.6)
No	467 (83.7)	948 (94.1)	1415 (90.4)
Total	558 (100.0)	1007 (100.0)	1565 (100.0)
χ-square = 0.0215 N.S.			

Comparison between users and non-users of family planning with spontaneous abortion (yes/no) shows that there is no significance between these experiences (χ-square 0.0159, not significant), similarly comparison between users and non-users of family planning methods with induced abortion found to be not significant (χ-square 0.0215, *N.S.*). Hence, the prevalence of abortion among the rural women in the study area was not influenced by use and non-use of family planning methods, but not statistically significant. From Table 9 it has been observed that there were 150 (9.6%) women who had undergone induced abortion. Information further elicited regarding the reasons for induced abortion (Table 10). Reasons for induced abortion by order of pregnancy revealed that nearly 31 per cent of women had induced abortion after knowing the sex of the foetus (female). Among the women who had induced abortion, 51 per cent (Table 10) underwent induced abortion at first pregnancy, who had ultrasound test. One women with seventh pregnancy revealed that she had undergone sex selective abortion. The analysis reveals that, in the study area, sex-selective abortion are prevailing and ultrasound test (sonography) for sex determination is common. To examine the imbalance on sex ratio, it has been calculated by considering women who had undergone 'test' and or not. The results show that (Table 11) sex ratio by order of birth found to be more or less half in women who had undergone ultrasound test than women who had not. Further, sex ratio declines with the increase in birth order found to be more among women who had induced abortion after the 'test'.

Table 10

Reasons for Induced Abortion by Order of Pregnancy

Reasons	*First*	*Second*	*Third*	*Fourth*	*Fifth*	*Sixth*	*Seventh*	*Total*
Sex of child	21	11	10	—	2	1	1	46 (30.7)
Wrong position	40	15	9	—	—	1	—	65 (43.3)
Child health	12	3	7	4	2	—	—	28 (18.7)
Abnormal	2	1	4	—	1	—	—	8(5.3)
Mother's health	2	—	—	—	1	—	—	3(2.0)
Total (%)	77(51.3)	30(20.0)	30(20.0)	4(2.7)	6(4.0)	2(1.3)	1(0.7)	150 (100)

Table 11

Variations in Sex Ratio by Women Who had Ultrasound Test

Birth order	*Sex Ratio at Birth*	*Sex Ratio*	
		With Ultrasound Test	*No Ultrasound Test*
First	880	698	898
Second	769	455	786
Third	731	400	742
Fourth	634	*	646
Fifth	695	*	693
Six and above	589	*	767
All	779	593	795

*Observations are small to calculate proper rates.

Conclusions

This study is based on a survey conducted in the rural areas of Salem district of Tamil Nadu. The reproductive history of 1,565 currently married women revealed that 20 per cent of them had abortion. Around 30 per cent women with less than 10 years of marital duration had experienced abortion. The prevalence of abortion increases with the order of pregnancy. Induced abortion found to be more among women who had previous outcome was live birth. It has been observed that induced abortion found to be more among current users of family planning method. From this study, it was evident that the practice of induced abortion found to be high and mostly for desired sex selection. The increase in induced abortion by order of pregnancy, previous live birth and current users of family planning, gives indirect evidence that it was for want of male offspring. During the survey, it has been observed that apart from sex-selective abortion, female infanticide found to be prevailing in these areas. To prevent the practice of sex selective abortion it is necessary to implement policy decisions which will uplift the rural communities. Government of Tamil Nadu has introduced "Cradle Baby Scheme" to prevent infanticides and foeticides. However, efforts are not reaching the villages to stop the practices. Planners should focus on programmes related to improving women status, formal education of women, and counselling for social stigmas related to dowry system. Community education programmes related to gender equality should be organized. Income generating schemes which will enhance women's status should be implemented in these rural areas to bridge the gender gap.

Notes

1. This survey was conducted during the third quarter of 2002 with a follow up at the end of the year. This survey was funded by the International Institute for Population Sciences under research projects for the year 2002–03.

References

Arnold, F., S. Kishor and T.K. Roy (2002). Sex-selective Abortions in India, *Population and Development Review*, December, 28(4), pp. 759–85.

Booth, B.E., M. Verma and R.S. Bari (1994). Foetal Sex Determination in Infants in Punjab, India: Correlations and Implications, *British Medical Journal*, 309, pp. 1259–61.

Chunkath, S.R. and V.B. Athreya (1997). Female Infanticide in Tamil Nadu: Some Evidence, *Economic and Political Weekly*, April, 32(17).

Chhabra, R. and S.C. Nuna (1993). *Abortion in India: An Overview*, Veerendra Printers, Delhi.

Das, N.P., G. Desai and R. Patel (2000). Incidence of Induced Abortion in India: A Study of Socio-cultural Aspects from NFHS Data, *Demography India*, July-December, 29(2), pp.149–64.

Das Gupta, M. and P.N. Mari Bhat (1997). Fertility Decline and Increased Manifestation of Sex Bias in India, *Population Studies*, 51, pp. 307–16.

George, S.M. and R.S. Dahiya (1998). Female Foeticide in Rural Haryana, *Economic and Political Weekly*, August 8, pp. 2191–98.

Jamshedji, A. and N. Kokate (1990). Medical Termination of Pregnancy and Concurrent Contraceptive Acceptance, *Journal of Family Welfare*, XXXVI (3), September.

Khan, M.E., S. Basu and Thilip (1996). Abortion in India: An Overview, *Social Change*, XXVI (3 and 4), September.

Nanda, A.R. (2000). Abortion Services and Health Care, *ISSRF Newsletter*, January, (3):1, pp. 3–4.

Rao, N.B. and R. Kanbargi (1980). *Medical Termination of Pregnancy: An Analysis of Trends and Differentials in Legal Abortions in Karnataka*, Himalaya Publishing House, Bombay.

Retherford, R.D. and T.K. Roy (2003). Factors affecting Sex-selective Abortion in India and 17 Major States, *NFHS Subject Reports No. 21*, IIPS, January, pp. 7–8.

Sachar, R.K., J. Verma, V. Prakash, A. Chopra, R. Aklaka and R. Sofat (1990). Sex-selective Fertility Control: An Outrage, *Journal of Family Welfare*, 36 (2), pp. 30–35.

Sayeed, Unisa, C.P. Prakasam, R.K. Sinha and R.B. Bhagat (2003). Evidence of Sex-selective Abortion from Two Cultural Settings of India: A Study of Haryana and Tamil Nadu, International Institute for Population Sciences, Mumbai.

Sudha, S. and S.I. Rajan (1999). Female Demographic Disadvantage in India 1981–1991: Sex-selective Abortions and Female Infanticide, *Development and Change*, July, 30(3), pp. 585–618.

Varkey, P., P.P. Balakrishna, J.H. Prasad, S. Abraham and A. Joseph (2000). The Reality of Unsafe Abortion in a Rural Community in South India, *Reproductive Health Matters*, November, 8(16), pp. 83–91.

SIX

Traditions in Transformation

Emerging Son Preference Attitudes among the Nairs of Kerala

S. Sudha, S. Khanna, S. Irudaya Rajan and R. Srivastava

This study examines whether son preference (systematic preference for male children) arises in a society previously considered free from this phenomenon. In a qualitative study among the Nair caste of Kerala state in southern India, we analyze whether the rise of male-centric kinship, family and marriage systems, along with socio-economic development that prioritizes productive roles of males over females, may relate to rising son preference attitudes and practices. Findings indicate that key societal transformations in Kerala (the move away from matriliny, and lack of female occupational chances, despite the spread of education) appear to be linked with the rise of son preference attitudes among middle and lower socio-economic sub-groups of Nairs. However, practices such as the use of prenatal sex-selection technologies appear very limited.

Son preference or parents' systematic preference for male children, often leads families to deter the birth and survival of unwanted daughters. Son preference has persisted in several societies in South and East Asia despite socio-economic development that includes factors such as the spread of education, new work opportunities, or other factors that may be expected to improve women's societal position (Das Gupta et al., 2003). The effects of son preference are seen in the century-long masculinization of India's population sex ratio, in contrast to societies where this manifestation of gender bias is absent (Mayer, 1999). Persistent son preference is thus a troubling indicator of gender inequality linked to millions of 'missing women' whose existence has been averted or cut short (Klasen and Wink, 2002; Sen, 1990). Newer technologies to 'weed out' unwanted daughters such as prenatal sex selection, supplement or substitute ancient methods such as female infanticide, abandonment, or selective neglect (Goodkind, 1996). Analyzing son preference thus remains an important field of inquiry (Bhat and Zavier, 2005).

Persistent son preference reflects societal gender inequality at the level of the family. Within the family, parents strategize about which child to invest in for education, occupation, and life chances, based on their assessment of sons' vs. daughters' perceived role in the family and in society (Sudha and Rajan, 2003). This assessment, and thus son preference, is influenced by both kinship and marriage systems, and socio-economic factors (Kishor, 1993).

The influence of kinship and marriage systems on son preference is illustrated by the contrast between girls' vs. boys' life chances in northern vs. southern India (Dyson and Moore, 1986). Northern India shows lower and more gender-unequal female education, paid work, and life chances compared to the South. Northern India is broadly characterized by patrilineal (descent traced from fathers to sons) and village-exogamous (marrying into a family from a different village) kinship and marriage systems among major religion and caste groups. In these systems, daughters are seen as temporary sojourners in their parents' houses who carry resources (dowries) away to their husband's home and contribute work there, while sons bring assets into the family and perpetuate the family name. In southern India, by contrast, girls' school, work and life chances are higher and more gender-egalitarian. This region has had more bilateral (descent incorporates elements from the mother's and father's lines) kinship regimes among major groups, where girls remain closer to natal families and marital gift exchanges are more equal between families. However, South Indian kinship systems have undergone substantial transformation in recent decades, shifting toward similarities with those of the North. The impact of these transformations on son preference has been less studied, but it is suggested that they may be linked to increasing son preference in South India (Rahman and Rao, 2004).

Socio-economic factors also influence families' perception of male and female children, and thus son preference. This study considers how men's and women's education and work participation relate to son preference. Women's work participation reduces son preference as it raises female economic worth and agency. Regions such as northern India where women's productive involvement was lower have had higher son preference (Miller, 1981). The role of female education however is mixed. Overall it appears to increase female agency and lower son preference (Murthi et al., 1995). But, in contexts of limited female economic opportunity and patrilineal kinship, women with some schooling discriminate more efficiently against daughters, because formal schooling increases instrumental knowledge of medical services but does not transcend societal gender inequality (Das Gupta, 1987; Clark and Shreeniwas, 1994). Neither male education nor employment improves the position of daughters (Murthi et al., 1995). Socio-economic development does not automatically reduce son preference as might be expected. Urbanization and increased parental education decrease overall child mortality, but do not improve life chances of girls relative to boys.

However, most prior research has not examined son preference in settings that have experienced major changes in kinship patterns along with socio-economic development. In the present study, we examine a cultural context, the Nair community of Kerala state in southern India, that has experienced socio-economic development hand in hand with kinship changes, to clarify whether and how these changes link with son preference attitudes and practices. We first detail the theoretical perspective underlying our inquiries, followed by a brief ethno-historical description of the context, research methods, and then present results and the concluding discussion.

Theoretical Perspective

Theorists within the 'gender and development' framework have suggested that gender inequality may widen during socio-economic development despite rise in overall prosperity, education and income, unless it is deliberately addressed during the planning process (e.g., review by Razavi and Miller, 1995). Specifically, Blumberg (2004) has argued that women's position in agrarian societies diminishes when social change leads to the separation of spheres of women and men, enhances productive roles of men but not of women, and promotes a male-centric kinship organization. On the other hand, gender equality is enhanced when women have control over economic resources and are involved in the production process. These conditions typically exist within kinship systems that permit women to inherit property, reside near female natal kin, and emphasize women in descent. Such kinship systems are considered more female-centric. The interplay of kinship systems with socio-economic patterns is highlighted, as women's inheritance of property and control over productive resources play a key role. Socio-economic development has been frequently found to displace women from their prior productive roles. For example, mechanization makes women's labour obsolete and in the absence of alternative paid work creates widespread female unemployment. Often, efforts to promote development have targeted males rather than females regardless of a region's pre-existing gender pattern of production (Tinker, 1990). Thus, formal education alone (though necessary) may not be sufficient to promote gender equality. Though absolute levels of prosperity may rise with development, the relative position of women may worsen.

There has so far been little opportunity to examine son preference in contexts where kinship regime transformations and socio-economic development have both occurred. We address this gap by examining whether the decline of female-centred kinship systems and the rise of socio-economic changes that enhance the productive roles of men more than women, will be associated with the emergence of son preference. We examine these possibilities among the Nair caste of Kerala state in southern India.

Our analysis comprises two levels. First, at the cultural level, we describe historical patterns in the Nair community focusing on past kinship systems, the position of women in the family, and legal changes in kinship. We briefly describe socio-economic development in recent decades. Second, using qualitative interviews with individual Nairs in contemporary Kerala, we explore whether emerging marriage and family patterns, and developments in male and female education and roles in family and work may be linked with son preference attitudes or practices.

Ethno-history of Nair Families

Nairs, comprising several subcastes, were the dominant caste (Srinivas, 1962) in much of Kerala in economic, social and political power. They were a mostly landowning and military group who practised matrilineal (from mothers to daughters) descent and inheritance and matrilocal residence (women live with mothers and maternal kin, even after marriage) (Jeffery, 1976). Although variations existed, the traditional household, or *tharavadu,* in the 19th century usually comprised women, daughters, maternal uncles, brothers and sons. Married (sometimes polyandrous) women continued to reside in their natal home while husbands visited from their own homes. While father-child bonds were acknowledged, property, residence and family name were rarely derived from fathers. Though household administrative power was often vested in the seniormost male, or *karanavar,* senior women often had similar authority (Arunima, 2003).

Under matriliny women had comparatively higher status compared to under patriliny (Jeffrey, 1992; Renjini, 1998; Saradamoni, 1999). Descent and inheritance in the female line defined daughters as key members of the family. Dowry was absent. There was no structural basis to view daughters as liabilities; "the value of a female child was relatively high in matrilineal families" (Jeffrey, 2005: 657); and "a female baby eagerly welcomed in every *taravadu,* and if no such baby was born, a girl was adopted" (Saradamoni, 1996: 138). No historical discussion of son preference practices such as female infanticide or abandonment exists in Kerala, in contrast to British observers' focus on such practices in northern and north-western India (e.g., Sen, 2002). Also, no rituals, customs, or proverbs reflect greater value of a son versus daughter (in marked contrast to regions with son preference). On the contrary, in a traditional song performed in Kerala folk theatre, or *Theyyam,* a mother of ten sons yearns for a daughter who will inherit the vast family wealth and provide her spiritual liberation (Kodoth, 1998). The historical picture thus does not indicate systematic son preference attitudes or practices in Kerala during the late 19th to early 20th century.

One of the most fundamental social changes in Kerala was the legal abolition of matriliny over the late 19th to mid-20th century, by British administrators with the support of most Nair men. The former aimed to standardize administrative and legal procedures across India and also viewed matrilineal arrangements as irregular. The latter perceived advantages to gaining direct control over property and inheritance through stronger father-son and conjugal bonds, as traditional occupations and inter-caste links declined and modern political and socio-economic conditions emerged. Matrilineal practices were deemed as out of step with these modernizing realities, and they were sensitive to outsiders' derogatory comments on these practices (Kodoth, 2001). In the public arena, some Nair women and men supported continuing matriliny, but most women appeared silent on this issue, even though they wrote and spoke widely on other topics (Saradamoni, 1996). Kodoth (2001: 384) suggests that women's silence was likely a 'strategic erasure' by Nair males, seeking to "redefine women and children in a dependent relationship within a patrilineal framework". In the private arena some women under matriliny perceived advantages to living in a conjugal family system free from *taravadu* household politics and *karanavar's* domination (Saradamoni, 1996).

In sum, historical patterns among Nairs indicate a favourable position for women within the female-centric kinship and family structure, despite overall societal patriarchy (Jeffrey, 2005). These structures gave women ownership of property, residence in proximity to female kin, relative authority and control over their lives. They facilitated women's access to formal education, though women did not participate in wider economic activities to the extent that men did. There is little or no evidence to suggest that Nairs historically preferred sons to daughters.

Socio-economic development since independence has shown high achievements (near 100% literacy and long life expectancy) in Kerala despite low income, largely due to successful redistribution campaigns and state provision of education and public health (Dreze and Sen, 1998; Parayil and Sreekumar, 2003). Kerala also shows excellent outcomes for women, e.g., near-complete female literacy, and 'normal' population sex ratios, etc. These are attributed to high women's status stemming from the prior matrilineal traditions of major subgroups (including Nairs) comprising over 40 per cent of the population (Jeffrey, 2005; Nair, 1989). However, despite overall progress, Kerala women's relative position on key dimensions appears to have worsened. These include poverty and access to resources (Saradamoni, 1994; Omvedt, 1998), female unemployment nine times higher than the national average (Kannan, 2005), low political participation (Erwer, 1999), and violence against women and spreading dowry customs (Eapen and Kodoth, 2003). Here, we examine whether son preference attitudes or practices have emerged among Nairs in Kerala in the wake of these kinship and socio-economic changes.

Method

Research Strategy

To compare with the ethno-historical description, we conducted interviews among contemporary Nairs, to describe current beliefs about roles of males and females in family, work and education, and to determine whether son preference now exists in this community. We gathered qualitative data during 2002–03 in and around Thrissur city—an important commercial and religious centre of Kerala with significant Nair representation.

Qualitative Data Collection Method

We used qualitative methods to address the multiple levels of enquiry in our study, comparing contemporary individuals of a specific social group with historical descriptions of this community (Ambert, Adler, Adler and Detzner, 1995). To address underlying motivations for possible son preference, and potential demographic behaviour, we used an adaptation of ethnographic rapid assessment method (Scrimshaw and Gleason, 1992)—a research technique originally developed to produce a speedy community assessment for public health or policy related issues. This method involves a team of trained investigators rather than a solo researcher. It is well suited for interdisciplinary enquiries involving a combination of larger-scale health-related information and in-depth understanding of the cultural meanings ascribed to behaviours (Lambert, 1998). Our adaptation used a longer time frame for data collection compared to rapid assessment methods, but kept the strategy of a collaborative research team.

Interview Process and Content

The research team comprised two of the four authors of this paper (one female and one male) and six interview staff (three men and three women to facilitate gender matching of interviewer and participant). The staff and the male author were natives and/or long-term residents of Kerala, with spoken and written fluency in both the local language of Malayalam and English. All authors have native familiarity with India and its cultural contexts.

Interview documents were drafted in English a language familiar to all members of the research team and the language of most published research on our study topic. They were translated into Malayalam by the team to give participants a choice of languages. Translation was facilitated by the ongoing work of local researchers, professionals, and media, and widely accepted and appropriate translations existed for all terms. Interviews, conducted in Malayalam or English depending on the participant's preference, were transcribed, and translated into English by the research staff. The team held weekly meetings to monitor interview experiences, data, emergent themes, and ensuing interview revisions. This enabled all team members to participate in the research process and promoted inter-interviewer consistency and reliability.

The length of interviews was determined by interview dynamics; they averaged 1.5 hours. There were two components: a structured household survey and an in-depth interview. The household survey obtained demographic, household, and socio-economic information including the participant's age, sex, numbers and sex of children, spouse and household residents, education, occupation and marital status of household members and children and siblings elsewhere, and household asset ownership (home/property ownership and major consumer goods). Women's reproductive histories (numbers of pregnancies and births, dates of births, use of health care during pregnancy and delivery) were ascertained.

Our strategy was based on an adaptive theory approach, a variation of grounded theory that accommodates research issues identified from the existing literature and those emerging from the data (Layder, 1998). This guided interview process and content. To explore son preference, we laid the foundation by examining kinship, family and marriage practices; men's and women's education; work and household activities and ideologies, to assess male and female roles in family and society. These themes led to topics on son preference: ideal family size and sex composition; views on sons and daughters; and knowledge, attitudes, and use of sex selection technologies. Emergent data suggested further lines of enquiry. For example, discussions on customs around marriage payments (e.g., what was usually given at the time of marriage, to whom and by whom, the expectations from bride's and groom's families, how the amount was determined, could a marriage take place without giving such payments, etc.) opened a discussion on dowry. Upon probing, the finding emerged that that even those who said they did not pay dowry or disapproved of it, often viewed substantial 'gifts' to the bride or couple as necessary, and how dowry and gifts differed from inheritance. On education, we asked if education was important for Nair girls as well as boys; were girls encouraged to get higher education; how was it determined how high a child should study; etc. On work, we asked views on Nair women working outside the home for money (before and after marriage); taking up a night shift or travelling far to take up a job; etc. These exchanges seemed non-controversial and open, leading to discussions on appropriate male and female roles within and outside the home. Data suggested limitations on women's work, and emergent themes indicated the importance of notions of female chastity in restricting women's work choices and mobility. Discussion on family size, sex composition, and views on sons and daughters began with family planning among Nairs; followed by desired numbers and sex of children; if a couple could have children of only one sex, which would be preferred, and why; issues in raising daughters versus sons; and differences from earlier days. Participants freely discussed attitudes to son preference, and knowledge and attitudes of prenatal sex selection techniques. Actual practices had to be ascertained with specific probing questions, springboarding from discussions on their reproductive histories and those of their children, where appropriate.

Data Analysis

In keeping with rapid assessment approaches, preliminary data analyses were conducted by the entire interview team in periodic meetings during the data collection phase. Guided by adaptive theory, these focused on existing research themes, identifying emergent themes, and data quality checks. We focused on the main lines of enquiry laying the foundation for son preference. These included first, changes in kinship and marriage practices from female to male-centred by emergent data on dowry, gifts, costly wedding celebrations and female inheritance. Second, questions on male and female education and work were guided by prior studies and emergent data on the theme of chastity as a further limitation on women's work. Third, questions on ideal family size, sex composition, son preference attitudes and practices, and use of reproductive technology (for family planning and prenatal sex selection) were guided by prior literature and emergent data on reasons for preferring sons or daughters.

Subsequent data analyses focused on coding themes in the data and summarizing and presenting results, through use of the NuDist qualitative data analysis software programme (QSR International, 2003–2005). Major themes on the topics described above were coded line by line by one author and one other author reviewed the codes.

Very few discrepancies were found, and were settled by discussion. Negative cases were discussed by these two authors only with regard to their frequency and significance for inferences. The software was used only to efficiently summarize information from the numerous interview transcripts, specifically to assess frequency of attitudes and patterns, and identify specific quotations.

Participants

Participants were selected by snowball techniques that began with personal acquaintances of the research staff, who were then asked to suggest other interviewees. We grouped men and women into three age groups (18–39, 40–59, and 60+ years), and three broad socio-economic strata (higher, middle, and lower). The age groups aimed to broadly delineate younger adults (unmarried or married with younger children), midlife adults (those with older children), and older adults. To construct the socio-economic groups, we followed a strategy similar to that of the National Family Health Survey-2's (NFHS–2) "standard of living index" (Indian Institute for Population Sciences and Macro International, 2001: 27). We enumerated the assets (land acreage, housing size and quality, fuel source, drinking water source, and major durable goods, e.g., household appliances, car, motorcycle, etc.) reported by each household. We assigned a value from 1 (low) to 4 (high) to each category, depending on level of ownership, and summed the values. We grouped households into one of three strata based on summed values 0–14, 15–24, 25+. In our data these groups overlap broad occupational categories of the head of the household (professional/ technical/managerial, clerical/sales/skilled trade, blue-collar/ manual labour). We thus take the strata as indicating household socio-economic status. Approximately 26 per cent of our study households were in the lower, 39 per cent in the medium, and 35 per cent in the higher group. In comparison, the NFHS–2 had 18 per cent in the lower, 54 per cent in the medium, and 28 per cent in the high standard of living groups for the all-Kerala sample.

We made efforts to include additional members of groups whose numbers appeared low by seeking introductions in specific neighbourhoods. Numbers of participants were determined by the need to ensure adequate representation of both sexes among different socio-economic and age strata, and to follow up emerging themes. We continued adding participants until saturation was evident, i.e., no new information appeared forthcoming and repetition of prior themes occurred. In each household we interviewed every adult present at the visit—a strategy facilitated by sending paired teams of male and female interviewers to the residences. There were no cases of refusal as respondents seemed eager to participate. We interviewed 215 individuals belonging to 179 households. In 152 households, one member was interviewed, two members in 19 households, and three members in the remainder.

Our research team also interviewed 14 key informants including four Nair community leaders and two researchers. We did not ascertain household demographic and socio-economic information from them, but focused on views of Nair marriage and family practices, education and work patterns and attitudes, whether Nair parents nowadays prefer sons rather than daughters, and if so, what methods they might use to meet their family goals. We also included eight medical practitioners (OB/GYNs, radiologists, lab technicians, and traditional and folk medicine practitioners) to probe sex-selection practices from the health provider's perspective.

Participants' Profiles

Tabulations are presented to provide information on the participants, not to draw inferences to generalize to a wider population. Table 1 shows the age, education and work distribution of the 215 men and women in our data (not including key informants). Few persons reported no schooling, with little sex difference in the levels of education attained. In comparison, NFHS–2 data for Kerala state (Indian Institute for Population Sciences and Macro International, 2001) indicate 2.4 per cent illiteracy among ever married women aged 15 to 49 and 1.8 per cent among husbands of 'other castes' (a residual group of castes including Nairs). Our data show greater male than female work participation. Eapen and Kodoth's review (2003) shows that in the mid-1990s, women's labour force participation in Kerala ranged from 20 to 23 per cent and men's ranged from 54 to 56 per cent. A few women who reported not working were engaged in part-time home-based income-generating activities, such as tutoring or tailoring.

Table 1

Distribution of Male and Female Study Participants by Age, Education and Work Participation

	Males (92)	*Females (123)*
Age group		
Per cent in age group 18–39	39.1	35.0
Per cent in age group 40–59	28.3	41.5
Per cent in age group 60 and above	32.6	23.6
Education		
Per cent reporting no schooling	1.1	2.3
Per cent reporting up to HS	52.5	56.2
Per cent reporting college	32.7	29.3
Per cent reporting post-graduate, professional, other education	13.7	12.3
Work participation		
Employed full time	54.7	16.5
Employed part-time	3.9	2.0
Retired	12.3	4.6
Unemployed	2.7	4.3
Housewife	0.5	47.7
Student	24.4	22.6
Other	1.7	2.4

The data also indicated lower fertility among younger women (average children borne 1.72) compared to midlife (2.56) or older ages (6.17), illustrating Kerala's well-known fertility decline (e.g., Zachariah and Rajan, 1997). In India, though lower fertility appears to be linked with decreasing son preference, the majority of unwanted births are still girls, increasing demand for prenatal sex selection (Bhat and Zavier, 2005). In Kerala, the spread of medical technology related to reproduction is indicated by contraceptive use (mostly sterilization) rates of 53 per cent, 52 per cent and 23 per cent among older, middle and younger age group respectively and prenatal care use of 85 per cent, 77 per cent and 60 per cent, respectively. Prenatal care included weight and blood tests, inoculations, vitamin/iron tablets, and ultrasound scans to check fetal development and position and that can reveal foetal sex. Only one participant reported undergoing amniocentesis, permitted in India only when specific risk factors for birth defects exist. By law, practitioners are barred from revealing the sex of the foetus.

Results

Prior literature and emergent information from the interview process identified aspects of kinship and family practices, and men's and women's education and work roles and attitudes, as most relevant to son preference. Our presentation of the results thus follows this progression, beginning with the kinship, education and work patterns that underpin son preference, and then data on son preference attitudes and practices.

Contemporary Kinship, Family and Marriage Practices

We investigated contemporary practices in family (residence, descent) marriage, and property (dowry and inheritance) organization, to examine women's changing position in these domains. Emerging themes indicated that gift payments made at marriage bore similarities with dowry, and that these payments co-existed with women's inheritance.

Family organization: Participants' residence patterns showed mostly nuclear families as now common in Kerala. About 79 per cent of the 179 households comprised married couples with unmarried children or siblings of the husband. The remainder included the parents either of the husband or the wife; or married brothers co-residing. There were no instances of currently married sisters living together. Some older participants recalled matriliny, but young adults had no personal experience of it. The views of matriliny also varied by gender. Female views were typified by a 55 year-old woman, living with her husband, parents-in-law and unmarried daughter. She and her husband had both grown up in matrilineal households:

> Now, ... in the nuclear system, we will not get any support from our families. We have to find our own food and shelter. But in the *Tharavadu,* we were staying with sisters, cousins, etc., and they will help us very much ... looking after family matters and also in the kitchen. Food was not at all a problem.

Another 54 year-old woman said, "We [women] got importance in the family life. But the seniors took all the decisions". The contrasting male viewpoint was illustrated by an older man who said, "In the old system, women were dominant. That was not good, things are better now". A midlife man said, "At that time there was not much ... connection between fathers and children. Now it is more natural that children live with both father and mother".

Changes in naming practices reflect increasing centrality of males. Where previously daughters had carried on the lineage, now, the father's name has gained prominence. A 52 year-old woman said, "Nowadays, we all have to fill out forms for everything ... and we have to write according to the modern system: first our own [given] name, and then father's name". A young woman said, "In these days, children are addressed with father's *tharavadu* name, though they belong to the mother's *tharavadu*". After marriage now, women often take their husband's name which historically had never been the case. Most respondents knew their *tharavadu* name, and kept in touch with kin for social and ritual occasions, such as weddings or death ceremonies.

Marriage practices: Among the most striking changes in marriage customs has been the shift away from former simplicity toward lavish expenditure mostly borne by the bride's family. This is illustrated in contrasting descriptions from participants of different age groups. Older participants' accounts were typified by that of a 98 year-old woman living in her ancestral house with her married son and daughter-in-law:

> In those days ... a few people only would come from that side, only the groom and one or two people ... It would be considered shameful if a lot of people came from their side to eat at the bride's house. The actual wedding was very simple ... a small ceremony with a lamp in the middle ... with the family elders present. Even their clothes were quite simple. Then there would be just a small feast.

This contrasted with typical accounts of current customs such as by a 45 year-old woman:

> Wedding expenses are borne by the girls' family ... marriage celebration, banquet, marriage hall, ornaments for the bride, etc. ... we are inviting a lot of people ... . Otherwise people will say "oh that marriage took place without anybody". Minimum 2 *payasam* [a sweet dish] should be there ... people are giving 24 types of curries.

This view was widely echoed among the participants. A 57 year-old man with an unmarried daughter reported regarding marriage expenditures that "people can't avoid luxuries ... [because] they fear public opinion".

Dowry, gifts and inheritance: The data also revealed the penetration of the dowry custom into this formerly matrilineal community, similarity between dowry and gifts, and a distinction between dowry/gift and women's inheritance. Participants described dowry as a newer custom among Nairs. Daughters are now typically given substantial assets at marriage, comprising jewellery, cash, and household goods, which usually pass to the control of the in-laws. Reflecting the fact that dowry is barred by law, some respondents spoke disapprovingly of it, as did a 74 year-old man with two sons: "Morally and intellectually it is bad. At any cost we cannot support dowry". However, when discussing payments relating to their own or their children's marriages, some participants said they did not ask or pay 'dowry', but gave 'gifts' to the bride instead. There appeared a blurred distinction between 'dowry' and 'gift'. A 34 year-old male lawyer said, "there is no dowry in the Nair community" but added "without giving any gifts, there is less chance to get married". A midlife man said, "even if it is not demanded we should give something to our daughters. Nobody calls it 'dowry'". These gifts represent a very widespread practice as, according to a retired police officer; "no marriage can take place without gold" (a saying echoed by several participants). Other respondents spoke more openly about dowry and strategies for obtaining it. A 71 year-old woman said:

> Dowry is now very common. People may not ask directly but they say the groom's brother got so much gold and cash etc. My neighbor got 50 sovereigns of gold [one sovereign = 24 gm of gold, at the time of research about $ 18,000] and Rs 50,000 [about $ 1,100] ... we should give some gold to our daughter according to our financial status ... Inheritance share is separate from dowry.

Reciprocal gifts from the groom's side were of much lesser value, typically comprising a sari and gold chain for the bride, though the notion was expressed that the bride would share all the groom's possessions in her new life. This substantial transfer of wealth at the time of marriage is in stark contrast to former matrilineal practice when assets were not given to the groom's family at the time of marriage but often paid to the bride's family.

Dowry was widely viewed as distinct from inheritance; participants stated that women would get inheritance in addition to dowries or gifts. A retired government officer said, "The gold and cash given at the time of marriage are not considered as inheritance. They [daughters] get inheritance afterwards". This applied to gifts too, as in the words of a 43 year-old businessman, "Gift is not the same as inheritance. Women will get their share after the death of parents or at the time of partition". A 41 year-old homemaker said, "My parents gave me dowry in the form of gifts" and added, "Women will get an equal inheritance share apart from dowry". The role of women's husbands in securing female inheritance was suggested by a 57 year-old man in the following words: "Inheritance share has to be given apart from dowry. If the groom is a decent man he won't demand inheritance share but it happens often". All children inherited equal shares of property.

Younger generation's perspective: We further investigated whether marriageable Nair youth may resist developments such as dowry, especially in a society with a high level of formal education and keen awareness of class inequalities and social struggles. We explored the possibility of individual agency as avenues out of marital constraints. Respondents underscored the strict role of marriage and kinship rules in linking and shaping family and personal life. Marriages are typically arranged by parents or family elders, considering hypergamy in caste, education, age, etc. 'Love marriages', though more common than the past, are still infrequent. Even in love marriages, the couple usually negotiates family approval, and choice tends to fall within broad bounds of religion, class and caste. Respondents cautioned about the dangers of marrying out of caste to evade dowry. A 33 year-old man of lower socio-economic status with two daughters said, "Nairs will not encourage girls to marry from another community under any circumstances … . They will not allow that girl back in the house. They may think of her as dead". A young, unmarried, middle socio-economic group woman said, "I want to encourage women to remain single if they cannot find a partner willing to marry without dowry. I have no objection in finding a husband in some other community. But finding [one] from our community is preferred because intercaste marriage will create problems. The Nair girl would be isolated [from] her family. One of my friends is facing [this]". Even in the younger age group, there appeared little flexibility in marriage choices. A key informant said, "Most marriages are arranged by the family because youngsters are not ready to take risk".

Almost every respondent considered the idea of a woman marrying a man younger than herself (to widen her choices) as unthinkable. Remaining single for either sex was admitted as a theoretical possibility, but seen as a very undesirable life situation. In India, marriage is considered almost compulsory for men and women (except for religious renunciates), as 'samskara' (life cycle event) for Hindus, and as a status which confers social adulthood (e.g., unmarried men and women are usually referred to as 'boy' and 'girl') in all communities. Unmarried persons, especially women, are typically viewed with suspicion.

In sum, contemporary family and marriage practices among Nairs indicate marked contrasts with prior customs under matriliny. Contemporary practices reveal increasing centrality of males, decline of women's earlier connection to family and property, and thus, erosion of the kinship forms associated with greater gender equity. Where formerly daughters carried on the lineage and inherited and bequeathed property, they now create expenses in terms of lavish marriage celebrations, dowries or gifts, and inheritance claims, and convey assets to husbands' families—practices associated with son preference elsewhere. Marriage is near-universal, a key marker of personal and familial status, and younger generations do not have much greater flexibility to marry outside familial restrictions.

Male and Female Roles in Education, Work and Family

Son preference is linked with limited female work participation, with a mixed effect of female education. We explored women's and men's views of education and work participation, and the meshing of work and family responsibilities, to investigate possible limitations on women's economic productive roles, despite access to education. Emerging themes suggested that concerns about women's chastity posed additional work restrictions for them.

Education: Participants reported valuing education for both sons and daughters among all socio-economic strata. In a typical response a retired male accountant said, "Of course we are encouraging women to get good education and employment ... no difference between daughter and sons". For some families in the lower socio-economic group however, financial constraints limited daughters' education. A male labourer said, "We can't send our women for education. We don't have much money ... poor families are like that". A 54 year-old woman labourer said, "My elder daughter did not get education due to financial difficulties ... now she depends on others to write a letter ... . I encouraged my younger daughter to study up to SSLC [high school] but ... the miserable [financial] condition of our family ... put an end to her education".

Work and family: Across the socio-economic spectrum paid work was valued for women and men. As a 38 year-old woman labourer said, "It is good that women are working ... . Nowadays we can lead a smooth life only if both women and men work". A 28 year-old middle socio-economic group woman said, "Double income is necessary for average families nowadays". A 21 year-old female student said women should work because "she will become independent [and] get equal importance and respect in the family".

However, participants thought that women should withdraw from outside work if family needs arose. A 33 year-old married man said, "Who will look after the children? ... that's their [women's] duty. I will not allow my wife to work out side". A 65 year-old housewife said, in words echoed by many others, "for daughters, marriage is more important than employment". A lower socio-economic group widow said, "men can take up manual work, but women are meant to look after children". A 21 year-old male student said, "I don't like women to go for job. There is no need of women earning in my family. I don't see any advantage ... only disadvantages. We have to arrange for a servant. Children will not get sufficient care".

Views of male and female roles further illustrated that employment was seen more as a male domain. An older woman said that if one person in the married couple needed to stay home, it had better be the wife because "it is shameful for a husband to live on his wife's earnings", another widely held view. A labourer woman reported that while she herself worked for pay, she did not want her daughter-in-law to do so, as "the girl that we brought to our house must stay at home. The reason is that if men don't work for a day, they have to live with their wife's high attitude". She perceived that in the past both men and women worked in agriculture, but "now men work in other jobs and women concentrate on housework".

Chastity: The theme of chastity emerged to suggest further work restrictions for women, coded in mentions of safe working conditions for women. A young unmarried woman said that "men are allowed to take up night shifts and to move to a far away place to take up jobs ... my parents won't allow me to move ... because ... we have to mingle with other people". A midlife man said that he encouraged his daughter to become a teacher because in an office job she would have to "mingle with others".

In sum, men appear to function as providers and women focus on the household domain to maintain the appropriate gender balance of roles and relationships. Though education and work are highly valued for both men and women, women's work roles may be curtailed to reflect family priorities or perceptions regarding chastity.

Son Preference Practices and Attitudes

We further examined whether son preference attitudes and practices have arisen in this community due to the kinship and socio-economic changes described above.

Regarding attitudes however, initially it appeared there was preference for a balanced family: a son and a daughter. A 33 year-old man said, "If we have a boy then we wish for a girl and if the first one is a girl we wish the second is a boy". The upper socio-economic group appeared relatively free of son preference. A retired professor with three daughters said, "Nairs prefer girls because ... it is traditionally believed that having only a son will end the lineage. A daughter is necessary to continue it". A 29 year-old homemaker said, "We prefer daughters because we believe daughters are more attached to parents".

However, about 35 per cent of the participants, mostly among middle and lower socio-economic groups, revealed attitudes preferring sons, when asked what they preferred, or if they could have children of only one sex, which they would prefer. A middle socio-economic group woman was blunt, "Most Nair families prefer sons. If they have two sons they are happy. But if it is two daughters, they are sad". In a similar vein, a 48 year-old low socio-economic group woman said, "Some of my family members are in a worry because they have no sons".

The attitudes reflected assessments of sons' vs daughters' roles in family and society. An older woman of the middle socio-economic group said, "Nairs prefer sons, because now daughters have to stay at their husband's home". Another of the same group said, "A son is necessary ... suppose anyone in the family gets a heart attack or something, who will take care of them? I don't think that in the night any girls can help". A 69 year-old lower socio-economic group man said, "Male children have many advantages for poor people". A woman of the same group said that though she loved her daughter and granddaughter, she was "eagerly ... wishing for a male baby for my son ... [because he] has a girl child and it would be a burden if it is another girl, as he has no proper employment. If he has a boy then it will be helpful for him".

In addition, about 74 per cent of respondents felt it was more difficult to bring up girls than boys due to the higher expenditures needed for daughters, or to sons' and daughters' work and family roles. A 43 year-old woman of the middle socio-economic group said, "For daughters, you have to educate them and prepare for their marriage ... compared to boys bringing up girls is difficult just due to marriage cost". A 68 year-old man from the higher socio-economic group said, "Bringing up girls is more difficult [than boys] because we have to take extra care to keep girls safe". A key informant highlighted the changed assessment of daughters among the formerly matrilineal Nairs in the followed words: "There is preference for sons. Parents frankly say to their young daughters that they have to go to another house and they have to be given dowry".

However, the study did not reveal widespread practices indicative of son preference. Participants reported no differences in ceremonies and celebrations connected with the birth of girls vs. boys.

Regarding prenatal sex-selection techniques and practices, almost all respondents had heard of them (mainly ultrasound, a few were also aware of amniocentesis). Most strongly disapproved of finding out the sex of the baby prior to birth, and condemned sex-selective abortion. Again, however, nuances emerged on further conversation.

A 55 year-old male labourer said, "I don't think it is bad. If a family has one or two girls and they came to know the next child is also a girl, and they have no economic resources to afford one more girl, then there is no problem to abort that child". A 23 year-old upper socio-economic status man reported:

> My relative's neighbour underwent abortion as soon as they found out that the baby is a girl … . They could not afford a second girl. They belong to low-income group … . Though abortion charge is high people do it fearing dowry. They had done it from Thrissur Medical College. I think everybody can do this if we give more money to doctors or nurses.

Several participants felt that finding out the foetus' sex was bad because it would lead to disappointment if it was a girl. A woman of lower socio-economic status said, "It is better not to come to know the sex of the baby during pregnancy, as if it is a girl, the mother will face trouble from the in-laws".

A midlife lower socio-economic group woman said, "No medical practitioner will tell the sex of the baby during pregnancy because it is illegal. But if the doctor is very close to you, [or] if you have enough money to pay a private doctor, they will surely tell you". A male upper socio-economic group retiree said, "Female foeticide is done in Thrissur Nursing Home and also in some other clinics … . The cost of abortion can be Rs 1,500. Both high-income and low-income groups practise female foeticide". A 19 year-old male computer science student said, "I have heard that female foeticide is practised here. But I don't know any individual case. If people want to abort they can do it. I support it".

In sum, our study revealed son preference attitudes more among middle and lower socio-economic groups of Nairs in Kerala, linked to perceptions of roles of sons and daughters in the family, and expenses of raising girls. However, it did not reveal widespread use of sex-selection practices, though a few participants reported them.

Health Care Providers' Perspectives

All medical practitioners interviewed for this study reported high professional compliance with laws forbidding revealing the foetus' sex. They were proud of the wide adherence to medical rules and ethics in Kerala, and stated that the Indian Medical Association has strongly opposed female foeticide. Despite this a gynaecologist in a major local hospital said, "I have no direct experience of female foeticide … and I have not heard of such cases from my colleagues. But there is always a preference for boys. Some women are disappointed when they deliver a girl. They are not happy even if that is her first delivery". A gynaecologist in an infertility clinic reported:

> Many people come to find the sex of the baby ... . Parents are eager to know ... and I am not against [this ... Some doctors are ready to do this and these practices are increasing in number. Now parents are unhappy when they come to know their second child is also a girl. Most commonly if the third child is also a girl they terminate ... . I am also directing some people to some doctors. They do these things for money. Both private and government doctors ... but I can't reveal the name of the hospitals.

A retired health supervisor reported, "As I was a health supervisor, I know female foeticide is practised here. In every community, including Nairs, some people having one daughter scan the next pregnancy, and if they find out if it is a female, surely get depressed. But many would not go for foeticide because they believe it is a sin. Female foeticide is practised in every hospital, including the government hospital".

An ayurvedic doctor mentioned medicines that could be prescribed prior to conception to ensure a male foetus. A traditional medicine practitioner stated that while some families may be curious about the foetus' sex, he was not aware of any prejudice against girl children or prenatal sex selection in his area. During the study the research team observed several new maternity clinics, radiology facilities, etc., in the Thrissur area. These indicate the spread of the privatized modern medical sector in Kerala (as in most of urban India) and suggest that motivated families seeking a sex-selection facility may be able to find one.

Discussion

Using data from qualitative interviews contrasted with historical studies, we examined the proposition that in the Nair community of Kerala, India, where transformations in kinship systems and socio-economic changes have occurred, son preference may emerge. Our findings indicated that after matriliny ended, kinship and family systems that often prioritize the interests and needs of men over those of women have arisen. Descent now emphasizes the male line, women reside after marriage with husbands, and bring substantial assets from their natal homes. Nair women's relations to family and property appear transformed. Such kinship systems resemble those described as 'patrifocal' by Mukhopadhyay and Seymour (1994). Our findings indicate that despite high education for both sexes, women's productive roles are limited due to lack of job availability, and perceptions of female family roles. Theoretically, such social change is expected to be associated with a rise in gender inequality (Blumberg, 2004), despite overall gains for both sexes in education, health, and other arenas. Our findings suggest that son preference attitudes are an added indicator of relative gender inequality emerging mostly among lower and middle socio-economic sub-groups of Nairs in the wake of these changes. Prior studies indicated that changes in kinship systems lowered the status of adult Nair women (Saradamoni, 1994) through the process of 'housewifization' (Renjini, 1998), but did not examine son preference. Prior studies of son preference examined cultural groups where it is an entrenched practice. The present study suggests the rise of son preference attitudes in the context of social change in a group where it did not previously exist.

Participants emphasized the value of education for both sexes, yet many also reported curtailing women's work due to perceptions of female household roles and chastity. While gender role specialization previously existed in Nair society, findings suggest that the emergent forms of family and economy have widened gender inequity in paid work. Widespread formal education and extra-familial paid work are socio-economic changes associated with modernization. Modernization is often assumed to lead to the decline of 'traditional' inequalities, including those of gender. With modernization, Kerala women and men have made major gains in domains such as education and health, but in other arenas such as employment and dowry, women's relative position appears to have worsened. The interlinked changes in kinship, economy and gender roles create the perception that daughters are expensive and are no longer core members of the natal family. Modernization in India has not diminished but has enhanced the reliance on male-focused kinship networks, male dominance of the occupational sphere, and female specialization in the domestic arena, for family advancement (Khanna, 2001). We found that the younger age group's marriage-related views and practices were not more progressive than their seniors'. Our findings extend those of Srinivasan and Lee (2004), who found a mixed effect of modernization on Bihar women's attitudes, especially that younger women did not disapprove of dowry. Our study thus accords with 'gender and development' perspectives.

The abolition of matriliny was part of a community strategy led by Nair men to advance within a modernizing wider society, a tactic that "hinged on a rejection of the woman-centered 'otherness' of their matrilineal past" (Arunima, 2003: 195). Women's private adaptations or resistance to these changes are less documented, but Renjini (1998) suggests that some women welcomed the shift to conjugal families, hoping for greater personal autonomy and freedom from extended family controls. Men acquired the roles of providers and heads of families, and women those of homemakers and auxiliaries (Eapen and Kodoth, 2003). These patterns resemble those in regions of India where son preference historically existed. In those regions, contributions of wives may be valued, but daughters are viewed as expensive outsiders whether or not dowry is paid (Das Gupta et al., 2003). The fact that son preference attitudes appear to have emerged among middle and lower socio-economic Nair groups accords with Basu's (1986) observation of poverty-driven demographic innovations in Kerala, but not with studies in North India showing that families with some wealth rather than poorer ones discriminate against daughters (Miller, 1981; Das Gupta, 1987).

Our findings accord with numerous studies of the spread of dowry into communities in southern India where it was not previously the norm, accompanied by the decline of endogamous marriage patterns, and increase in consumerism and expenditure on weddings (e.g., Caldwell, Reddy and Caldwell, 1983; Osella and Osella, 2000; Rao, 1993a and 1993b). India's post-1992 economic liberalization has led to increased consumerism where aspirations for consumption are high but relatively few can afford the expense (Kothari, 1997). The rise of costly wedding celebrations paid for by the bride's family indicates another way in which the position of daughters has become more vulnerable in the modern Nair family. Eapen and Kodoth (2003) argue: "Gender-based inequality in the context of marriage practices emerges ... by norming specific kinds of consumption ... . By generating expectations on a wide scale through lavish marriages ... women are objectified in dangerous ways" (p. 14). Though the authors place a positive interpretation on the fact that dowry does not exhaust women's inheritance claims, by contrast, our study suggests that the practice may increase the perceived expensiveness of daughters, especially when costs of education are added.

Though the Kerala legacy of matriliny paved the way for high female education and a unique and pervasive consciousness of women's entitlements (Jeffrey, 2005), education does not automatically enable women to overcome gender inequality, especially if the content and context of schooling promote social conservatism rather than transformation (Longwe, 1998). In the context of limited work availability for women, many females in Kerala spend longer in formal education as a socially acceptable venue to wait for marriage (Eapen and Kodoth, 2003). While this certainly facilitates women's occupational opportunities, it also leads to their seeking husbands with higher qualifications, which has implications for dowry payments. High education expenses together with higher dowry, inheritance claims, and a relative scarcity of paid work—all contribute to the rising perception of daughters as expensive outsiders, especially in a social climate where marriage is a strict necessity. Thus, our findings suggest that female education, a widely advocated policy prescription to address a variety of social dilemmas, is not sufficient to overcome societal disadvantage faced by women. To overcome these barriers female employment appears important. In South Asia, women's economic participation, even at low wages, can radically transform women's value in the household, reduce familial gender inequality, and challenge patriarchy (Ahmed and Bould, 2004).

Our study suggests that key societal transformations in Kerala (the move away from matriliny, and the limitation of female work chances, despite the spread of education) are linked with the rise of son preference attitudes among middle and lower socio-economic sub-groups in the Nair community. However, these findings must be understood within the scope of the study with the following limitations. It was a challenge to address this extremely sensitive topic during fieldwork, especially the private nature of decision-making around son preference. We made strenuous efforts to meet these challenges through rapport-building during interviews. Second, our research focused on a single time point. We did not follow respondents periodically to learn about their choices and strategies when faced with life situations involving sons, daughters, and themselves.

Instead, we asked contemporary Nairs in Kerala about marriage and family, male and female education and work roles, and son preference. By contrasting their responses with what is known historically about this community's beliefs and practices, we examined social and economic transformations. Finally, the study refers only to the situation among Nairs in Kerala, not elsewhere, and not for any other formerly matrilineal castes. The study was the first effort in this area, and future studies on this topic need to investigate these gaps. Despite its limitations, it contributes toward examining processes of gender inequality among a culture usually lauded for high women's status.

References

Ahmed, S.S. and S. Bould (2004). One Able Daughter is Worth 100 Illiterate Sons: Reframing the Patriarchal Family, *Journal of Marriage and Family,* Vol. 66, December, pp. 1332–41.

Ambert, A., P.A. Adler, P. Adler and D.F. Detzner (1995). Understanding and Evaluating Qualitative Research, *Journal of Marriage and the Family,* 57, November, pp. 879–93.

Arunima, G. (2003). *There comes Papa: Colonialism and the Transformation of Matriliny in Kerala, Malabar c 1850–1940,* Orient Longman Pvt. Ltd., Hyderabad.

Basu, A.M. (1986). Birth Control by Assetless Workers in Kerala: The Possibility of a Poverty-induced Fertility Transition, *Development and Change,* 17(2), pp. 265–82.

Bhat, P.N.M. and F. Zavier (2005). Fertility Decline and Gender Bias in Northern India, *Demography,* 40(4), pp. 637–57.

Blumberg, R.L. (2004). Extending Lenski's Schema to hold up both Halves of the Sky: A Theory-guided Way of Conceptualizing Agrarian Societies that Illuminate a series of Puzzles about Gender Stratification, *Sociological Theory* 22:2, June.

Caldwell, J.C., P.H. Reddy and P. Caldwell (1983). The Causes of Marriage Change in South India, *Population Studies,* 47, pp. 343–61.

Clark, A. and S. Shreeniwas (1995, March). Questioning the Links between Maternal Education and Child Mortality: The Case of Gujarat, paper presented at the Population Association of America Annual Meeting, San Francisco.

Das Gupta, M. 1987. Discrimination against Female Children in Rural Punjab, India, *Population and Development Review,* 13(1), pp. 77–100.

Das Gupta, M., J. Zhenghua, L. Bohua, X. Zhenming and W. Chung (2003). Why is Son Preference so Persistent in East and South Asia? A Cross-country Study of China, India and the Republic of Korea, *Journal of Development Studies,* December, 40(2), pp. 153–187.

Dreze, J. and A. Sen (1997). *Indian Development: Selected Regional Perspectives,* Oxford University Press, New Delhi.

Eapen, M. and P. Kodoth (2003). "Family Structure, Women's Education and Work: Re-examining the High Status of Women in Kerala", in S. Mukhopadhyay and R. Sudarshan (eds.), *Tracking Gender Equity under Economic Reforms: Continuity and Change in South Asia,* Kali for Women and IDRC, New Delhi, India, pp. 227–67.

Erwer, M. (1999). Development beyond 'the status of women': The Silence of Agency in the Political Space in Kerala, India, paper presented at the 7th Interdisciplinary Congress on Women, Tromso, Norway, June 20–26.

Goodkind, D. (1996). On Substituting Sex Preference Strategies in East Asia: Does Prenatal Sex Selection Replace Post-natal Discrimination? *Population and Development Review,* 22(1), pp. 111–25.

International Institute of Population Sciences and ORC Macro (2001). *National Family Health Survey (NFHS-2) India, 1998–99, Kerala,* IIPS, Mumbai.

Jeffery, R. (1976). *The Decline of Nayar Dominance: Society and Politics in Travancore, 1847–1908,* Holmes & Meier Publishers, Inc., NY.

—— (1992). *Politics, Women and Well-being: How Kerala became 'a model',* The Macmillan Press Ltd., London.

—— (2004/2005). Legacies of Matriliny: The Place of Women and the 'Kerala Model', *Pacific Affairs,* Winter 77, 4, pp. 647–64.

Kannan, K.P. (2005). Kerala's turnaround in Growth: Role of Social Development, Remittances and Reform, *Economic and Political Weekly,* February 5th, pp. 548–54.

Khanna, S.K. (2001). Shahri Jat and Dehati Jatni: The Indian Peasant Community in Transition, *Contemporary South Asia,* 10(1), pp. 37–53.

Kishor, S. (1993). May God give Sons to All: Gender and Child Mortality in India, *American Sociological Review,* 58(2), pp. 247–65.

Klasen, S. and C. Wink (2002). A Turning Point in Gender Bias in Mortality: An Update on the Number of Missing Women, *Population and Development Review,* June, 28(2), pp. 285–312.

Kodoth, P. (2001). Courting Legitimacy or Delegitimizing Custom? Sexuality, Sambandham and Marriage Reform in Late Nineteenth Century Malabar, *Modern Asian Studies,* 35(2), pp. 349–84.

—— (2001b). Gender, Family and Property Rights: Questions from Kerala's Land Reforms, *Indian Journal of Gender Studies,* 8(2), pp. 291–306.

—— (1998). Women and Property Rights: A Study of Land Tenure Structure and Personal Law in Malabar, 1880–1940, Unpublished Dissertation, Department of Economics, University of Hyderabad.

Kothari, S. (1997). Whose Independence? The Social Impact of Economic Reform in India, *Journal of International Affairs,* New York, Summer, 51(1), pp. 85–117.

Layder, D. (1998). *Sociological Practice,* Sage Publications, London.

Longwe, S.H. (1998). Education for Women's Empowerment or Schooling for Women's Subordination? *Gender and Development,* July, Vol. 6 # 2, pp. 19–26.

Mayer, P. (1999). India's Falling Sex Ratios, *Population and Development Review* 25(2), pp. 323–43.

Miller, B. (1981). *The Endangered Sex: Neglect of Female Children in Rural North India,* Cornell University Press, Ithaca.

Mukhopadhyay, C.C. and S. Seymour (eds.) (1994), *Women, Education and Family Structure in India,* Westview Press, Boulder.

Murthi, M., A. Guio and J. Dreze (1995). Mortality, Fertility and Gender Bias in India, *Population and Development Review,* 21, pp. 745–82.

Nayar, P.K. (1989). "Kerala Women in Historical and Contemporary Perspective", in K. Mahadevan (ed.), *Women and Population Dynamics: Perspectives from Asian Countries,* Sage Publications, New Delhi, India, pp. 205–20.

Omvedt, G. (1998). Disturbing Aspects of Kerala Society, *Bulletin of Concerned Asian Scholars,* Symposium on Kerala, October-December, 30 (3), pp. 31–33.

Osella, F. and C. Osella (2000). *Social Mobility in Kerala: Modernity and Identity in Conflict,* Pluto Press, London.

Parayil, G. and T.T. Sreekumar (2003). Kerala's Experience of Development and Change, *Journal of Contemporary Asia,* 3(4), pp. 465–492.

Rahman, L. and V. Rao (2004). The Determinants of Gender Equity in India: Examining Dyson and Moore's Thesis with New Data, *Population and Development Review,* 30(2), June, pp. 239–268.

Rao, V. (1993a). Dowry Inflation in Rural India: A Statistical Investigation, *Population Studies,* 47(2), pp. 283–93.

—— (1993b). The Rising Price of Husbands: A Hedonic Analysis of Dowry Increase in Rural India, *Journal of Political Economy,* 101, pp. 666–77.

Razavi, S. and C. Miller (1995). From WID to GAD: Conceptual Shifts in the Women and Development Discourse, Occasional Paper No. 1, *UN*

Fourth World Conference on Women, February 1995, United Nations Research Institute for Social Development, Palais des Nations 1211 Geneva 10 Switzerland.

Renjini, D. (1988). *Nayar Women Today: The Disintegration of Matrilineal System and Changing Status of Nayar Women in Kerala,* Classical, New Delhi, India.

Saradamoni, K. (1994). Women, Kerala and Some Development Issues, *Economic and Political Weekly* XXIX (9), pp. 501–09.

—— (1996). Women's Rights and the Decline of Matriliny in Southern India, in C. Risseew and R. Palriwala (eds.), *Shifting Circles of Support: Contextualizing Gender and Kinship in South Asia and Sub Saharan Africa,* Altamira Press, Walnut Creek CA.

—— (1999). *Matriliny Transformed: Family, Law and Ideology in Twentieth Century Travancore,* Sage Publications, New Delhi, India.

Scrimshaw, N.S. and G.R. Gleason (eds.) (1992). *Rapid Assessment Procedures: Qualitative Methodologies for Planning and Evaluation of Health Related Programmes,* International Nutrition Foundation for Developing Countries (INFDC), Boston, MA, USA.

Sen, A. (1990). More than 100 million Women are Missing, *New York Review of Books,* December, 20, pp. 61–66.

Sen, S. (2002). The Savage Family: Colonialism and Female Infanticide in Nineteenth Century, *Journal of Women's History,* Autumn, 14(3), pp. 53–79.

Srinivas, M.N. (1962). *Caste in Modern India and Other Essays,* Asia Publishing House, Bombay and New York.

Srinivasan, P. and G.R. Lee (2004). The Dowry System in Northern India, Women's Attitudes and Social Change, *Journal of Marriage and Family,* 66, pp. 1108–17.

Sudha, S. and S. Irudaya Rajan (2003). Persistent Daughter Disadvantage in India: What do Estimated Sex Ratios at Birth and Sex Ratios of Child Mortality Risk Reveal? *Economic and Political Weekly,* Special Issue on Sex Ratios in India, 38, pp. 4361–69.

Tinker, I. (ed.), (2000). *Persistent Inequalities,* Oxford University Press, Oxford.

Zachariah, K.C. and S. Irudaya Rajan (eds.), (1997). *Kerala's Demographic Transition: Determinants and Consequences,* Sage Publications, New Delhi, Thousand Oaks (California) and London.

SEVEN

Status of the Girl Child and Son Preference in Madurai

Mumtaj Begum and Christianna Singh

The Indian Census report of 2001 clearly shows that there is a significant decline in the child sex ratio. The birth of a girl child often goes unreported and unregistered. This factor assumes greater significance where large numbers of female children are not even allowed to be born. They are either killed in the womb itself or soon after birth. The declining child sex ratio is an indicator of accelerated disequilibrium. There are many socio-cultural and economic reasons for this disturbing trend. These issues pertain to inbuilt social bias against the girl child. An aura of second-class citizenship pervades the life of a girl emanating from even before her birth, tormenting her all through her life until death. There is something inherent in the Indian socio-economic and cultural environment that is deep set and hard to eradicate which, in spite of all the progress made on several frontiers locally, nationally and internationally, still subjugates the natural vivacity of a female child. It causes the Indian girls to grow up with a deep-rooted sense of fear and insecurity coupled with inadequacy to meet the challenges of daily life on their own. It also often psychologically cripples them to face the hardships of life in general and resist gender-based discrimination in particular. In an attempt to stem the rot, female foeticide, female infanticide, selling of a girl child, girl child prostitution and any form of violence against a woman is strictly forbidden by law drawing heavy penalties on violation. Like a deadly virus that develops resistance to the vaccine, the discrimination against the females continues to manifest itself in more subtle forms, one of which is the continued preference for sons in society. Unless an attempt is made to continuously monitor, understand and eradicate the factors contributing to 'son preference' and 'daughter aversion' and stop the disease at its roots, more resistant strains of the disease will develop, making it very difficult to rid the country of a serious population imbalance. Even now, it appears as if this 'disease' has already spread to its secondary stage affecting the welfare and growth of the economy in spite of the industrial and technological revolution in the context of globalization and liberalization and is that much more difficult to cure.

The strong preference for sons over daughters and resulting discrimination against daughters in India is well known (Mathur and Sen, 1974; Sarma and Jain, 1974; Williamson, 1976; Bhatia, 1978; United Nations, 1981, 1985; Cleland, Verrall and Vaessen, 1983; Khan and Prasad, 1983; Kanitkar and Naravan, 1984; Sarma, 1988; Basu, 1989; Khan and Gupta, 1987; Arnold, 1996, 1997) though it is not uniformly observed across different regions of the country.

Biologically, female children have longer life. Despite such statistical and scientific reasons, the sex ratios at birth as well as in general are unfavourable to girl children. Sex differentials in child mortality (Pakrasi, 1970; Graves, 1978; Dyson and Moore, 1983; Gurusamv, 1990; Klasen, 1994; Dreze and Sen, 1996; Sen, 2001) result in the smaller number of females compared to males. Dreze and Sen (1996) have termed the low sex ratio in India as a 'missing women' phenomenon: on the basis of sub-Saharan ratios, the number of 'missing women' in India, as estimated by them is between 35–37 million.

The studies on son preference are innumerable both in the international and national contexts. These studies are usually based on National Sample Surveys (secondary data). Studies based on regional data are limited. Regional studies are much needed to throw light on specific regional peculiarities and behaviour. Hence, the present study has been taken up to identify factors determining the status of the girl child and son preference at a regional level—Madurai district in Tamil Nadu.

Data and Methodology

To meet the above objectives, primary data on the selected socio-economic, demographic and cultural variables was collected from the households of Madurai district.

Rationale behind Choosing Madurai District as the Study Area

Madurai is the second largest district in the state of Tamil Nadu, comprising people from varied socio-economic and cultural backgrounds. Moreover, it reflects the characteristics of modern life strongly combined with traditional outlook. There are strong emerging cross-cultural forces that will surely surface in other regions as well within the country as more and more rural areas get exposed to the global world with the onslaught of the IT revolution and globalization. Hence, such a socio-economic study of Madurai district will offer a platform on which policy making is facilitated on a macro level for the country as a whole.

Sampling Design

To pursue the objectives of the present study, primary data on the selected socio-economic, demographic variables were collected from 300 households—157 from the urban and 143 from rural areas of Madurai district. The district comprises of seven taluks and 13 blocks. The required samples were chosen by adopting a three-stage stratified sample design with taluk as the first stage, block as the second stage and household as the third stage sample unit.

Data Collection

The study is limited to married women having at least one live birth and living with their husband. In almost all cases, the wife from the selected household was interviewed. The questionnaire was administered in August 2005. A pilot study was conducted to test the validity and suitability of the questionnaire.

Data Analysis

The socio-economic and demographic variables collected in the survey are classified and tabulated for the purpose of analysis. One-way and two-way frequency tables and summary statistics give insight into the profile of the respondents.

To countercheck the findings of the direct questions on son preference, the following indices were developed using the figures for ideal number of boys in the family (IB), ideal number of girls in the family (IG), ideal number of children of either sex (IE), and the ideal total of children including specific sex preferences and otherwise (IT). The relationship between the components is given as IB + IG + IE = IT. From this relationship, an index of extent of son preference or daughter aversion was developed as follows:

Index for Extent of Son Preference Using Ideal Number of Children

Criterion	*Extent of Son Preference*
1. IG = IE = 0, then IB = IT	Absolute son preference/daughter aversion
2. IB ≥ IG	Strong son preference
3. IB = IG ≠ 0	Equal son preference
4. IG ≥ IB	Weak son preference
5. IB = IE = 0, then IG = IT	Absolute daughter preference/son aversion
6. IB = IG = 0, then IE = IT	No preference

A cross-tabulation of the data pertaining to son preference from the three different investigative approaches was made after suitable coding: 0 = no son preference, 1 = strong son preference. In the case of the extent of son preference, items 5 and 6 above were coded as 0 and the others as 1 (because of the existence of definite preference for sons) respectively.

Women's autonomy is ascertained by considering the decision-making power of the women in domestic, socio-economic and reproductive matters. Nine statements related to these matters were given to the respondents to indicate whether decisions were made by self or others (decisions made by 'self' implies all situations in which the woman is actively involved in decision-making even if the decisions are taken jointly by the couple or family members). Every decision made by 'self' is given a score of 1 and 'others' zero. On the basis of the total score obtained by each respondent, their autonomy is then classified as low if total score is less than or equal to 3, medium if it is between 4 and 6, and high if it is higher than 6.

Binary Logistic Regression is applied to find out the influence of select variables on the son preference of the respondents. Logistic regression is a technique used to analyze situations in which there are one or more independent variables which determine an outcome that is measured with a dichotomous variable in which there are only two possible outcomes. The preference for sons depicted by a binary variable takes a value of unity if a son is preferred and 0 otherwise.

The son preference model estimated in the present study is as follows:

$$Y = 1 \text{ if } Y^* > 0$$
$$= 0 \text{ otherwise}$$

$$Y = \beta_0 + \beta_1 X_2 + \ldots + \beta_n X_n$$

where Y is son preference (a dummy variable) and Xs are the explanatory variables.

Explanatory Variables

The set of explanatory variables considered in this model are as follows:

- Current Age of Wife
- Age at Marriage of Wife
- Religion (Categorical Variable)
- Caste (Categorical Variable)
- Family Type (Nuclear = 0, Joint = 1)
- Education of Wife (in years)
- Current Residence (Rural = 0, Urban = 1)
- Occupation of Wife (Low = 0, Medium = 1, High = 2)
- Employment Status of Wife in Comparison to Husband (Low = 0, Medium = 1, High = 2)
- Total Family Income
- Number of Living Boys
- Number of Living Children
- Number of Boys Born
- Age at First Delivery
- Difference between Age at First Delivery and Age at Marriage
- Induced Abortions
- Current Pregnancy
- Adoption of Family Planning
- Knowledge of Contraceptives

- Ideal Number of Children
- Ideal Number of Boys
- Expected Expenditure on Children
- Daughter as a Liability (No = 0, Yes = 1)
- Family Head (Others = 0, Self = 1)
- Perceived Self Status in the Family (Low = 0, Medium = 1, High = 2)
- Women's Autonomy (Low = 0, Medium = 1, High = 2)

MLE method is applied to estimate the son preference function in the chosen area of study.

Socio-economic and Demographic Background of the Respondents

- *Religion and caste:* Hindus are in large majority (90.7%), followed by Christians (6.7%) and Muslims (2.7%). Similarly, in the caste analysis, the number of respondents in the backward community forms the clear majority (66%), followed by Scheduled Castes and Scheduled Tribes (19.7%) and relatively minor representations from MBC and FC categories.
- *Family type:* The breaking up of the traditional joint family is obvious in the current study with 86 per cent of the respondents belonging to nuclear families.
- *Literacy:* The respondents and their husbands are moderately literate on an average, with only 11.7 per cent of the husbands and 24 per cent of the wives in the sample classified otherwise. However, the average level of literacy among the men is higher with the average man going beyond higher secondary level of education and the corresponding level for women being high school.
- *Residence:* Urban households (52.3%) marginally outnumber the rural households.
- *House ownership:* Most of the respondents (55.7%) live in their own houses, followed by those who live in rented houses (33.7%). The remaining (10.7%) have leased a house. This indicator of status is positively skewed.

- *Occupation:* The occupational status of the husbands on an average belongs to the middle strata of employment which includes non-casual workers, small shopkeepers, telephone operators and other clerical cadres for the sample. The corresponding mean occupational status of the women in the sample is very low with 78.3 per cent of the respondents reporting as unemployed and the remaining 7.7 per cent employed in low-status jobs. When comparing the status of employment of the husband and wife, the wife's employment status is low.
- *Income:* The main breadwinner of the family is the husband. Most of the reported income·for the sample is income from employment. The lower middle income group earning Rs 50,000 to Rs 2.5 lakh annually forms the main income class of the sample. The economic consideration of being able to financially support a large family is definitely a limiting factor as regards to the size of the family.
- *Current age:* The respondents and their husbands are on an average middle-aged (35 years for women and 41 years for men). Some of the criteria for selection in the sample was that the respondent should be married and with at least one child. Hence, there is no undue weightage on either end of the age scale.
- *Age difference between the couple:* The data reveals that on an average, the husband is about 5 to 6 years older than the wife. This is once again reflective of a common phenomenon. Seniority in age is strongly correlated with decision-making and higher status (deserving of more respect) traditionally.
- *Age at marriage:* On an average, the men in the sample are about 26 years of age at the time of marriage and the women are about 21 years. This happens to be the traditionally accepted ideal age for marriage of men and women, the chief criterion for men being the age at which they are well-settled in a job after completion of higher studies or professional training and for the women, it is the age prescribed by the government and other health welfare services as the ideal minimum age for marriage versus the legally valid 18 years.
- *Number of children:* The sample average of one boy and one girl per family has a wide variation and is skewed in favour of boys.

The ratio of boys and girls living to boys and girls born is slightly in favour of the boys (1.14 : 1.00). The mean percentage of girls reported dead to total female births (6.5%) within a family is more than that of boys (4.8%). The biological life expectations are more for girls than for boys. Yet, the figures pertaining to death ratios also reveal that more deaths occur among females. In other words, the sample data seems to be corroborating the existence of son preference and daughter aversion. The living child sex ratio (714) of the sample is less than its child sex ratio at birth (892). This could possibly imply female infanticide and neglect of health care for the girl child and also be an indicator of son preference.

- *Ideal number of children:* The mean of the ideal number of boys per family, as given by the respondents, is greater than that of girls—indicating a preference for sons. The ideal size of the family is two children, with at least one boy and one girl on an average. Only 8.6 per cent of the respondents had absolute son preference, not wanting any daughter and also clearly expressing that they were not indifferent as to their choice of the sex of their child ideally. The largest grouping of 42.3 per cent wished for an equal number of boys and girls. About 29.3 per cent maintained that they were indifferent as to the sex of the child, not showing any strong or weak preference for either sex, whereas 13.7 per cent and 1.3 per cent showed strong and weak son preferences, respectively. On the whole, excluding those who showed absolute daughter preference and those who were truly indifferent to the sex of the child, 66 per cent of the respondents did indicate a preference for sons of varying degrees.
- *Age at first delivery:* The mean age of the respondents at first delivery is 22 years. Most women bear their first child within the second completed year of marriage. The fertility period of the women is thus fairly long within the sample. The scope for multiple pregnancies is large. However, the mean number of children born per family is only 2.26. This is an indicator that the Family Welfare Scheme working within this district (coupled with the economic criterion of small income families) has met with moderate success in the overall Indian context and that the respondents are, on an average, aware of family planning methods.

- *Induced abortions:* The possibility that a woman goes in for aborting a pregnancy according to the sample data is 0.073.
- *Current pregnancy:* The respondents who reported being currently pregnant were only 7.3 per cent of the sample population.
- *Desire for more children:* Only 28 per cent of the respondents desire to have more children. The majority have come to terms with the prevalent child sex ratio. Hence, it implies that the sample is less prone to drastic child sex ratio changes.
- *Sex preference of child:* While 56.7 per cent of the respondents claimed to be indifferent to the sex of the child, marking their choice as 'either sex', 23.3 per cent preferred sons and only 20 per cent quoted a daughter preference. This indicates a denial of strong son preference when directly questioned and the need to adopt an indirect method of enquiry.
- *Family planning knowledge and use:* Due to cultural inhibitions, only 50 (16.67%) women responded to the query on use of contraceptives to avoid pregnancy (among these, 32 per cent had not used contraceptives to avoid pregnancy). Yet, when questioned about methods used, an increased number of 48 per cent admitted knowledge and use of contraceptives. The most popular method of contraception was condom (44%), followed by tubectomy (26%). Fewer men opted for permanent methods (1.4%). Of the 49 per cent of the respondents who gave reasons for adoption of family planning methods, 61 per cent quoted both reasons of prevention and spacing pregnancy. Only 38 per cent had used methods of contraception exclusively for prevention and 0.9 per cent exclusively for spacing. In yet another indirect attempt to find the usage of contraceptives, when the respondents were asked to list the methods of family planning they had knowledge about, 86.7 per cent were not willing to answer the question or claimed ignorance in spite of the fact that some of them had admitted usage of at least one method. The most popular reason for not using contraceptives was that it was not needed (54%) and not lack of knowledge (22%). This is a clear indicator that many respondents were ill-at-ease with disclosing matters relating to knowledge and use of contraceptives to the student investigators, though the students had been given adequate training to make these enquiries.

- *Son preference:* After queries about the ideal number of children in a family the respondents were more emphatic about stating their preference for sons. About 77 per cent stated that they would like to have at least one son in the family. The most common reason cited is security in old age (51.1%). The other significant reasons are economic motivation (14.16%), religious obligations (10.73%) and continuation of the family lineage (10.30%). The less significant reasons in order of priority are help in business/farm/household activities and lastly, emotional support.

Table 1

Reason for Preferring Son by Current Residence

Reason for Preferring Son	*Current Residence (in percentage)*		
	All	*Rural*	*Urban*
Old age security	51.1	50.0	52.3
Economic motivation	14.2	12.3	16.2
Religious obligations	10.7	18.0	2.7
Continuation of the family line/name	10.3	9.8	10.8
Help in business/ farm/household activities	8.2	7.4	9.0
Emotional support	5.6	2.5	9.0
Total	100.0	100.0	100.0

Table 1 indicates that, in general, apart from the major motive of old age security, the greater reason for son preference among urban families is economic in nature, whereas among rural families it is due to religious reasons.

- *Daughter preference:* Daughter preference is not considered as mutually exclusive to son preference. Just as son preference denotes a desire for a son, daughter preference is the desire for a daughter. About 66.3 per cent of the respondents have indicated daughter preference which is however much less than the percentage expressed for son preference. This throws up the much stronger desire of the two-son preference. While the respondents look for social and economic security from their son, they seek emotional security from their daughters (48.8%).

Table 2

Reason for Preferring Daughters by Current Residence

Reason for Preferring Daughter	*Current Residence (in percentage)*		
	All	*Rural*	*Urban*
Emotional support	48.8	57.1	41.8
Old age security	23.4	24.2	22.7
Help in business/farm/household activities	10.4	4.4	15.5
Religious obligations	6.0	6.6	5.5
Continuation of the family line/name	6.0	3.3	8.2
Economic motivation	5.5	4.4	6.4
Total	100.0	100.0	100.0

Table 2 brings to light the similarities and dissimilarities in the attitudes of rural and urban families in their reasons for preferring daughters. Irrespective of area of residence, the major reasons for daughter preference are the same, viz., emotional support and old age security. However, the more progressive attitude due to exposure and awareness is evident among urban families in their stronger indication of the belief that a daughter is also capable of carrying on economic activity, at home or outside and in the continuation of family name. This could be the key to the problem under study.

- *Relative expenditure on children:* Most respondents (52.3%) claim that the expenditure incurred in bringing up children of either sex is the same.
- *Favoured treatment at home:* About 65.7 per cent of the respondents say that equal treatment is given to children of both sexes. Those who claim that special treatment is given on the basis of sex, admit that the special treatment is more in favour of boys. The boys have access to better educational facilities (92.31%) and develop outside the boundaries of the home, whereas, the girls get more privileges also in education (27.6%) and better social activities (25.73%), being equipped both for the hearth and for the home.
- *Daughter as a liability:* Even if the respondents appreciate the worth of their daughters, when it comes to work premises, most of them (56.7%) opine that the daughter is a liability. However, 43 per cent did not cite any reasons for considering daughters as

liabilities. The key issue raised by 35 per cent of the sample population was that any investment on them is a loss to the family as they marry and go out of the family line. Strangely, while the daughter is considered a liability for not offering economic support in the long run, the son is not considered a liability for failing to offer emotional support!

- *Family head:* Only 33 per cent of the respondents perceived themselves as head of their families by seniority.
- *Perceived status of the women in family:* Most of the respondents (58%) perceive themselves to have a medium level of status in the family primarily because of their decision-making power (33.67%).
- *Improvement of women's status:* 81.7 per cent of the respondents strongly believe that their status improves when they give birth to a child. While 47.7 per cent feel that their status improves after having given birth to a son whereas only 15 per cent believe that the birth of a daughter improves their status. When the first child born is a boy, 34 per cent of the women feel that their status in society becomes higher. An almost equal percentage of respondents (about 63%) feel that their status does not lessen with the birth of a boy or a girl.
- *Women's autonomy:* More than 50 per cent of the women make decisions in matters relating to what to cook, purchase of household goods for daily needs, purchasing of consumer durables, obtaining healthcare, going and staying with friends and relatives, use of contraception, whether to have a child or not and whether to have sex. Only in the context of earning and spending money, 51 per cent of the decision-making is by others. Hence, the autonomy index shows that 86 per cent of the respondents have an average or above average level of decision-making power.

Results and Discussion

Cross-tabulation of Study Variables with Reference to Son Preference

The reasons for conscious or unconscious preference for sons (daughter aversion) is analyzed by cross-tabulation of the demographic, socio-economic and psychological variables of the study.

Religion: Son preference is greater among the Hindus (80%) and Muslims (75%) whereas among the Christians it is only 50 per cent.

Caste: Among the various caste categories, son preference is highest among the SCs/STs (89.8%), followed by MBCs (82.1%), BCs (73.7%) and FCs (66.7%). There appears to be an inverse relationship of son preference with caste hierarchy. Since the most quoted reason for son preference in the sample study was old age security, it could be that caste and higher levels of education go hand in hand as is often the case in India with the higher caste Brahmins being the most scholarly. Education and exposure may lead them to seeking old age security from investments in the finance market and in the form of other property assets rather than expecting the same from the offspring, particularly sons.

Family type: Preference for sons is higher in joint families (81.4%) than in nuclear families (76.7%). Culture and tradition play a stronger role in the joint family environment and are less prone to change. Hence, the traditional choice of son preference is stronger.

Education of husband and wife: Higher the level of literacy, less the preference for sons. Among illiterates, son preference is as high as 91.4 per cent but as the level of education of the husband increases to the professional level, the preference for son among the respondents declines to 66.7 per cent. Similarly, among the respondents themselves, as their level of literacy increases from illiteracy to professional qualifications, the percentage of son preference decreases from 86.1 per cent to 62.5 per cent. It is obvious that the women find the old age and other security that they are looking for less in their sons with increase in educational qualification of parents.

Current residence: Son preference is higher in rural areas (85.3%) than in urban areas (70.1%) since the rural environment is more shielded from modern influences.

House ownership: Those living in rented houses have a higher percentage of son preference (81.2%), whereas the corresponding figures for those in leased houses is (75%) and own houses (75.4%). The marginal increase in son preference for those owning houses to those living in leased houses could be due to the inheritance factor—to keep property within the family, in view of the fact that the daughter is considered to belong to her husband's family.

Occupation of husband and wife: The degree of son preference reduces with increase in the occupational level. While those with husbands in low level occupations have a son preference of 88.8 per cent, for those with husbands in high level occupations the corresponding figure is only 69.6 per cent. For those women who are unemployed and in low levels of occupation, the level of son preference is almost the same at about 80 per cent, whereas the women in the highest levels of occupation have a son preference of only 58.3 per cent in comparison.

Employment status of respondent in relation to husband: A strange phenomenon is observed in this analysis. Son Preference, which is at 79.1 per cent for those with lower employment status than their husbands, decreases to 63.4 per cent for women on an equal employment status. This is reasonable in that it can be explained that respondents find themselves on equal footing with their husband, gain confidence and are empowered enough to prefer sons less. However, when the level of employment is higher for the wife, i.e., for those with high employment status in relation to husband, the preference for sons is 100 per cent. Probably the women are not comfortable with facing the world or are ashamed that their husbands are not on an equal footing with them (or better) when it comes to jobs. Having sons gives them the prestige that their husband's employment does not.

Income: In general, when income levels increase, the strong son preference decreases. This is true for income of wife, income of husband and family income. The only exception is for a single household of very high income category which has an absolute son preference of 100 per cent. The income earner in this case is the husband. There are two points of significance to be noted from the sample data. Firstly, at every level of income, the women income earners have a lower level of son preference than the level of son preference at the corresponding levels of income taken from husband's earnings and total earnings of the family. This is a positive indicator of reduction in son preference with increase in women's earnings. Secondly, women who have no income of their own have absolute son preference.

Relative expenditure on children: Son preference is lowest among those respondents who say that the relative expenditure on children of both sexes is the same (73%). Ironically, among those who are of the opinion that the relative expenditure for girls is higher, son preference is 75 per cent, whereas the corresponding figure is 88.7 per cent for those who say that bringing up sons is more expensive. Even if the expenses incurred are likely to be more, the preference for sons is still greater in the context of other factors like old-age security. Those who prefer more sons do not mind spending more on them. Any expenditure on a son is considered to be worthwhile since it is an investment for the family and is considered to remain within the family.

Current age of husband and wife: As the current age of the husband and wife increases, son preference appears to decline. Son preference is lowest for respondents and their husbands whose age is above 50 (58.2% and 69.2%) respectively. As the woman grows older, her preference for sons declines.

Age at marriage: Son preference is considerably lower for those who belong to the age group of 31–40 years. In fact, the women who belong to the 31–40 years category at marriage have absolutely no son preference, being happy with whatever child they have.

Age at first delivery: As the age at first delivery increases, the preference for sons is lower but not very significant. While the women are happy with the birth of a child of any sex, they still hope that the child to be born is a male child. This analysis did not throw up significant results as expected because preferences change with time and circumstances. Hence, the present preference for a child is not significantly linked with the age at first delivery.

Difference between age at first delivery and marriage: While one can expect son preference or sex preference to be weakened when the first child is born after many years of marriage, the data shows that there is 100 per cent son preference even among those who had to wait six years or more to have their first child.

Number of living children: As the number of living boys increases, the respondents have claimed a higher preference for sons. The son preference among those not having a living male child is only 53.7 per cent whereas it is 100 per cent for those with four living sons. Strangely, these women feel the need for a daughter less as the number of sons increases. Their level of indifference to sex is also low. This could be because they take their daughters for granted and take great pride in having sons.

A similar study among those with living daughters reveals that among those with no living girl child, the son preference is as high as 80.2 per cent. These mothers obviously do not prefer daughters. For those with one or two living daughters, the son preference is less at 76.2 per cent and 71.2 per cent respectively obviously keeping the size of the family and affordability in mind. However, for those with three to four living daughters, the son preference is as high as 91.7 per cent and 100 per cent indicating that the size of the family does not matter to them as long as they have at least one son.

When the number of living children is taken in total and compared with the responses for son preference, son preference is lowest among those with less living children. As the number of living children increases from one (the minimum criterion for the respondent to qualify for inclusion in the sample) to six, the preference for sons increases from 67.9 per cent to 100 per cent. This is explained by large size families occurring in those sections that find security in having many children to take care of them in old age—the less literate, those at the lower echelons of the caste structure, with lower levels of occupation and income.

Table 3

Proportion of Living Female and Male Children in Families

Number of Living Children	*Proportion of Children (in percentage)*	
	Female	*Male*
1 (81)	62	38
2 (252)	54	46
3 (84)	33	67
4 (28)	25	75
5 (10)	20	80
All (641)	53	47

Note: The figures in parentheses indicate total number of living children.

The proportion of male children in the family is higher among families with a greater number of living children.

Number of children born: When a study of number of boys born is made in relation to the preference for sons, it becomes obvious that the preference for sons decreases with the increase in the number of sons born. This is a rational decline. The remarkable feature however is that son preference is only 49 per cent among those who have not given birth to boys (it is even less than the 50% son preference of the respondents who have had four boys). A preference of less than 50 per cent indicates a daughter preference or indifference to the sex of a child and a level of contentment with the child that they have.

A cross-tabulation of number of girls born with preference for sons indicates that when the number of girls born is four or more, the preference for sons is absolute at 100 per cent. That the reverse is not true (an absolute preference for daughters when the number of boys born is higher than three) is to be noted and is an indication of the strong son preference that exists in the society. As the number of girls born increases, the son preference becomes stronger in general, except in the case where there are other considerations to limit the size of the family. About 82.9 per cent of those with no girls born still prefer sons.

When the number of children born is taken in totality, for those with larger families the son preference is stronger. It ranges from 72.6 per cent in families with one baby born to 87 per cent in families with four children born and 100 per cent in families with children born greater than four.

Number of children died: Although the data suggests a strong son preference (about 78%) even when there are no deaths, for the category with one boy dead, the son preference is higher whereas in the category with one girl dead, the son preference is lower. Probably the 'replacement' factor is significant in the minds of those respondents who have lost children. However, it should be noted that when a girl child dies, the related son preference is less than the corresponding figure for boys, but it is still strong in that it is greater than 50 per cent.

In the event of child deaths in the family, 65 per cent of families who have lost daughters and 75 per cent of families who have lost sons indicate a preference for sons.

Table 4

Preference for Son in Case of Child Death

Child Deaths	*Preference for Son (in percentage)*		
	No	*Yes*	*Total*
Female	35	65	100
Male	25	75	100
Total	31	69	100

Table 5

Perception of Daughter as a Liability

Girl Deaths	*Daughter as a Liability (in percentage)*		
	No	*Yes*	*Total*
No	44	56	100
Yes	30	70	100
Total	43	57	100

Where there are no girl child deaths in the family, the perception of a daughter as a liability is lower.

Induced abortions: The son preference is stronger among those who have gone in for induced abortions (85%) than those who have not (76.8%). Although sex-selective abortion is illegal, this may still be in occurrence.

Current pregnancy: Among those who are currently pregnant, 81.8 per cent prefer sons as against 77 per cent who are not currently pregnant but still have an overall preference for sons. Considering the fact that a currently pregnant woman can be expected to give a more correct answer of sex expectations of a child to be born, it is obvious that the son preference factor looms large.

Adoption of family planning: There is not much of a difference between those who have adopted family planning techniques to those who have not in terms of son preference (about 75%).

Desire for more children: In the context of the present study, those who desire to have more children are significant. It is to be noted that among those who desire more children, the preference for sons is stronger (85.7%) than those who do not (74.1%).

Ideal number of children: As the ideal number of boys per family increases, the preference for sons also increases ranging from 78 per cent when ideal number of boy is one to 100 per cent when the ideal number of boys is more than three.

In the case of ideal number of daughters, the son preference should decrease as the ideal number of daughters per family increases. It does follow the rule with son preference at 79.9 per cent when the ideal number of girls is one to 50 per cent when the ideal number of girls is three.

For those who claim that they cannot define an ideal number of children in a family in terms of ideal number of girls and boys and for those who chose the 'either' category, son preference decreases from 75 per cent to 66.2 per cent when number of children increases from one to two. However, a definite pattern cannot be established beyond this.

Table 6 reveals that while most rural and urban families visualize an ideal family as that comprising of one son and one daughter, the greater demand for sons is among rural families.

Table 6

Ideal Family Size of the Respondents by Current Residence

Ideal Family Size	*Current Residence (in percentage)*	
	Rural	*Urban*
1 son	6.3	7.7
2 sons	6.3	2.9
1 daughter	2.1	4.8
1 son 1 daughter	40.6	72.1
1 son 2 daughters	—	3.8
2 sons 1 daughter	27.1	—
2 sons 2 daughters	8.3	1.9
2 daughters	—	5.8
3 and above sons	9.4	1.0
Total	100	100

Preferential treatment to children: In bringing up children, among those who have opted for special treatment to girls, there is 59.5 per cent son preference. However, in comparison, among those who favour special treatment given to boys have a son preference of 95.1 per cent. Even those who claim to give equal treatment to both children, have a son preference of 75.6 per cent.

Daughter as a liability: For those who feel the daughters to be a liability, son preference is stronger at 88.8 per cent. However, even those who claim that daughters are not liabilities have a strong son preference of 62.3 per cent instead of the rational 50 per cent or lower. This reflects societal attitudes towards daughters.

Perceived status of women in the family: As the perceived status of the woman in the family increases from low to medium to high, preference for sons declines marginally from 80 per cent to 79.5 per cent to 74 per cent. As the woman feels that a better status is accorded her in the family, her strong preference for sons declines, albeit marginally. Women who accord their higher family status to their decision-making status have the lowest level of son preference at 69.3 per cent.

Women autonomy: Those respondents who have the highest level of autonomy within their families also have the lowest son preference 65.9 per cent.

The above analyses are highly suggestive (and not conclusive) of a strong son preference and the missing girl child.

Multivariate Analysis: Binary Logistic Regression

Binary logistic regression is applied to find out the influence of the chosen socio-economic, demographic and psychological variables on son preference among the residents of Madurai district. The results are presented in Table 7, which show that caste, expenditure per month, special treatment to children, liability of daughter, perceived status of women in the family and women autonomy were found to be significant factors in determining the preference for son. Odds ratio suggests that while the variables—caste, expenditure per month, special treatment to children and liability of daughter—increase the odds of son preference, perceived status of women in the family and women autonomy decrease the odds of son preference. Those women who consider daughters as liability are more likely to prefer sons (nearly four-fold) whereas women who have autonomy in domestic decision making and those who perceive higher status in the family are less likely to prefer sons.

Table 7

Logistic Regression Results Showing the Effect of Selected Variables on Son Preference

Selected Variables	*Exp(B)*	*Sig.*
Current age of the wife	0.973	0.277
Age difference between the spouses	1.057	0.485
Age at marriage of the wife	0.975	0.860
Religion	1.020	0.965
Caste	1.726	0.045*
Family type	1.281	0.661
Education of wife	1.148	0.676
Current residence	0.612	0.224
Occupation of wife	1.034	0.892
Total income of the family	1.000	0.738
Expenditure per month	1.600	0.002*
Number of boys living	2.040	0.356
Number of boys born	0.853	0.827
Age at first delivery	1.000	0.999
Induced abortions	1.898	0.468
Desire for more children	1.409	0.440
Ideal number of boys	1.399	0.230
Expenditure on children	1.691	0.101**
Bringing up children	3.308	0.004*
Liability of daughter	4.925	0.000*
Perceived status of women in the family	0.742	0.049*
Women autonomy	0.456	0.007*
–2 Log likelihood	211.851	
Nagelkerke R Square	0.465	
Cox & Snell R Square	0.305	

Note: Dependent variable: preference for son (0 = No; 1 = Yes).
* Significant at 5 per cent; **Significant at 10 per cent.

Measure of Son Preference as an Indicator of Daughter Aversion

The pilot study that was done to check the carefully prepared schedule of questions revealed the need to use indirect questioning methods to study the status of the girl child and son preference. The level of awareness among the sample units was high enough to make them realize that they ought not to give responses lowering the status of the girl child. Thus, it was required that the respondents state their views on son preference (daughter aversion) from different perspectives with varying lead questions.

After the initial household demographic and socio-economic background survey of the family, the respondents were asked the maternity history, abortions and current pregnancy followed by a question on child sex preference. Most of the respondents claimed to be indifferent to the sex of the baby, and only a marginal number indicated sex preference with son preference still outweighing daughter preference.

In yet another component of the schedule on the respondents' attitude towards size of the family and child sex preference, the respondents' perception of an ideal family sex composition, desire for more kids and reasons for preference of and special treatment given to children of either sex was asked. In this part of the survey, the respondents revealed a very strong preference for sons and lesser preference for daughters.

To countercheck the findings of the direct questions on son preference, an index to measure the extent of son preference or daughter aversion was prepared.

Table 8

Crosstab of the Three Responses on Questions of Son Preference

Question on Child Sex Preference	*Question on Son Preference*	*Calculation of Extent of Son Preference*		*Total*
		No son preference	*Son Preference*	
No son preference	No son preference	30	34	64
	Son preference	59	107	166
Son preference	No son preference	3	1	4
	Son preference	10	56	66
Total	102	198	300	

The figures in the table above indicate pure and consistent preferences either for son preference or for absence of son preference. The comparison of these two figures reveal that the absolute preference for son is higher than the other (56 > 30). All other cells indicate frequencies of those who have mixed up choices of pure and mixed responses relating to son preference. Apart from the 86 who have shown a pure and consistent choice of son preference or the absence of it, the remaining respondents (300 – 86 = 214) give inconsistent answers in different contexts. However, even among these inconsistent answers, the representation is maximum in those cells for which at least two of the responses are indicators of clear son preference. Hence, even in this inconsistency, the element of son preference appears to be strong.

The inconsistency that is depicted above is not merely taken as an indicator of confused and erratic responses but as the extent to which the women in the sample practise son preference and son preferential treatment (gender discrimination) without being aware of having done so.

Conclusion

Madurai district is progressive in nature and also belongs to one of the rapidly developing states in India. Much development in various sectors has been recorded in the last decade. In spite of the economic advancements, rapidly increasing female and overall literacy rates and increased decision-making ability among women, the census data reveals that women work participation rates are lower. In a tradition-bound society, this has been viewed as a sign of progress. However, this study reveals that the women income earners are those with lowest levels of son preference and daughter aversion. It is thus essential to encourage women to take part in more social and economic activities outside the home front.

With the opening up of frontiers for development as a result of globalization, the world is becoming smaller for an educated Indian male. In contrast, in Madurai district, the educated woman who is qualified for jobs is encouraged to be a home-maker if she can afford to do so. Hence, she remains dependent on the husband's earnings. In spite of her decision-making status within the family, she still maintains the dependence on the male members of the family. Even if incomes were to increase, resulting in a more secure future, the women will still be confined to the home and be largely dependent. This ultimately results in the lower status of her girl child because the girl is also brought up in such a retrogressive tradition limiting the space of an educated girl to her home. Higher societal values are placed on the women who remain out of public sight.

Strategies to empower women need to start from empowering girls and improving their status. Cultural factors that limit opportunities for girls need to be identified and appropriately dealt with through suitable policy formulations. Educational institutions may be encouraged to compulsorily offer exposure/training off and on campus to reduce gender-role stereotyping for both boys and girls. This will go a long way in reducing disparities between boys and girls which in turn, in the long run, will eliminate the evils of patriarchy especially the liabilities of raising a girl child (dowries, jewels and gifts to raise her status, marriage expenses, social ceremonies, etc.) Progressive religious practices should be adopted by the clergy and supported by the government. Media advocacy to remove cultural taboos restricting girls should be supported and monitored by the government. Girls who grow up in an environment that gives them equal opportunities at home, at school and in the workplace will eventually become truly empowered women much like a tree whose roots are strong.

References

Arnold, F. (1985). Measuring the Effect of Sex Preference on Fertility: The Case of Korea, *Demography,* 22, pp. 280–88.

—— (1997). Gender Preferences for Children, *Demography and Health Surveys Comparative Studies*, 23, pp. 1–56.

Chunkath, Sheela Rani and V.B. Athreya (1997). Female Infanticide in Tamil Nadu: Some Evidence, *Economic and Political Weekly,* 32 (17), pp. 21–28.

Gulati, S.C. (1987). Some Reflections on Son Preference and its Influence on Additional Desired Fertility, *Demography India,* Vol. XVI, No. 2, pp. 207–19.

Kenley, Barret (2004). Determinants of Female Autonomy and its Demographic Implications, http://www.arts.cornell.edu/econ/75devconf/PrelimSes.doc

Hatti, Neelambar, T.V. Sekher and Mattias Larsen (2004). Lives at Risk: Declining Child Sex Ratios in India, *Lund Papers in Economic History,* No. 93. www.ekh.lu.se.

Shelley, Clark (2000). Son Preference and Sex Composition of Children: Evidence from India, *Demography*, Vol. 37, 1, pp. 95–108.

Yagya Prasad, Subedi (2005). Factors Associated with Women's Autonomy in Nepal, unpublished research report, IIPS, Mumbai.

EIGHT

Implications of Declining Sex Ratio on Marriage Squeeze of India

Priyajit Samaiyar and William Joe

In the year 1990 Amartya Sen remarked on the fact that parts of Asia and Africa have greater sex ratio imbalances and compared to the total number of males the females were almost 11 per cent lesser. Being a major country of this region, India shares the bulk of this misfortune. Notably, the 2001 Census indicates that this problem has further assumed disquieting proportions with steep decline in the child sex ratio in different parts of the country. Although, the tendency of sex ratio imbalance persisted in India even during the 1950s (see Table 1) but in the past half a century what has emerged as an issue of major apprehension is the rate at which sex ratios have declined, particularly the child sex ratio. Although the 2001 figures revealed that there has been marginal improvement in the overall sex ratio over the 1990s but the worsening child sex ratios in the same period do not appear to be natural and perhaps are indicative of some kind of artificial interference in regulating births in India. In states of Haryana, Punjab, Delhi and Gujarat the child sex ratio has fallen below 900 girls per 1,000 boys. Distressing figures are recorded in almost 70 districts of India wherein the child sex ratio has declined by more than 50 points during the decade of 1990s and has resulted in stark inter-district differences. To get a hint regarding the severity of the problem one just needs to compare the child sex ratio of districts like Kurukshetra in Haryana (CSR of 770 girls per 1,000 boys) with districts of Kerala (having a balanced sex ratio).

Table 1

Overall Sex Ratio (OSR) and Child Sex Ratio (CSR) in India, 1951–2001

Sex Ratio	*1951*	*1961*	*1971*	*1981*	*1991*	*2001*
Overall Sex Ratio	946	941	930	934	927	933
Child Sex Ratio	983	976	946	962	945	927

Note: Here, OSR is defined as number of females per thousand males and CSR is defined as number of girls (less than six years of age) per thousand boys.

Source: Registrar General of India, Census of India (various years).

Owing to such findings, the issue of 'missing women' has received global attention and has received top priority by various governments and international developmental agencies as a vital area for policy research and action. There is an agreement among researchers and developmental community that worsening sex ratio signifies a dent in overall social development. In this regard, another related matter of concern arises from the fact that the Indian districts (especially in northern India), which are performing poorly in terms of sex ratio profiles, happen to be among the most prosperous areas of the country. For instance, the south-west district of Delhi has one of the highest income profiles and better literacy level compared to many other states but its child sex ratio is noted to be at a lower level of 845 girls per 1,000 boys (UNFPA, 2003).

In the recent past, the issue of declining child sex ratio in India and its socio-economic and demographic consequences are being extensively researched. Some studies have argued that in India birth of more male children compared to female is mainly due to a strong preference for sons and higher levels of child mortality (Arnold et al., 1998). Such a preference for males is embedded in the Indian society because of a number of socio-economic and cultural aspects. For instance, the patriarchal nature of Indian society looks upon son as an agency of familial line continuity. The society has also generated the expectations that sons would be the sole or at least the major source of support for ageing parents not only in terms of economic resources but also in terms of cultural favours, such as religious rites at the time of cremation. This very nature of the society, consequently, has presented a lower status to the women as it believes that women are economically unproductive and are a liability to the family. Moreover, the insecurity of a female child is increased manifold because of certain social practices, such as prevalence of dowry.[1] But in the wake of declining number of females, can it have any potential impact on their social status and for that matter will it affect the marriage prospects of these relatively large numbers of males. The answer to the former question would be uncertain at this point of time however, it could be argued that sex ratio decline would invariably have a significant bearing on the marriage market.

Sex Ratio and Marriage Market

This particular issue of women's status and marriages in India has been extensively studied by sociologists and anthropologists. In the context of a declining child sex ratio, several empirical studies have highlighted the importance women's social status and its implications on marriage market scenario. For instance, Agnihotri (2003), Bhat (2002), Patel (2004) and Premi (2001) discuss the status of women due to the decline in child sex ratio. These studies have mainly focussed on the various aspects of discrimination against females in India, while studies by Bhat et al. (1999), Rajan et al. (2002 and 2003), and Griffiths et al. (2000) explain the implications of declining sex ratio on issues like fertility, child survival and marriage squeeze. However, there is a dearth of literature that primarily focuses on the consequences of distortions in child sex ratio on marriage market. In demographic literature, any imbalance in the sex ratio of prime marriageable[2] males and females is defined as 'marriage squeeze'. In other words, when the number of males (females) in the prime marriageable age group surpasses the number of females (males) in the same age groups at certain point of time in a particular geographical area, then, this phenomenon is called 'male (female) marriage squeeze'.

The phenomenon of marriage squeeze primarily arises out of the demographic transition which every country undergoes at different points of time. Due to mortality transition the successive birth cohorts become larger and under the assumption that males seek younger females to get married it can be concluded that mortality decline will result in more females chasing lesser number of males for marriage resulting in female marriage squeeze. This phenomenon can ease when the fertility transition starts and results in smaller successive birth cohorts, that is, less females chasing more males resulting in male marriage squeeze. Society, then, adjusts for such scarcities of eligible mates by increasing the waiting time for males and females to get married and also by increasing the age gap between spouses. That is, both the age at marriage as well as age difference between spouse increase.

The phenomenon of marriage squeeze also has implications on the societal norms like dowry payments in India. In fact, it has been empirically supported that marriage squeeze has played a significant part in causing dowry inflation (Rao, 1993). Marriage squeeze also seems to play a role in increasing the difference in the age at marriage of men and women since, females will have to wait if there is scarcity of males in the market. Alternatively, they have to search for their mate in age cohorts other than the desired one to get married in the case of female marriage squeeze. Apart from the felt scarcity among overambitious bride-givers in India the real numerical deficit in the availability of eligible men due to mortality transition has resulted in the increase in marriage transactions (Bhat et al., 1999) though its impact on the phenomenon of dowry cannot be captured unambiguously.

One of the earliest works on the availability of males and females for marriage market was carried out by Akers (1967). This study applied a simple sex ratio approach to measure their availabilities in the marriage market. Since then, researchers have come a long way and have devised several different methods to measure the availabilities of males and females for marriage. Some of the earlier studies on marriage squeeze in India have observed a female marriage squeeze which due to fertility transition is expected to ease later in first decade of 21st century (Bhat et al., 1999; Rao, 1993). In this regard, a recent study by Verma (2003) explains the scenario of marriage squeeze in India and has developed and applied a different method of computing 'Availability Index' which takes into consideration the number of males and females so as to obtain a clear understanding of marriage squeeze. This study notes that India was experiencing a male marriage squeeze right from 1961 and since then there has been a consistent increase in the tightness of male marriage squeeze which contradicts the findings of the earlier studies.

Notwithstanding the role of demographic transition in marriage squeeze, this paper argues that the recent worrisome declines in the child sex ratios have added another dimension to the discussion on the phenomenon of marriage squeeze. As we know, the present child sex ratios are indicative of availabilities of males and females in the future marriage market and with improvements in the mortality rates and narrowing sex differentials in child mortality, the impact of declining child sex ratio on male marriage squeeze could be faster than what it would have been otherwise. In this regard, scholars have argued that marriage squeeze arising from an adverse sex ratio is capable of producing significant changes in both the levels and distribution of marriage and it appears to have such implications mainly in Third World countries (Schoen, 1983). Undoubtedly, a declining child sex ratio in India would have serious implications on the marriage market in terms of male marriage squeeze. Therefore, it is of relevance to examine how the declining sex ratio can intensify male marriage squeeze in India. However, from this study it would be very difficult to comment on whether the progressing male marriage squeeze will help in enhancing the status of females in India.

Data and Methods

This paper sifts the information from the censuses conducted during the years of 1991 and 2001. In particular, we have used the Socio-Cultural Tables of Census 1991 and 2001 published by the Registrar General and the Census Commissioner of India. From these tables the data on the never married male and female population have been used for the years 1991 and 2001. This data is utilized to compute two different indices based on a simple sex ratio approach.[3] The first index is called as Differential Proportion of Never Married (DPNM) and is defined as the difference between the never married male (female) below certain age 'i' [i= 19, 24, 29, 34, 39 and 44], as a proportion of total never married male (female) population which are at the risk of marriage. Although, these risks could be specified in relation to certain relevant socio-economic and individual correlates such as religion and age but, for simplicity, here risk of marriage is defined in terms of a single age-based criterion wherein all the individuals within the range of 15 to 49 years of age are considered to be at risk. This criterion is relevant because in India most of the individuals get married between this broad age group of 15 to 49 years marriages generally take place. The individuals aged less than 15 years are not considered for the analysis because the risk of their marriage is almost zero per cent—a fact which is also evident from their statistical distribution.

Based on the above conceptualization, the index of DPNM for females can be formally written as (1):

$$\text{(1)} \qquad \text{DPNM}_i^f = \left[{}^{2001}\!\left(\frac{{}_{15}\text{NM}^f_{\leq i}}{{}_{15}\text{NM}^f_{49}} \right) - {}^{1991}\!\left(\frac{{}_{15}NM^f_{\leq i}}{{}_{15}NM^f_{49}} \right) \right]$$

and for never married males it could be written as (2):

$$\text{(2)} \qquad \text{DPNM}_i^m = \left[{}^{2001}\!\left(\frac{{}_{15}\text{NM}^m_{\leq i}}{{}_{15}\text{NM}^m_{49}} \right) - {}^{1991}\!\left(\frac{{}_{15}\text{NM}^m_{\leq i}}{{}_{15}\text{NM}^m_{49}} \right) \right]$$

where, the superscripts 'f' and 'm' of DPNM refer, respectively, to female and male whereas the subscript 'i' refers to age group considered for the particular DPNM computation when [i= 19, 24, 29, 34, 39 and 44] years. The advantage of this index is that it can capture the shifts, if any, in age at marriage between the two census years of 1991 and 2001. For interpretative purposes, a positive (negative) value of the DPNM index would signify that the proportion of never married individuals (males or females) for a particular age group 'i' have increased (decreased) during the decade of 1991 to 2001 whereas a value of zero would imply that the proportions have remained unchanged between the two time points.

The second index developed in this paper is called Differential in Marriage Possibility (DMP) for males. This indicator employs the sex ratio approach in a different manner. Specifically, a cumulative approach is adopted here to compute the sex ratio. This measure takes into consideration the sex ratio of the females of age less than 'i' as a proportion of males in the age groups more than 'i' but less than maximum marriageable age, which is assumed to be 49 years.[4] The computation begins from the age group of 15–19 years and cumulates the subsequent age groups and stops at 45–49 years. This type[5] of cumulative technique allows for the possibility that a female can get married to any individual belonging to her age group or and other age group which is greater than her age group. It should be clear that this approach will find a greater number of females for males belonging to the last age group (45–49 years) but this would not affect our analysis and conclusions because our primary interest is to know the differentials in the marriage possibility for males between 1991 and 2001 census years. These results will highlight the differences in marriage possibility, if any, occurring during the decade. This index broadly measures the possibility of marriage for population belonging to different age groups. In simple terms, DMP values would reflect the changes in the availability of never married females per one thousand never married males during the decade 1991 and 2001.

$$(3) \qquad DPNM_i^f = \left[{}^{2001}\left(\frac{{}_{15}f_{\le i}^{NM}}{{}_{\ge i}m_{49}^{NM}} \right) - {}^{1991}\left(\frac{{}_{15}f_{\le i}^{NM}}{{}_{\ge i}m_{49}^{NM}} \right) \right] \times 1000$$

Further, the two concepts of DPNP and DMP are related and tested with the help of regression analysis keeping DPNP for females as independent and DMP as the dependent variable in the model for different age group separately over the major states of India.

$$(4) \qquad DMP_i = a + b\,(DPNM_i^f) + \in$$

Results and Discussion

Never married (NM) males in the age group 15–19 (i=19), as a proportion of total NM males in the broad age group 15–19, has declined during the decade 1991 to 2001 by around five NM males per one thousand NM males in India (see Table 2). This can be either due to increase in marriage rate during the decade or due to a higher rate of increase in the total NM males in the broad age group 15–49. Further probe into the data suggests that the rate of increase in population in the age group 15–19 is higher than the rate of increase in total NM male population in the broad age group 15–49. That is, there has been a higher rate of increase in total NM males in the age group 15–49 (which is the denominator in the index) during the decade or it can be said that more males have remained unmarried during the decade 1991–2001.

Older age groups show an increase in NM males as a proportion of total NM males (in the age groups 15–49). This indicates that there has been a shift in age at marriage for males to older ages during the decade. This can be further made clear from Table 4 which shows the distribution of NM males in different age groups during the two census years of 1991 and 2001. The distribution of NM males in the younger ages has increased by almost 1 per cent which is a significant change depicting the mean age at marriage in India. In the older age groups the NM male population has declined

Table 2

Decrement in Male Never Married Proportion ($DPNM_m$) 2001–1991

Age Group	*i=19*	*i=24*	*i=29*	*i=34*	*i=39*	*i=44*
AP	0.4285	0.5431	0.5763	0.5826	0.5846	0.5857
Assam	0.0088	–0.0054	–0.0115	–0.0053	–0.0004	0.0001
Bihar & Jharkhand	–0.0040	0.0042	0.0065	0.0048	0.0042	0.0017
Gujarat	–0.0125	–0.0040	–0.0002	0.0011	0.0017	0.0007
Haryana	–0.0252	–0.0062	–0.0001	0.0006	0.0011	0.0005
HP	–0.0649	–0.0303	–0.0021	0.0015	0.0017	0.0008
Karnataka	–0.0154	–0.0105	–0.0023	0.0007	0.0011	0.0004
Kerala	–0.0126	–0.0205	–0.0089	–0.0020	–0.0005	–0.0004
MP and Chhattisgarh	–0.0079	0.0024	0.0060	0.0058	0.0048	0.0023
Maharashtra	–0.0074	–0.0001	0.0063	0.0056	0.0033	0.0013
Orissa	–0.0291	–0.0324	–0.0068	0.0030	0.0032	0.0010
Punjab	–0.0011	0.0096	0.0104	0.0073	0.0048	0.0021
Rajasthan	–0.0014	0.0064	0.0047	0.0033	0.0026	0.0013
Tamil Nadu	–0.0199	–0.0137	–0.0006	0.0029	0.0026	0.0012
UP and Uttaranchal	–0.0147	0.0048	0.0086	0.0070	0.0058	0.0026
West Bengal	0.0178	0.0028	–0.0025	–0.0021	–0.0006	–0.0001
All India	–0.0045	0.0000	0.0030	0.0032	0.0028	0.0012

significantly by almost 1 per cent showing that the marriages among later age groups have increased.

In the case of females there is a negative sign of $DPNM_f$ in all the ages (see Table 3). This can be either due to higher rate of increase in the number of NM females in a particular age group compared to the total NM females in the age group 15–49 or due to a decline in the total NM female population. The distribution of NM females in the different age group shows that there is decline in the share of NM females in the age group 15–19 over the decade. If we compare the distribution of NM females over the ages the concentration is higher in almost all the ages in 2001 compared to 1991 (see Table 5). In both the census years the share of NM female population starts declining significantly from the age 25 (see Table 5) whereas for males this decline starts after age 30 (see Table 4). Overall the implication which can be derived is that more marriages of older males are happening and females are getting married relatively earlier than the males thus suggesting an increase in the age gap between the spouses during the decade.

Table 3

Decrement in Female Never Married Proportion ($DPNM_f$) 2001–1991

Age Group	*i=19*	*i=24*	*i=29*	*i=34*	*i=39*	*i=44*
Andhra Pradesh	–0.0261	–0.0067	–0.0027	–0.0017	–0.0008	–0.0004
Assam	–0.0293	–0.0255	–0.0159	–0.0092	–0.0042	–0.0016
Bihar and Jharkhand	–0.0129	–0.0022	–0.0003	–0.0001	0.0014	0.0004
Gujarat	–0.0194	–0.0043	–0.0020	–0.0014	–0.0006	–0.0004
Harayana	–0.0184	–0.0021	–0.0004	–0.0003	0.0001	0.0001
Himachal Pradesh	–0.0727	–0.0149	–0.0044	–0.0023	–0.0009	–0.0003
Karnataka	–0.0278	–0.0115	–0.0056	–0.0038	–0.0023	–0.0011
Kerala	–0.0047	–0.0140	–0.0122	–0.0086	–0.0054	–0.0029
MP and Chattisgarh	–0.0129	0.0002	0.0017	0.0017	0.0025	0.0015
Maharashtra	–0.0222	–0.0078	–0.0031	–0.0019	–0.0011	–0.0005
Orissa	–0.0648	–0.0227	–0.0078	–0.0041	–0.0017	–0.0007
Punjab	–0.0357	–0.0090	–0.0023	–0.0014	–0.0008	–0.0004
Rajasthan	–0.0165	–0.0034	–0.0016	–0.0007	0.0001	0.0002
Tamil Nadu	–0.0411	–0.0156	–0.0072	–0.0047	–0.0026	–0.0012
UP and Uttaranchal	–0.0265	–0.0036	0.0002	0.0006	0.0012	0.0007
West Bengal	–0.0098	–0.0104	–0.0090	–0.0078	–0.0044	–0.0020
All India	–0.0183	–0.0063	–0.0029	–0.0019	–0.0006	–0.0003

Table 4

Distribution of Never Married Male Population

Age Group	*1991*		*2001*	
	Never Married Males	*%*	*Never Married Males*	*%*
15–19	3,85,62,659	51.88	5,12,50,979	51.95
20–24	2,26,74,750	30.51	3,03,11,923	30.73
25–29	84,89,324	11.42	1,15,71,068	11.73
30–34	24,70,589	3.32	32,64,521	3.31
35–39	9,79,858	1.32	12,06,340	1.22
40–44	6,88,207	0.93	6,37,523	0.65
45–49	4,64,012	0.62	4,04,919	0.41
Total	7,43,29,400	100.00	9,85,47,272	100.00

Source: Socio-Cultural Tables, Census of India, 1991 and 2001.

Table 5

Distribution of Never Married Female Population

Age Group	1991		2001	
	Never Married Females	%	Never Married Females	%
15–19	2,38,64,041	72.91	3,48,85,235	71.13
20–24	63,36,480	19.36	1,00,10,817	20.41
25–29	14,62,975	4.47	23,73,388	4.84
30–34	5,09,590	1.56	8,10,444	1.65
35–39	2,36,028	0.72	4,58,256	0.93
40–44	1,93,559	0.59	3,04,689	0.62
45–49	1,26,454	0.39	2,02,431	0.41
Total	3,27,29,127	100.00	4,90,45,261	100.00

Source: Socio-Cultural Tables, Census of India, 1991 and 2001.

Furthermore, under the assumption that NM males marry NM females, the availability of NM females per thousand NM males has declined for all the age groups during the decade (see Table 6). It implies that in general the marriage possibility for NM males has declined during the decade and would have adverse implications if the disturbing sex ratio trends are not reversed.

The simple regression analysis based on equation (4) suggests that at younger ages marriage possibility of NM males is explained more by the availability of NM females. However, the explanatory power (value of R^2) of the change in the NM females during the decade in explaining the change in the marriage possibility for males declines as the age group increases except for the group i=24 (see Table 7). The regression results for group i=20 shows a sudden decline in the R square value and then it increases to decline further in the subsequent groups. Here, the sudden decline in the explanatory power of availability of NM females in explaining the marriage possibility for NM males can be linked with CSR. Since male belonging to age 24 will search for females less than age 24 who will belong to the birth cohort of 1978 or after when there was a better supply of females due to higher births of females. As reported earlier in Table 1, 1981 is crucial from the viewpoint that it was only during this census that the CSR had improved which otherwise was showing a declining trend. Such findings are indicative of a

Table 6

Difference in Marriage Possibility (DMP) 2001–1991

Group	*i=19*	*i=24*	*i=29*	*i=34*	*i=39*	*i=44*
Andhra Pradesh	–148	–147	7,726	36,132	87,838	2,22,433
Assam	39	–63	–1517	–6,038	–1,578	23,661
Bihar and Jharkhand	233	1,541	9,758	31,998	1,03,264	2,82,875
Gujarat	–162	–463	–320	2,912	17,683	48,998
Harayana	–183	–429	1,223	5,070	20,413	50,898
Himachal Pradesh	–590	–2292	–2,006	5,806	20,861	50,914
Karnataka	–90	–341	–882	3,996	28,113	77,795
Kerala	–121	–690	–3,126	–7,341	–12,570	–43,365
MP and Chattisgarh	146	1197	8,421	28,113	71,010	1,89,844
Maharashtra	–36	107	5,151	25,680	61,629	1,57,690
Orissa	–230	–1503	–4,595	23,320	1,08,281	2,65,350
Punjab	–57	626	4,704	10,501	21,038	52,765
Rajasthan	231	2100	7,739	16,669	38,605	1,04,435
Tamil Nadu	–145	–444	–299	7,878	31,765	89,222
UP and Uttaranchal	81	1424	6,723	16,002	36,719	97,798
West Bengal	117	173	–110	–1,346	–947	1,615
All India	–33	–274	–2,422	–10,937	–34,930	–96,391

Table 7

Regression Results

Groups	*Standard Coefficients*	*R Square*
i=19	0.726**	0.526
i=24	0.616**	0.379
i=29	0.721**	0.519
i=34	0.677**	0.459
i=39	0.588**	0.346
i=44	0.577**	0.332

significant relationship between CSR and marriage market in India and suggests that any distortion in CSR can have very serious implication on the marriage prospects for males. If the CSR declines further to lower levels, then, males will have to wait more for getting married or they may have to search for mates in other than desired age cohort which can increase the age gap between spouses or may even alter the norms regarding marriage age and spousal age gaps.

Fertility Norms, Sex-Selective Abortion and Sex Ratio: Some Concerns

After highlighting the importance of sex ratio imbalance and its implications on marriage market, in this section, we reiterate our concerns regarding the implications of declining fertility norms in the society on the CSR. In fact, the implications could be much more serious in a society where there is a preference for birth of a particular sex.

To elaborate, here we illustrate that under circumstances of sex-selective abortions, how the promotion of two-child norm can further aggravate the imbalances in CSR to higher levels. For example, if there is a dominant preference for male child and every couple wishes to have at least one male child in their family. By taking the prevailing preference for number of live births as 'n' the implication can be explained with the following method of calculating overall sex ratio (see equation 5) under the assumption that abortion is carried out successfully, i.e., aborted female foetuses are replaced by equal number of male foetuses. Also, the mortality of foetuses is replaced randomly without selecting any sex.

$$(5) \qquad SR = \left[\left(\frac{(n \times 2^{n-1} - F_a)}{(n \times 2^{n-1} + F_a)}\right) \times 1000\right]$$

In equation (5), F_a is the number of missing girls for a given couple either due to sex-selective abortion or infanticide owing to the assumption of strong preference for males. Now, consider that there is a prevalence of three-child norm (n=3) in the society and every couple wants to have at least one male child (F_a = 1) in their family. In such case the society can have sex ratios as low as 846 females per thousand males (see Table 8). Here, F_a is taken as one since the risk of getting aborted for a female foetus having two sisters is highest (Arnold et al., 1998). Furthermore, if the government policies are formulated for motivating people to have two children in their family or if the couples decide to restrict their number of children to two then with a given preference for male child, female foetuses who already have one sister are at the highest risk of abortion. Under such circumstances, the sex ratio can, statistically, go as low as 600 females per thousand males (see Table 8).

Table 8

Table Illustrating the Sex Ratio Outcomes when Female Foetus Having One Sister in Case of Two-Child and Two Sisters in Case of Three-Child Norms are Aborted

Child Norm	*Possible Combinations of Children*	*Sex Ratio Outcome after Sex-selective Abortion*
2	MF, FM, MM, FF	600
3	MMM, MMF, MFM, FMM, FFM, FMF, MFF, FFF	846

Since we know that society consists of individuals with differing norms and principles regarding family composition in terms of sex of the child and numbers we may a require a more generalized expression to capture the overall sex ratio. For this purpose, we provide equation (6) which can be applied for the population as a whole to calculate the overall sex ratio depending on the different child norms prevailing in different states of the country.

$$\text{(6)} \qquad \text{OSR} = \left[\frac{1}{1000 \times G} \sum_{i=1}^{G} \left(\frac{(n_i \times 2^{n_i - 1} - F_{ai})}{(n_i \times 2^{n_i - 1} + F_{ai})} \times 1000 \right) \right]$$

In equation (6), G represents total number of different groups having different child norms. It should be clear from the equation that restriction of family size without altering the male preference structure would only deteriorate the sex ratio imbalance. Therefore, government policies should place greater emphasis on the imposition of the laws against the sex-selective abortions and strictly monitor the sex differentials in infant mortality. A control over these issues and further measures to strengthen the social status of women may prevent further distortions in the overall sex ratio whose implications so far though unambiguous but can be severe. In fact, in this paper, we were able to highlight that if these distortions are not checked and the number of females gets further reduced, then, it can have very serious implications on the marriage market in the near future.

Unsurprisingly, the parts of India having lower levels of child sex ratio are also the regions in which females have lower status compared to males. It is rather disconcerting to observe that this low status of females is prevailing in these regions despite their prosperous economic profiles. In order to change the perception regarding social importance of females policies are required to identify and target the peculiar characteristics of these regions and intervene through altering the major determinants of female status. For instance, these regions are found to have higher gender differentials in literacy levels (see Table 9). Perhaps bridging Table 9 this gap will strengthen the capabilities of females to be independent and will eventually help in increasing the status of females. Policies should be formulated to motivate females to attain higher educational standards which will further increase their employment prospects. Similarly, one can also look at the development of service sector in these regions which has the potential of generating employment for females eventually increasing there status in the society.

Table 9

Gender Differential in Literacy

States	*Male Literacy*	*Female Literacy*	*Gender Differential*
Himachal Pradesh	86.02	68.08	17.94
Punjab	75.63	63.55	12.08
Uttaranchal	84.01	60.26	23.75
Harayana	79.25	56.31	22.94
Rajasthan	76.46	44.34	32.12
Uttar Pradesh	70.23	42.98	27.25
Gujarat	80.5	58.6	21.9

Source: Population Data Sheet, Census of India 2001.

Conclusion

This paper analyzed the impact of different child norms prevailing in the society and its implications on sex ratio. This imbalance in CSR directs us to believe that there has been some kind of artificial interference in regulating the child births in India and in spite of national laws against sex-selective abortions, discrimination against female foetus persists. This declining sex ratio has direct and serious consequences on the marriage market. This study shows that the shortage in the availability of never married females over the decade of 1991 to 2001 has begun to affect negatively to the marriage prospects of young males. Consequently, males are now required to prolong their marriages. If the present trend in the sex ratio imbalance continues, the marriage prospects of males can further get dampened and they might be required to postpone their marriages to higher ages. Conclusion can also be drawn that at the higher ages other factors (e.g., economic) become important to determine the marital status of a male. Therefore, there should be an urgency to rectify this imbalance for which the low social status of the females needs to be uplifted. The paper further demonstrated that how the cultivation of small family (two or three child) norm without giving due considerations to the problem of sex-selective abortions can actually aggravate the problem of sex ratio imbalance in the country. This study finds that the regions showing higher imbalance in the sex ratio were also the regions marked with higher gender differentials in literacy. Identification of such region-specific factors and targeting them through policy initiatives can go a long way in redressing the problem of adverse sex ratio and marriage prospects in the future.

Notes

1. Dowry is synonymous to a disproportionately hefty sum (of gifts and payments) which is often unwillingly forwarded by the bride's family to the groom's family and relatives during the wedding ceremony.
2. Prime marriageable age groups of marriages are chosen by setting the mid points of prime age range very close to the median age at first marriage and surrounding this particular age they are equidistantly expanded in both sides in such a way so that it can cover a high proportion of all marriages.
3. The main assumptions behind adopting these methods are that males are always elder than females in the formation of married couples in India and that never married males always marry never married females. In fact, in the Indian context, these assumptions largely hold true as it is observed that widow remarriages still account for a much smaller fraction of the total marriages in India.

4. In fact, data reveals that almost all the individuals get married before the age of 49 years and the proportion of as never married population beyond age of 49 years is negligible.
5. Some studies have adopted a much stricter assumption behind cumulative approach. For instance, Bhat et al. (1999) assume a spousal gap of five years which in the Indian context is arguably a more restrictive assumption.

References

Agnihotri, S. (2003). Survival of the Girl Child: Tunnelling Out of the Chakravyuh, *Economic and Political Weekly*, October 11.

Agnihotri, S. et al. (2003). Sex Ratio and 'Prosperity Effect': What do NSSO Data Reveal? *Economic and Political Weekly*, October 11.

Akers, D.S. (1967). On Measuring the Marriage Squeeze, *Demography*, 4 (4), pp. 907–24.

Arnold, F., M.K. Choe and T.K. Roy (1998). Son Preference, the Family Building Process and Child Mortality in India, *Population Studies*, 52, pp. 301–15.

Clark, S. (2000). Son Preference and Sex Composition of Children: Evidence from India, *Demography*, 37(1), pp. 95–108.

Griffiths, P. et al. (2000). Understanding the Sex Ratio in India: A Simulation Approach, *Demography*, Vol. 37, pp. 477–88.

Guillot, M. (2002). The Dynamics of the Population Sex Ratio in India, 1971–96, *Population Studies*, 56, pp. 51–63.

Mari Bhat, P.N. (2002). On the Trail of 'Missing' Indian Females, I: Search and Clues, *Economic and Political Weekly*, December 21.

Mari Bhat, P.N. and S.S. Halli (1999). Demography of Bride Price and Dowry: Causes and Consequences of the Indian Marriage Squeeze, *Population Studies*, 53, pp. 129–48.

Mayer, P. (1999). India's Falling Sex Ratio, *Population and Development Review*, 25(2), pp. 323–43.

Patel, T. (2004). Missing Girls in India, *Economic and Political Weekly*, Commentary, February 24.

Premi, M.K. (2001). The Missing Girl Child, *Economic and Political Weekly*, May 26.

Rajan, S.I. et al. (2002). Fertility Decline and Worsening Gender Bias in India: Is Kerala No Longer an Exception? *Development and Change*, Circa.

Rao, V. (1993). Dowry Inflation in Rural India: A Statistical Investigation, *Population Studies*, 47(2), pp. 283–93.

Registrar General, India (1991). Socio Cultural Tables, Census of India.

—— (2001). Population Data Sheet, Census of India.

—— (2001). Socio-Cultural Tables, Census of India.

Schoen, R. (1983). Measuring the Tightness of Marriage Squeeze, *Demography*, 20(1), pp. 61–77.

UNFPA (2003). Mapping the Adverse Child Sex Ratio in India, June.

Verma, S. (2003). Marriage Squeeze in India, *Demography India*, Vol. 32(2), pp. 181–99.

NINE

Active and Passive Elimination of Girl Child

Findings from Rural Haryana

Sutapa Agrawal and Sayeed Unisa

The most alarming finding of the 2001 Census is the sharp decline in the sex ratio among the children in the 0–6 years age group. The sex ratio of the child population has declined by 18 points from 945 in 1991 to 927 in 2001. The sharpest decline in the child sex ratio (CSR) after independence was observed during 1991–2001. Masked by the national ratio, far grimmer ratios prevail in selected parts of India in relatively prosperous states such as Haryana. In Haryana the CSR has gone down to 820. Several authors have expressed this continuing disparity between males and females in terms of total missing females. Behind this lies a story of sex-selective discrimination by active elimination through abortion of the female foetus and passive elimination through neglect ultimately leading to the death of the female child. Very little is known about the reasons and circumstances under which a woman discriminate her own child. It may be possible that there may be a life course impact on the woman's behaviour regarding her sex preference, family size preference and sex-selective discrimination. There is dearth of studies which explored the relationship between woman's autonomy and sex preference or her marital instability and sex preference or any influence of her own childhood experience with her reproductive behaviour and its linkages with the ultimate process of active and passive elimination of females. Again, any policy measures must not focus primarily on restricting technology used to female's detriment, but also the root causes of devaluation of women.

India supports a plural or heterogeneous society consisting of numerous stratifications based on religion, caste and class. Dual structure of law exists side by side, under which the religious sanctions condoned against constitutional ones. Yet one finds that preference for sons runs high amongst all religious groups and social classes. This preference is due to shared civilization patterns in the Indian subcontinent and the underlying principle of a patrilocal, patrilineal and patriarchal society. Women in such societies always occupy a low status and are neglected. As women are considered a burden, female infant mortality exceeds that of males, notwithstanding the fact that a female child is biologically stronger at birth. A girl faces deprivation throughout her life. Preference for sons is obvious from the brutal traditions that are prevalent in India (Bambawale, 1992).

India has a unique demographic situation concerning the extent and impact of son preference on the ultimate sex structure of its population (Kishor, 2002). With scientific inventions, new methods are available that are extremely useful to choose the sex of the child at the time of conception (Unisa, 2002). Now, son preference may be expressed prenatally through sex-selective abortion. The advent of sex-selective abortion has added a new and definitive means for acting on prejudice against girls. The female infanticide and sex-selective abortions that are caused by son preference have led to imbalances in sex ratios characterized by millions of females 'missing' from populations in Asia, China and North Africa. Despite the significant contributions of women to the social and economic progress in India and China, female foetuses are being aborted at startling rates. According to economists and demographers, this practice may be due to a particular form of patriarchal family common in most parts of both regions (Dugger, 2001).

The largest sex differential in morbidity and mortality appear to be found in countries of South Asia. Numerous studies have documented excess mortality among females in India, Bangladesh and Pakistan, and investigated its association with educational differentials, with parental discrimination resulting from family-building strategies and marriage patterns, and with differential treatment operating from the selective allocation of food and medical care (D'souza and Chen, 1980; Chen, 1982; Miller, 1984; Koenig and D'Souza, 1986; Das Gupta, 1987; Bairagi, 1988; Stanton and Clemens, 1988; Bhuiya and Streatfield, 1991; Bourne and Walker, Jr., 1991; Coale, 1991; Muhuri and Preston, 1991). Statistics suggest that discrimination against daughters in feeding, treatment, and care is likely to depend in part on the number and sex composition of living children that a couple already has (Mishra et al., 2004).

Discrimination against the girl child is an old tradition in India, as it has been all over the world. Forms of discrimination have undergone changes over time, and in many parts of the world open and obvious forms of discrimination have disappeared. However, in India and a few other countries around it, not only the open forms of discrimination continue but also are getting exacerbated through use of new technologies and with the connivance of professionals.

In this study, we have attempted to investigate qualitative and less explored factors which can influence child sex ratio. For this the Heise (1998) ecological model of gender discrimination has been used. As a first dimension in gender discrimination study, individual perpetrator is considered, i.e., women who has seen discrimination, marital violence, being abused as a child and is named here as 'childhood experience'. It is very strongly argued that attention to a mother must start not after she has become a mother, not even when she is just about to become a mother, but when she is herself an infant and a child, because what happens to her during her own childhood which will eventually determine the adequacy of her physical and mental state as a mother (Gopalan, 1985).

Another dimension of gender discrimination in this study relates to marital conflicts, control of wealth and decision-making in the family. Most of the time it is found that women's fertility is culturally produced and controlled by marital arrangement. Hence, importance of married life in demographic analysis cannot be ignored as women spend major part of their life in marital union and their behaviour is greatly influenced by married life characteristics. It has often been argued that women's status is an indicator of the level of development in societies. Women's autonomy is likely to have a significant impact on demographic and health-seeking behaviour of couples by altering women's relative control over fertility and contraceptive use, and by influencing their attitudes and abilities (Sen and Batliwala, 1997).

In the above perspective, the broad objective of the study is to investigate into the interlinkage between the different aspects of woman's life course with sex-selective discrimination. However, specifically, the study examined the son preference and disfavour of daughters among women in rural Haryana during the prenatal and postnatal periods. Also, it deals with selective abortion (passive elimination) and female child neglect leading to their death (passive elimination).

Data and Methods

This paper is an outcome of a follow-up study of a community-based research project carried out by the International Institute for Population Sciences (IIPS), Mumbai, in Jind district of Haryana in 2000–2002 (Unisa et al., 2003). In this project, a secondary data analysis of child population (0–4 and 5–9 years) was done for 1981 and 1991 censuses in the state of Haryana by districts (Office of the Registrar General and Commissioner, 1986, 1987 and 1998). Jind district in Haryana exhibited a very high child sex ratio. The district map was prepared using the child population (0–6 years). There were many villages with sex ratio of 125 and above in the district. One of the concentrations of such cluster was selected in the district. From the cluster of villages with high child sex ratio, five villages were selected randomly. Complete enumeration of all the households in the selected villages was done. A total of 2,590 households were covered. Around 2,646 ever-married women in the reproductive ages were interviewed. Information was collected on household characteristics, pregnancy histories, antenatal care utilization and obstetric morbidity for each pregnancy.

In this study a subset of women was identified who had experienced a pregnancy outcome after the year 1995. Overall, there were 1,329 women who had given birth after 1995 in the selected five villages. A sample of 418 women was drawn from this subset of women with any of the following characteristics:

- women who had first two births as female children, or
- women whose first child was a female and had experienced an abortion or female child death.

It is assumed that when a woman has first female child or first two female children then she is likely to undergo sonography for subsequent pregnancies followed by sex-selective abortion if foetus is female. Also, these women may have neglected female children in terms of nutrition or immunization or treatment which may result in the child death.

A combination of both qualitative and quantitative approaches has been used in the study. Data was collected through face-to-face interview method. A semi-structured interview schedule containing both closed and open-ended questions was developed for this purpose. The questions included in the schedule were aimed at obtaining detailed information on the background characteristics of women, such as their childhood experience, various dimensions of women's autonomy, characteristics of married life including perception of married life by women at different stages of their marriage and some evidence of violence within marriage, women's sex preference and family size preference, and active and passive elimination process of the girl child. Also, case studies have been carried out for those women who had gone for induced abortion.

Both bi-variate and multivariate statistical methods have been used for data analysis. In the multivariate analysis, logistic regression method has been used to examine the different covariates of the study.

Computation of Indices

Childhood Experience Index: Women may perceive their childhood status in their natal family somewhat differently than what had actually happened to them. Therefore, a childhood experience index has been computed on the basis of some experiences, which women actually had during their childhood. A number of questions were asked to them relating to their experiences in their childhood days on certain aspects, such as freedom/mobility, unpleasant and distressed feeling at home, ever wished she had been born a boy and marriage considered burden or pleasure. The categories for each of them were 'always', 'sometimes' and 'never'. For 'never' a score of '0', for 'sometimes' a score of '1' and for 'always' a score of '2' was given. The index value ranges from 0 to 8, with a mean value of 3.11 and standard deviation (SD) of 1.66. Based on mean and SD, index value has been categorized into three as good, average and bad. Index value of 0–2 represents good childhood experience, 3–4 average childhood experience and 5 and above bad childhood experience.

Autonomy Indices: A set of situation-specific questions were asked to women in order to capture the different dimensions of autonomy among women in rural Haryana. Based on the responses given by women, autonomy indices have been created and weight was given to each response along with scores, means, standard deviation and cut-off points. The index value ranges from 0 to 21 with a mean value of 10.55 and standard deviation (SD) of 4.61. Based on mean and SD, index value has been categorized into three as low, medium and high. Index value of 0–6 shows low autonomy, 7–14 medium autonomy and 15–21 higher autonomy among women. In rural Haryana, a majority of the women (57%) fall into medium autonomy category whereas about 23 per cent in the high autonomy category.

Marital Instability Index: Although in general couples with children have a lower risk of divorce than do childless couples, the stabilizing effect of marriage may depend on the children's gender. In the present study marital instability among women has been examined on the basis of following three questions, asked to every woman during the time of personal interview: (i) Are you afraid of your husband? (ii) Did your husband ever beat or slap you during the last one year? (iii) Did your husband ever threaten to leave you or throw you out from home during the last one year? Based on the responses, a marital instability index has been constructed and weights were given to each response along with scores, means, standard deviation and cut-off points. The index value ranges from 0 to 6 with a mean value of 1.77 and standard deviation (SD) of 1.06. Based on mean and SD, index value has been categorized into three as low, medium and high. Index value of 0–1 shows low marital instability, of 2 medium marital instability and between 3–6 higher marital instability. The index values thus obtained show that in rural areas of Haryana 47 per cent women had a low marital instability, while 33 per cent women had a medium marital instability and 20 per cent women had a high marital instability.

Results and Discussion

At the outset it is important to know about the background characteristics of the respondents. The respondents primarily consist of middle-aged women (mean age 33.8 years ± 7.6 SD). Mean age at marriage is 14 years and consummation of marriage is 16 years. The mean number of children ever born is 4.52 while the mean number of surviving children is 3.74. Respondents mostly belong to Hindu religion. The caste composition shows that a higher percentage of women are from general castes (49%) and scheduled castes and other backward castes constitute almost 25 per cent each. More than 70 per cent of respondents are illiterate. Only 7 per cent have completed high school education. However, 20 per cent have completed education less than that. More than half the respondents are currently working and mostly in the agriculture. With regard to women's exposure to mass media, a very small proportion of them have such exposure. About one-third of the women listen to the radio at least once a week, followed by only 17 per cent who also watch television. The standard of living shows that 21 per cent live with a low, 44 per cent with a medium, and 36 per cent with a higher standard of living. Considering the living arrangement of the respondents, more than one-third are co-residing with their in-laws. Socio-economic characteristics of follow-up women and households were similar to large-scale community survey carried out by IIPS.

Active Elimination Process

Active elimination process has been examined in terms of women's experience of abortion according to some selected background characteristics as a life cycle approach.

Abortion by the Sex of the Surviving Children

A clearer picture emerges when we see the experience of abortion among women according to the sex of the surviving children. As shown in Table 1, a significantly higher proportion of women who had less number of children ever born with no male child experienced abortion than women who have one or more male child. However, no significant differential in the experience of abortion had been found among women who have more number of children ever born according to the survival status of the male child. Similarly, survival status of the female child has also shown significant differential in the experience of abortion among women. A significantly higher proportion of women who have only one female child had experienced abortion than women who have two or more surviving female child, irrespective of the number of children ever born. Thus, both the sex and the number of surviving children are important factors for abortion among women.

Table 1

Percentage of Women Experienced Abortion by Sex of the Surviving Child and Children Ever Born

Children ever born	Number of male child surviving			Number of female child surviving				Number of women
	0	1+	Total	1	2	3+	Total	
2 to 3	44.4**	24.7**	29.8**	44.8	24.6	21.4	29.8	104
4 +	21.4	19.2	19.4	50.0*	11.8*	20.6*	19.4*	222
Number of women	41	285	326	35	112	179	326	326

Significance level by Chi-square test: * at 10 per cent level; ** at 5 per cent level.

Abortion by the Sex of the Ideal Number of Children

Table 2 shows that a significantly higher proportion of women had experienced abortion (28%) who desired a small ideal number of children than those who desired a larger ideal number of children (19%). Also, the sex of the ideal number of children shows that considerably higher proportion women had experienced abortion who reported ideal number of daughter as none than those who reported ideal number of daughter as one or more. However, more women who reported only one ideal number of son were found to experience relatively higher abortion than those who have reported two or more ideal number of sons. Thus, the findings clearly indicate that more women who desire a small ideal family with no female children are experiencing abortion. This may be the result of a strategy to retain a small family size with the desired combination of sex.

Table 2

Percentage of Women Experienced Abortion According to the Ideal Number of Children by Sex

Ideal number of children by sex	Percentage of women who had experienced abortion	Number of women
Ideal number of children**		
Up to 2	28.1	139
3+	18.8	186
Ideal number of son*		
One	26.9	130
2+	20.1	194
Ideal number of daughter		
0	(37.5)	16
1+	22.0	309

( ) Based on less than 25 cases.
Significance level by Chi-square test: ** at 5 per cent level; * at 10 per cent level.

Abortion by Male Child Surviving and Ideal Number of Children

From Table 3 it is evident that among both the types of women (preferring small as well as large family size), experience of abortion significantly varies with the presence of a male child. A higher proportion of women not having a male child and who reported a small ideal family size, were found to experience abortion (35%) than those having one or more male children (27%). Also, a significantly more proportion of women not having male child (39%) and who reported a large ideal family size, were found to experience abortion than those having one or more male children (17%). This indicates that presence of a son as well as a desire for a small family size are most significant for abortion among women in rural Haryana.

Table 3

Percentage of Women Experienced Abortion According to Male Child Surviving and Ideal Number of Children

Ideal number of children	*Number of male child surviving*		*Total*	*Number of women*
	0	*1 and above*		
Up to 2	34.8	26.7	28.1	139
3 +	38.9**	16.7**	18.8	186
Number of women	41	285	22.7	325

Significance level by Chi-square test: ** at 5 per cent level.

Abortion by Childhood Experience, Autonomy Status and Married Life Characteristics

In Table 4, which presents the data regarding women who had experienced abortion according to their childhood experience, one can notice variation in the experience of abortion with women's childhood experience. Women's perceived status in the natal family has significant impact on abortion. More women who perceived their status in the natal family as better had undergone abortion than women who perceived their status as average or bad. A woman, age 31 years, mother of one son and three daughters, reported:

> *"Khud bahut dukh saha hai bachpan main, isliye mujhe ladki nehi chahiye tha. Lekin mujhe teen beti ke baad ek beta hua hai. Agar pehele agar ladka hota to, ek bhi ladki nehi chahiye the".* (I had a harsh life during my

childhood. That's why I did not like to have a daughter. But only after three daughters I had a son. If I would have a son before my daughters, then I certainly would not want any daughters.)

Table 4

Percentage of Women Experienced Abortion According to Childhood Experience, Autonomy Status and Married Life Characteristics

Characteristics	*Percentage of women who had experienced abortion*	*Number of women*
Childhood experience		
Good	24.5	143
Average	18.8	116
Bad	25.8	66
Autonomy		
Low	18.0	61
Medium	22.7	181
High	30.1	73
Perceived married life in present situation		
Happy	29.1	86
Satisfied	21.6	153
Sad	18.4	87
Marital instability		
Low	26.2	145
Medium	19.2	104
High	25.8	62
Total	22.7	326

A differential in the experience of abortion has been found with various autonomy indices. All the indices have a positive relationship with experience of abortion except decision-making autonomy. About 30 per cent women with a high combined autonomy had experienced abortion compared to 23 per cent women with medium autonomy, which further decreased to 18 per cent among women with a low autonomy. On the other hand, 26 per cent women with low decision-making autonomy had experienced abortion compared to 18 per cent women with a high decision-making autonomy. This indicates that it is only the decision-making autonomy of the women, which plays a significant role in mitigating the burden of abortion.

A noticeable differential has been found with the women's perceived married life and experience of abortion. More percentage of women perceiving their married life as very happy have been found to experience abortion than women perceiving their married life as sad. It may be said that the happiness in their married life may be the result of abortion by which they might have eliminated unwanted female children. Marital instability may be a key factor affecting the decision to abort pregnancies (Wadhera and Millar, 1997). However, in the present study, a significant variation in the experience of abortion has not been found with women's marital instability.

Correlates of Abortion

Table 5 presents the adjusted effects (odds ratio) of male and female children ever born, ideal number of children, location of women among their sisters, childhood experience, autonomy and marital instability and other socio-economic and demographic factors on abortion among women. Male and female children ever born and autonomy of women were found to be significant factors for women who had undergone an abortion. Women not having a male child were found to be almost three times more likely to experience abortion than women having one male child. On the other hand, women having more female children were significantly less likely to experience abortion than women having one female child. Moreover, women also reported that they have not gone for abortion because they have more female children. It is interesting to note that women having higher autonomy were significantly found to be four times more likely to experience abortion with reference to women with a lower autonomy.

Besides the sex of the children ever born and women's autonomy, none of the other background factors were found to be significant for women's experience of abortion. However, more women with a bad childhood experience were found to experience abortion with reference to women with a good childhood experience but the result is not statistically significant. Again, a higher proportion of women who want to limit their family size were found to experience abortion more likely than women who want three or more ideal number of children. Also, women with a high marital instability were found to be more likely to experience abortion than women with a lower marital instability.

Table 5

Logistic Regression Result Showing the Adjusted Effects (Odds Ratio) of Selected Predictors on Abortion among Women

Selected predictors	*Abortion*	
	Odds Ratio	*P value*
Male children ever born		
1[R]	1.000	
0	3.060**	0.030
2 +	0.917	0.812
Female children ever born		
Up to 1[R]	1.000	
2	0.214***	0.002
3 +	0.333***	0.022
Ideal number of children		
Up to 2[R]	1.000	
3 +	0.744	0.360
Has done sonography		
No	1.000	
Yes	1.784	0.231
Childhood experience		
Good[R]	1.000	
Average	0.909	0.797
Bad	1.267	0.565
Autonomy		
Low[R]	1.000	
Medium	1.866	0.175
High	3.788**	0.015
Marital instability		
Low[R]	1.000	
Medium	0.540*	0.089
High	1.281	0.563
Constant	0.652	
–2 Log likelihood	293.2	
Nagelkerke R Square	0.191	
Number of women	303	

Note: Dependent variable: Abortion 0=No and 1=Yes

The model also controls for age, education, ethnicity, women's occupation, husband's occupation, standard of living index, co-residence with in-laws and exposure to any mass media which are not significant

[R] Reference category

Significance level: * $p < 0.10$; ** $p < 0.05$; *** $p < 0.01$.

Thus, the results of logistic regression confirm that male children ever born is an important factor for women undergoing an abortion. Women without a male child have been found significantly more likely to experience abortion. On the contrary, more number of female children decreases the likelihood of abortion. This clearly explains that women desiring a small family size with a strong son preference are undergoing abortion.

Passive Elimination Process

In this section the passive elimination process of the girl child has been discussed by exploring the sex differential in child death by different demographic parameters, such as the survival status of the male children by birth order, gender differential in childhood mortality pattern in terms of morbidity, and treatment and immunization pattern of the dead child. The determinants of passive elimination, i.e., effects of some selected predictors, such as male children ever born, female children ever born, ideal number of children, women's childhood experience, autonomy, married life and other socio-economic and demographic factors on the death of female child are also examined.

Excess of Female Deaths over Male Deaths by Birth Order

Table 6 presents the percentage of child deaths by sex and excess of female deaths over male deaths according to birth orders. Overall, 15.6 per cent children had died of which 16.1 per cent were females and 14.7 per cent were males. However, a significant gender differential has been found in the deaths of the children according to birth orders. Percentage of deaths of female children is found to be increasing in the higher order births. On the other hand, percentage of male child deaths is found to be significantly low in the higher order births. It is also evident from the table that the excess of female deaths over male deaths drastically increases at the higher birth orders. The ratio of female deaths over male deaths is found to be less than one indicating more male deaths in the lower birth orders which increases to 1.8 indicating more deaths of female children in the higher birth orders. The extreme variation in child deaths by sex in higher birth orders may be the result of ignorance and neglect of the female child in the higher birth order, which eventually leads to their deaths.

Table 6

Percentage of Child Deaths by Sex and Excess of Female Deaths over Male Deaths According to Birth Order

Birth order	*Percentage of child death*			*Excess of female deaths over male deaths*
	Male	*Female*	*Total*	
Up to three*	21.6	15.5	16.9	0.7
More than three**	9.8	17.8	13.5	1.8
Total	14.7	16.1	15.6	1.1

Significance level by Chi-square test: * at 5 per cent level; ** at 1 per cent level.

Experience of Child Death by Women According to Sex and Number of Deaths

Table 7 presents the percentage of women who had experienced child death by the sex of the child and number of deaths. Mean child death indicates a higher proportion of female child death over male child deaths (0.46 and 0.22 respectively). Looking at the number of child deaths, again, a significant differential has been observed in the deaths according to the sex of the child. A higher proportion of women have lost at least one female child than male child (22% and 14% respectively). Further, in case of death of two or more children, also, noticeably a higher proportion of women lost more daughters than sons (9% and 4% respectively). Thus, the negligence of female children, which may be a strategy of passive elimination of girl children leading to their death, is confirmed.

Table 7

Percentage of Women Experienced Child Death by Sex and Number of Deaths

Number of deaths	*Only male child death*	*Only female child death*	*Death of both male and female child*	*Death of either male or female child*
1	14.1 (46)	21.3 (71)	3.5 (11)	26.1 (85)
2 +	3.7 (12)	9.2 (31)	0.6 (2)	16.2 (53)
Mean child death	0.22	0.46	0.05	0.69
Number of women	326	326	316	326

Figures in the parentheses denote number of women.

Experience of Female Child Death by Women According to Male Child Surviving and Children ever Born

Table 8 presents the percentage of women who had experienced female child death according to male child surviving and number of children ever born. Women with four or more children ever born had experienced a higher proportion of female child deaths although the number of male children surviving does not make a significant difference. However, women with two to three children ever born have experienced a relatively lower proportion of female child deaths. But, among women with two to three children ever born, number of male children surviving makes a significant difference in the death of the female child. About 19 per cent women experienced death of female children who have no male children surviving compared to 9 per cent women having one or more male child surviving. This indirectly indicates that women not having a male child and preferring small family size might be ignoring female children more.

Table 8

Percentage of Women Experienced Female Death According to Male Child Surviving and Number of Children Ever Born

Children ever born	*Number of male child surviving*		*Total*	*Number of women*
	0	*1+*		
2 – 3	18.5	9.1	11.5	104
4 +	42.9	40.4	40.5	222
Number of women	41	285	31.3	326

Gender Differential in the Morbidity Pattern of the Dead Children

Table 9 presents the gender differentials in the morbidity pattern of the dead children. It is evident from the table that the diseases, which can be prevented by childhood vaccinations such as tetanus and measles, were found to be more among female children. Moreover, iron deficiency diseases like anaemia were also found to be higher among the female children. Interestingly, none of these diseases were found among the male children. Further, premature birth had also been reported higher in the case of female children. However, general diseases like diarrhoea/jaundice/fever/typhoid/

pneumonia had been found predominant among male children. Thus, it is clear that there exists a remarkable gender differential in the morbidity condition of the dead children. Female children were found to suffer from those diseases, which could have been prevented by proper care.

Table 9

Gender Differential in Morbidity Pattern of the Dead Child

Disease after birth	*Male child*	*Female child*	*Total*
Tetanus/measles/anemia	(0.0)	(13.6)	12
Diarrhea/jaundice/fever/typhoid/pneumonia	76.5	47.7	55
Heart/kidney/respiratory problem/cancer	(5.9)	(12.5)	12
Premature birth	17.6	26.1	26
Total deaths	(17)	88	105

Gender Differential in the Treatment Seeking for the Dead Children

Table 10 shows a significant gender differential in the treatment-seeking behaviour for the dead children. About 44 per cent of the female children had not received any treatment compared to 18 per cent of the male children. Further, looking at the money spent on the treatment, all the male children had received paid treatment whereas in case of 12 per cent female children, the treatment was free.

Table 10

Gender Differential in Treatment Seeking of the Dead Child

Treatment-seeking behaviour	*Male child*	*Female child*	*Total*
Get any medical treatment for the disease*			
No	17.6	43.9	39
Yes	82.4	56.1	60
Total	17	82	99
Paid for treatment			
No	(0.0)	(12.2)	6
Yes	100.0	87.8	57
Total	14	49	63
The cost for treatment was paid by			
Husband	92.9	82.2	50
Others	(7.1)	(17.8)	9
Total deaths	(14)	45	59

Significance level by Chi-Square test: * at 5 per cent level.

Again, looking at another domain of treatment-seeking behaviour such as who paid the cost of treatment for the child, again, a gender differential has been noticed. In case of 18 per cent female children, the cost of treatment has not been borne by the father whereas it was only 7 per cent in the case of male children. This indicates relatively more negligence from the point of view of the father in case of a daughter than a son. Thus, the discussion brings out that there exists a gender differential not only in the treatment-seeking pattern of the child in terms of medical treatment of the disease but also in paid treatment as well as involvement of the father in child care.

Gender Differential in the Immunization Pattern of the Dead Children

Table 11 shows the gender differential in the immunization pattern of the dead child. The information on immunization pattern is mainly based on mother's report. All the vaccinations were found to be lower among female children than male children except BCG. A significant gender differential had been observed against polio vaccination. All the male children were immunized of polio whereas 26 per cent of the female children were not vaccinated even after the government's initiative of such a massive programme of pulse polio in India. Also, in the case of DPT and measles vaccines, 70 per cent of the male children were immunized compared to only 58 per cent and 51 per cent of the female children respectively. Deaths due to tetanus and measles have been found more among female children because of low immunization. The discussion clearly brings out that in rural Haryana, there also exists significant gender differential in case of immunization. It indirectly shows more disregard towards the female children because immunization facilities are readily available within or near the village.

Table 11

Gender Differential in the Immunization Pattern of the Dead Child

Received immunization	*Male child*	*Female child*	*Total*
BCG	70.0	77.3	53
Polio*	100.0	74.4	53
DPT	70.0	58.1	53
Measles	70.0	51.2	53
Total deaths	10	43	53

Significance level by Chi-square test: * at 10 per cent level.

Correlates of Passive Elimination

It is worthwhile to examine the correlates of passive elimination of girl child, which has been seen in terms of death of the female child.

Table 12 presents the adjusted effects of selected predictors, such as male children ever born, female children ever born, ideal number of children, women's childhood experience, autonomy, married life and other socio-economic and demographic factors on female child death.

Except female children ever born and age of women, none of the other factors are found to be statistically significant for female child deaths. Women with three or more children ever born are found to experience female child death four times more with reference to women with up to two female children ever born. Also, women of older ages (35–52 years) were significantly more likely (1.7 times) to experience female child death than women of younger ages (20–34 years).

In spite of being statistically insignificant, the other variables like male children ever born, women's autonomy and marital instability do have some impact on the death of a female child. Women without a male child and having high marital instability had experienced more female child deaths with reference to their counterparts. However, women with a higher autonomy had experienced fewer female child deaths than women with a lower autonomy. Thus, the results of logistic regression confirm that there is a significant impact of demographic factors such as female and male children ever born in female child death. Also, women's autonomy and marital instability play an important role on the death of the female child.

Summary and Conclusions

This present study examined the sex-selective discrimination by active elimination of female foetus and passive elimination of female child leading to their death and the role of different background characteristics like women's childhood experience, autonomy, married life and sex preference and family size preference of women in it. The study shows that there exists extreme sex-selective discrimination against girl child through conception to their rearing and bearing. Also, extreme discrimination by women sometimes results into the sex-selective abortion in the society in the desire for male child. It can be said that there exists women's life course impact on the discrimination against girl child. Woman who herself had a worst childhood experience (in terms of discrimination in all spheres including childhood status, food, education, mobility, etc.), feels

Table 12

Logistic Regression Results Showing the Adjusted Effects (Odds Ratio) of Selected Predictors on Female Child Death

Selected predictors	*Female child death*	
	Odds Ratio	*P value*
Male children ever born		
1[R]	1.000	0.942
0	1.517	0.192
2 +	1.039	0.942
Female children ever born		
Up to 2[R]	1.000	
3 +	4.243***	<0.001
Ideal number of children		
Up to 2[R]	1.000	
3 +	1.235	0.491
Childhood experience		
Good[R]	1.000	
Average	0.735	0.406
Bad	1.121	0.741
Autonomy		
Low[R]	1.000	
Medium	1.208	0.624
High	0.769	0.584
Marital instability		
Low[R]	1.000	
Medium	1.017	0.960
High	1.353	0.452
Age		
20–34	1.000	
35–52	1.717*	0.082
Constant	0.116	
–2 Log likelihood	314.976	
Nagelkerke R Square	0.249	
Number of women	303	

Note: Dependent variable: Experience of female child death (0 = no and 1 = yes).

The Model also controls for education, ethnicity, women's occupation, husband's occupation, standard of living, co-residence with in-laws and exposure to any mass media which are not significant.

[R]Reference category.

Significance level: * $p < 0.10$; *** $p < 0.01$.

high instability in her married life or perceives a sad married life, is more responsible for the discrimination against girl child from conception through her childhood leading to a vicious cycle of gender deprivation and gender discrimination.

Health sector has to play more positive role in Haryana. More efforts are required to immunize the female child. It has been found that women exposed to mass media are significantly experiencing less abortion. So, mass media exposure should be made more effective in rural Haryana by incorporating the health consequences related to late and frequent abortion on the part of women in addition to its legalization. This will help the women to become aware of the hazards of abortion. The negative effects of sex-detection technologies and abortion after the first trimester should be vigorously publicized in rural areas. Stronger messages are required to tell that female should not be blamed for the birth of female child, because biologically husband is responsible for the birth of the child of either sex. National and regional working groups may be established to formulate and promote action strategies to reduce sex preference and their negative impacts. It should be widely publicized that an imbalance in the sex composition not only means violation of the human rights of a girl child, but it can also lead to disastrous demographic and social consequences.

Acknowledgements

Authors are profoundly thankful to Praween Agrawal for his useful comments and suggestions on the earlier draft of this paper. Support for the fieldwork by the Parkes Foundation Small Grant Fund, Department of Biological Anthropology, Cambridge University, UK is greatly acknowledged.

References

Agrawal, S. (2004). *Interlinkages between Women's Childhood Experience, Autonomy, Sex Preference and Elimination of the Girl Child: A Study of Women in Rural Haryana* (unpublished Ph.D. thesis), International Institute for Population Sciences (IIPS), Mumbai.

Bairagi, R. (1988). Food Crisis, Nutrition and Female Children in Rural Bangladesh, *Population and Development Review*, 12(2), pp. 307–15.

Bambawale, U. (1992). Family Formation in India: Change and Continuity, *Social Change*, 22(3).

Bhuiya, A. and K. Streatfield (1991). Mother's Education and Survival of Female Children in Rural Area of Bangladesh, *Population Studies*, 45(2), pp. 253–64.

Bourne, K.L. and G.M. Walker Jr. (1991). The Differential Effect of Mothers' Education on Mortality of Boys and Girls in India, *Population Studies*, 45(2), pp. 203–19.

Chen, L.C. (1982). Where have the Women Gone? Insights from Bangladesh on Low Sex Ratio of India's Population, *Economic and Political Weekly*, 17(10), pp. 364–72.

Coale, A. (1991). Excess Female Mortality and the Balance of the Sexes in the Population: An Estimate of the Number of Missing Females, *Population and Development Review*, 17, pp. 517–23.

Das Gupta, M. (1987). Selective Discrimination against Female Children in Rural Punjab, North India, *Population and Development Review*, 13(1), pp. 77–100.

D'Souza, S. and L.C. Chen (1980). Sex Differentials in Mortality in Rural Bangladesh, *Population and Development Review*, 6(2), pp. 257–70.

Dugger, C.W. (2001). Modern Asia's Anomaly: The Girls who don't get Born, *New York Times*, May 6, p. 4.

Gopalan, C. (1985). The Mother and Child in India, *Economic and Political Weekly*, 20(4), pp. 159–66.

Heise, L. (1998). Violence against Women: An Integrated, Ecological Health Framework, *Violence against Women*, 4(3), pp. 262–90.

Kishor, S. (2002). *Putting India's Experience in Context: Population Sex Ratios and Sex Ratios at Birth from the Demographic and Health Surveys* (Unpublished), presented at the Symposium on Sex Ratio in India, January 10–11, 2002, organized by International Institute for Population Sciences, Mumbai and Ford Foundation, New Delhi, p. 22.

Koenig, M.A. and S. D'Souza (1986). Sex Differences in Childhood Mortality in Rural Bangladesh, *Social Science and Medicine*, 22(1), pp. 15–22.

Koenig, M.A. and S. D'Souza (1984). Daughter Neglect, Women's Work and Marriage: Pakistan and Bangladesh Compared, *Medical Anthropology*, 8(2), pp. 109–26.

Mishra, V., T.K. Roy and Robert D. Retherford (2004). Sex Differentials in Childhood Feeding, Health Care and Nutritional Status in India, *Population and Development Review*, 30(2), pp. 269–95.

Muhuri, P.K. and S.H. Preston (1991). Effects of Family Composition on Mortality Differentials by Sex among Children in Matlab, Bangladesh, *Population and Development Review*, 17(3), pp. 415–34.

Office of the Registrar General and Census Commissioner (1986). Census of India 1981, *Series 1, Part IV A. Social and Cultural Tables*, Registrar General and Census Commissioner, New Delhi.

—— (1987). Census of India 1981, *Series 5, Haryana Part IV A. Social and Cultural Tables*, Registrar General and Census Commissioner, New Delhi.

—— (1998). Census of India 1991, *Series 8, Haryana Part IV A Social and Cultural Tables*, Registrar General and Census Commissioner, New Delhi.

Sen, G. and S. Batliwala (1997). Empowering Women for Reproductive Rights: Moving beyond Cairo, paper presented at the Seminar on Female Empowerment and Demographic Processes: Moving beyond Cairo, IUSSP, Lund, Sweden, 21–24 April.

Stanton, B.F. and J.D. Clemens (1988). The Influence of Gender on Determinants of Urban Childhood Mortality in Bangladesh, *International Journal of Epidemiology*, 17(1), pp. 129–35.

Unisa, S. (2002). Opinion: Can Sex-selective Abortion be a part of Women's Right to Free Choice and Control over Reproduction? International Institute for Population Sciences (IIPS), *Newsletter* 43(1–2), p. 5.

Unisa, S., C.P. Prakasam., R.K. Sinha and R.B. Bhagat (2003). *Evidence of Sex Selective Abortions from Two Cultural Settings of India: A Study of Haryana and Tamil Nadu*, Unpublished Report, International Institute for Population Sciences, Mumbai.

Unisa, S., S. Pujari and R. Usha (2007). Sex-selective Abortion in Haryana: Evidence from Pregnancy History and Antenatal Care, *Economic and Political Weekly*, 42(1), pp. 60–66.

TEN

Across-Region Marriages

Poverty, Female Migration and Sex Ratio

Ravinder Kaur

The 2001 Census data suggests continuation of an alarming trend—the sex ratio (number of females per 1,000 males) has not only stayed low in several North Indian states but has actually deteriorated. Demographic, sociological and economic research has concentrated on analyzing the reasons for the low and declining sex ratio. While demographers have focused on the numbers of 'missing women' pointing to fertility decline and son preference as causes, sociologists have analyzed son preference in terms of the low status of women, caused by social practices of hypergamous and exogamous marriage systems. Other sociological factors contributing to the non-preference for women is their supposedly lower labour force participation and the consequent need for dowry as compensation. Women are socially constructed as the inferior, less valuable and a burden on the family. While sons are regarded valuable for various reasons (support to parents in old age, continuing the lineage, inheriting property), daughters are projected as being dispensable. Despite improvements in several social indicators for women (lower mortality, better education, increasing labour force participation, relative economic independence), son preference has not declined in Indian society. In fact, it appears as if the small and relatively educated and prosperous family is becoming inimical to the birth of girl children. Recent literature has focused on the correlation of low sex ratio with prosperity, pointing to the 'killing' role of technology in enhancing this negative trend.

The consensus is that technology is facilitating 'son preference' leading to the elimination of girl children before birth. Worryingly, the trends in the north are seen to be spreading to the other parts of the country as well. While the causes and practices leading to son preference and hence a low female sex ratio have been well researched, not many studies have paid attention to the manner in which this is affecting other social processes and patterns. Recently, and almost exclusively, in the popular media, attention has been on not the determinants of few women, but the consequences of too many men. Anecdotal evidence is linking the 'buying of girls for marriage' to the low sex ratio. A marriage needs both sexes in equal proportions, so what does the declining number of marriageable girls portend? The sex ratios in the neighbourhood of 800 for Haryana and Punjab imply that there are only four women available for every five men. Simply, this means that one of every five men will not have a local girl to marry. In China and South Korea, two other countries with a low sex ratio, the shortage of marriageable women is resulting in extreme measures to obtain girls. While the Chinese are resorting to abduction, kidnapping and even a return to the old practice of rearing a young girl child for subsequent marriage into the family, Koreans are importing ethnic Koreans from northern China and reaching out to the Philippines for wives (Dasgupta and Li Shuzhuo, 1999). Other literature from China is pointing to 'long distance' marriages where poor women are migrating to more prosperous areas through marriage (Fan and Huang, 1998).

Given the declining child sex ratio, a further shortfall in marriageable women in the low sex ratio areas of India is a foregone conclusion. How will communities handle the worsening shortage? What are the 'social' implications of this shortage for both men and women? Will more men be forced to remain bachelors? Will they resort to capturing and abducting women as in China or importing them for marriage as in South Korea? Will we see a return to polyandry with one woman being shared among several brothers? What will be the impact on marriage payments? Will dowry decrease (as predicted by Caldwell et al., 1983; Dasgupta, 1999) and will we see a spread of brideprice and a rise in its value? Will women be valued more due to their scarcity or treated worse if they are imported?

Few, if any, studies have examined the impact of the low sex ratio on marriage practices. Similarly, studies of marriage and kinship systems have not focused on the role of demographic variables in determining marriage. This paper examines the impact of the low sex ratio on marriage practices by documenting and analyzing an unusual response to the shortage of marriageable girls in the north. In the paper this phenomenon is described as 'across-region' marriage. The need for women, for productive and reproductive purposes, is being addressed through unconventional marriages that are uniting rural, illiterate Indians across boundaries of region, language, religion and even caste. Marriages are increasingly coming to note in which men from UP, Haryana, Punjab and Rajasthan are marrying women from West Bengal, Assam, Bihar, Andhra Pradesh and Tamil Nadu.

These unusual marriages are a consequence of a combination of factors like adverse sex ratio, acute poverty and the desire of parents to escape dowry. Poor parents are being driven to marry their daughters hundreds of miles away from home while men from the low sex ratio states of Haryana, Punjab, parts of UP and Rajasthan are 'importing' women from the eastern and southern states as marriage partners. Women, too, may be choosing this as a migration strategy to move from poorer to more desirable locations. Table 1 shows the much higher sex ratios in the states of Assam, West Bengal and Andhra Pradesh—states from which the brides are coming—and the low sex ratios in the receiving states of Punjab, Haryana and UP and also corresponding economic status figures). Evidence from the data gathered until now shows that the phenomenon of across-region marriages is not confined to lower castes only (who are expected to be less diligent in obeying prescribed cultural rules of marriage), but are occurring among all castes and income levels in these north-western states. Such marriages represent a hitherto undocumented type that cannot be explained adequately within the framework of categories available for understanding marriage and non-marriage transactions involving women, i.e., sexual trafficking, buying of women for marriage and brideprice marriage (the distinction between the latter two has often been debated in sociological literature—brideprice as a system of marriage payments is prevalent in many parts of the world and in several regions and among several groups in India and is hence differentiated from transactions in which women are purchased). The flow of women remains strictly unidirectional—women from Haryana/Punjab or UP are not given in marriage to families in

Table 1

Sex Ratio and Poverty in India

State	*Sex Ratio*		*Sex Ratio 0–4 Years*		*Poverty*
	1981	*2001*	*1981*	*2001*	*1999–2000*
Haryana	870	861	922	820	8.7
Punjab	879	874	925	793	6.2
Uttar Pradesh	882	898	965	916	31.2
Rajasthan	919	922	978	909	15.3
Assam	910	932	—	964	36.1
West Bengal	911	934	991	963	27
Andhra Pradesh	975	978	1000	964	15.8
Tamil Nadu	977	986	974	939	21.1
India	934	933	978	927	26.1

Notes: (1) Sex ratio is expressed in terms of females per 1,000 males.
(2) Poverty is represented as the proportion of the population whose monthly expenditure falls below the poverty line set by the Planning Commission, Government of India.

Sources: Census 1981 and 2001; NSS Household Expenditure Survey, 1999–2000.

Assam/West Bengal; being in short supply they are able to find spouses locally. In an inverted logic, the 'value' of the local women in the marriage market goes up—and this is seen in the demand for land in exchange for the girl by parents of women who are sought by grooms for a second marriage. In a society, where land is the pre-eminent good, and can only be transacted between males, this spells a shift in the position of local men and women in the marriage market. Parents of women in Haryana are being successful in marrying their daughters 'up' and ensuring that they do not get second rate grooms. While needy men bring lower ranked women from the east, local Haryana girls are sought to be married into the outlying areas of Delhi where property prices are on the rise, with an eye to ensuring their future prosperity. However, nowhere are these changes reflected in a lowering of son preference or attempts at ensuring that girl foetuses, children and young women are not eliminated or do not succumb to early mortality. The PNDT Act has only sent the detection process underground and made it more expensive and risky.

Given the century-long low sex ratio in the north, data being gathered reveals that 'across-region' marriages are not an entirely new phenomenon (Dasgupta, 1999; Blanchet, 2003). However, there have been gaps in the frequency of such marriages. Evidence from Haryana and Blanchet's study reveal that such marriages peaked about 20 years ago and again in the late 1990s. The renewed frequency of such marriages may be attributed to the continuing importance and necessity of marriage, a further decline in the sex ratio and the difficulty in poor areas in achieving marriage of daughters locally due to dowry demands. The persistence and spread of the poor sex ratio in the north-western states will logically keep up the demand for brides from elsewhere. Female migration for upward mobility is very possibly another factor contributing to such marriages.

The paper examines various attributes of across-region marriages. For example, do they represent a new pattern? How can one characterize such marriages if they do not fall into the categories of sexual trafficking, buying of women or brideprice? Are these 'deviant' or simply 'secondary' (not first) marriages? Do they flout traditional rules of marriage? How are such marriages achieved? What is the nature of marriage payments involved? On whom does the burden of adjustment lie? Is the burden on the women heightened as a result of the greater marriage distance? Is the violence towards women brought from outside greater? What are the sociological implications and consequences of such marriages for intergenerational change? Given the regional and cultural divide between the spouses, what are the integration dimensions of such marriage networks? The evidence provided by such marriages demands that conventional sociological assumptions about the 'sacred' and 'pure' nature of marriage in India be interrogated. The diversity of marriages being accepted by otherwise conservative caste-bound communities raises questions about the nature of changes that society is undergoing.

Contextualizing Across-Region Marriages

The average Indian marriage, especially in rural areas, is still perceived as governed by traditional rules of caste and community. These are rules of endogamy (marriage within one's own caste group although outside one's own 'gotra'—clan), hierarchy (bride-givers are inferior to bride-takers) and hypergamy (the woman must marry up, both socially and economically). The rule of caste endogamy is shared all over India. However, within the caste, isogamous (spouses of equal status) or hypergamous (spouses of unequal status) marriages may occur. In many parts of the North India, village exogamy is another rule, making it imperative for spouses to be from different villages. Dowry, since it has become near universal in the country, can be considered as another rule. According to high caste customs, an honourable marriage is one accompanied by dowry and not by brideprice (where the groom pays a sum of money to the bride's parents).

In general, patterns of kinship and marriage identified by Karve (1965), for the north and the south, with the rest of the country sharing a mix of the two, still prevail. In the south marriages often took place among close relatives due to which the brides were known to the family. Thus, real and classificatory 'cross-cousin' marriages and 'uncle-niece' marriages were quite common. In the north, however, people preferred to marry 'strangers'—those sufficiently removed in terms of both social and physical distance. The relationship between the bride-givers and bride-takers is more equal (isogamous) in the south and entirely hierarchical (hypergamous) in the north with the bride-takers having a permanent superiority here.

The first rule of caste endogamy is rarely infringed except in contemporary non-arranged marriages. Breakdown of endogamy may occur if a man is not able to find a spouse from his own caste—resulting in marriage with a woman from a caste inferior to his own. A woman is almost never allowed to marry beneath her caste and would face severe consequences if this were to happen. The need for strict conformity to endogamy and hypergamy (both social and economic) for the woman has been held responsible for the practice of female infanticide, especially among upper castes, such as Rajputs. The fear that a spouse of the appropriate status may not be found for the girl often led to her elimination soon after birth. Early marriage was also preferred (and still is in rural areas) to decrease the chances of women bringing dishonour to the family through inappropriate sexual behaviour. Dowry, additionally, reinforces the image of women as a burden. This is especially true in regions where they are made to practise seclusion, lowering their participation in the labour force or their labour is not counted as being remunerative.

The spread and spiralling costs of demand-led dowry further reinforce the sense of daughters as a burden.

Traditionally, marriages took place within a conventional social and physical distance, through the intercession of relatives, or through other social networks. For the urban and semi-urban dwellers, advertisements in newspapers have increased enormously the range of distance over which spouses meeting appropriate caste/class/community criteria can be identified. In the south the shift from matriliny to patriliny (in those areas where matriliny was prevalent) and a movement away from marriage among close relatives in patrilineal families are important changes affecting marriage patterns. Additionally, marriages among non-elite persons coming together in the urban work context are also broadening the marriage field.

'New' Trends in Marriage Patterns

In the post-independence period, demographic and social changes (declining fertility levels with a distorted sex ratio, education and reduced segregation of the sexes, rising age at marriage, changing work patterns, etc.) are leading to increasingly more differentiated and complex marriage and residence patterns. Although barriers of region, religion, caste and language have often been overcome by across-region marriages in India, this has been possible mostly for English-speaking, educated, professional Indians. Other across-region marriages have been characteristic of royal elites. However, rural Indians have rarely ventured outside the circles defined by rules of endogamy and exogamy.

The marriages being discussed here are 'arranged' across regions separated by hundreds of miles and do not occur through the agency of individuals brought together by the marriage, i.e., they are not 'love marriages'. Across-region marriages represent a pattern in which rural, often illiterate, people from different geographical and cultural regions are getting linked. Here, the marriage distance (defined as the distance between the bride's natal and conjugal home) can stretch to hundreds of miles taking a woman completely away from her familial, regional, linguistic and cultural contexts, compounding greater spatial distance with greater social distance. While the traditional North Indian marriage pattern typically emphasized physical, besides social, distance, this distance was within the parameters of an identifiable local community. The two opposing tendencies of endogamy (marriage within the caste) and exogamy (marriage outside the gotra and village—in the case of village exogamy) placed certain spatial and geographical limits to the spread of marriage networks. For example, Jats from Haryana would marry Jats from neighbouring UP or Rajasthan. In across-region marriages, on the other hand, a Jat or Chauhan from Haryana is now marrying a woman of indeterminate caste from Assam, Bengal or Bihar. The negative impact of marriage distance on women's status and autonomy (Dyson and Moore, 1983) is likely to be further heightened under such circumstances. More importantly, the specific cause of the spread of these hitherto uncharted marriage networks, across far-flung regions of the country, cannot be traced to marriage rules but lies in the linkages between female marriage migration, poverty and the sex ratio.

Although the statistical significance of such marriages remains to be established, there is increasing evidence of them among all castes and classes. Information is trickling in from the states of Haryana, Punjab, UP and Rajasthan at one end and from Assam, West Bengal and even Andhra Pradesh and Tamil Nadu, at the other. Blanchet's study provides information on the movement of Bangladeshi girls into UP for marriage. The present study takes up two distinct sets of networks, one between Haryana and Assam and the other between West Bengal/Bihar and UP, for study, providing anecdotal evidence of a Rajasthan-Andhra Pradesh network. Blanchet too mentions Bangladeshi women married into Rajasthan.

Fieldwork in two villages of Sonepat district in Haryana has revealed the occurrence of such marriages in almost every caste. Many of these marriages are between Haryanvi men and Assamese women, others with Bihari women. Some of the women have been settled in Haryana villages for as long as 20 years while others have come in the last 5–10 years with the trend still continuing. Further evidence is from marriages among several castes in a village of Etah district in UP (also being documented by the author). Here, the network is between UP men and women from West Bengal. While the Haryana-Assam marriages are 'rural', the UP-West Bengal ones while originating as rural marriages are further embedded in a rural-urban migration pattern with many such couples moving from their rural homes to cities like Delhi and possibly Mumbai. A third set of marriages coming to notice is between men from rural

Rajasthan and women from rural Andhra Pradesh. The occurrence of a single marriage leads to further marriages (not all of which are necessarily successful) resulting in a network. The married women bring other women—sisters, cousins, neighbour's daughters for marriage, creating fairly dense networks. Many women act as 'go-betweens', accompanying the grooms to their natal or neighbouring villages and getting the marriages performed. Most of the money is spent in travel and the celebration of the marriage with the go-between or 'marriage broker' saving a service fee for herself. A one-time go-between does not necessarily benefit economically; she may benefit socially, through expanding social networks. However, those who establish marriage brokering as a business for themselves seek to derive greater monetary benefits for themselves.

Marriage and Non-Marriage Transactions Involving Women

Reports in the national and vernacular media have been highlighting the increasing incidents of 'sale of girls' to the affluent but female-deficient states of Haryana and Punjab (*Tribune*, August, 3, 6, 13, 18, 19, 2003, September 1, 2003, *Outlook*, August 11, 2003; *India Today*, October 13, 2003). In these transactions, the girls are generally from poor families from West Bengal, Assam, Orissa, Chhattisgarh, and even the southern states of Andhra Pradesh and Tamil Nadu. Some of the journalistic reporting correctly correlates many such 'marriages' in the rural areas to the adverse sex ratio. However, the focus of the reports on sensational cases of sale and purchase of underage girls conceals the actual nature and range of marital and other transactions resulting from the poor sex ratio.

Before arguing that 'across-region' marriages present a distinct variant, there is a need to clearly distinguish the several types of transactions and 'marriages' being observed. First, the buying/selling of girls for marriage should be distinguished from sexual trafficking in women. Trafficking is purely for profit in which women are like any other commodity being bought and sold. Women and even underage girls are sent to brothels through touts or married to men much older than themselves. They are subjected to violence and repeated sexual abuse. This is clearly an illegal activity.

The second category is of marriage by purchase/sale. What distinguishes this category is that 'marriage' is a part of the transaction. Here, men who are unable to find wives and need them for their domestic, sexual and reproductive services buy women from poor families. The man pays the girl's parents to acquire a wife. These marriages are further differentiated from trafficking as the girl/wife is not passed on to others and is not one of several 'wives' thus acquired. More often than not, she makes a stable home with a particular man, fulfilling the roles of wife, mother and farm labourer. Poor men who are unable to attract marriage proposals buy a 'wife' from another poor family which sells a daughter for a monetary consideration. Buying is looked down upon by most rural communities.

Discussing what she calls 'deviant marriages' in the context of a Rajput village in UP, Minturn (1993) reveals that when a man is not sought after for marriage, it is usually due to "lack of education, poverty or scandal". She goes on to say, "Paradoxically, poor families who cannot attract wives and dowries for their sons may be forced to 'buy' their wives from families too poor to provide dowries for their daughters. The term 'buying a wife' is used to describe indirect dowry, the custom whereby the groom's family gives money to the bride's family, who use some of it provide dowry and keep some of it. Such marriages are disgraceful for both husband and wife, so purchased wives are often chosen from strange villages in order to minimize the resulting gossip" (p. 63).

While Minturn's evidence points to the groom financing his own marriage and the dowry, there is a difference between marriages in which the bride's family benefits monetarily and those in which no monetary benefit accrues to the parents—the case in across-region marriages. Further, marriages described by Minturn are between rich and poor families or between poor families of the 'same' community. The distinctive feature of across-region marriages is that not only are the brides from 'strange villages', but also from 'strange regions' with a different language and culture.

A third type of marriage exchange prevalent and accepted in India and elsewhere is the system of brideprice where the bride's family is compensated for the loss of her labour. Women as farm labourers are essential to most agrarian economies. Where their role in agriculture or their labour/income contribution to the household is 'visible' and 'acknowledged', brideprice is often the practice. Under this system, the family losing a productive worker gets compensated in cash or kind. A man may pay a certain sum of money to the bride's parents at the time of marriage or pledge his own labour on her parent's land for a specified period of time. Although on the decline, several communities in India have been known to favour brideprice. Brideprice marriages are not the same as marriages in which the women are 'bought'. Brideprice marriage is the accepted practice in an entire community and is not seen as 'buying' the bride.

The shortage of women can also potentially lead to a system of fraternal polyandry (sharing of one or more wives by several brothers), although there have been other reasons for its prevalence in areas where it was culturally accepted (Berreman, 1975). Some parts of Punjab and Haryana practised a 'surreptitious' polyandry induced by the low sex ratio and/or by economic considerations of controlling family size to prevent further sub-division of land.

Trafficking, buying of brides and brideprice marriages are thus analytically distinct phenomena. It is argued that the 'across-region' marriages discussed in this paper, however, do not fall into any of these categories. The crucial difference is that in none of the cases documented does the bride's family receive any monetary or other compensation from the groom. The couple is united in a 'proper' marriage ceremony either in the bride's or groom's village (usually in the bride's village). Money is spent by the groom on travel to and fro from his village, on a minimal trousseau for the girl and a feast for the villagers after the marriage ceremony—this legitimizes the marriage in the eyes of the villagers. It is specifically stated that the girl's parents do not want money in exchange for their daughter. At its end, the receiving family properly incorporates the bride into the family. Her status is not that of a concubine nor is she discarded after a while or passed into prostitution. The women go on to become mothers and even mothers-in-law. They settle down in their marital villages, continue to maintain contacts with their natal families and visits between the families take place even if they are not frequent (Blanchet's evidence of Bangladeshi women married into UP argues that the women are not allowed to maintain contact with their natal families and often choose to remain in Bangladesh when they are finally able to visit, sometimes abandoning their children and the husband—however, the evidence gathered for marriages within India is to the contrary). In several cases, a close relative of the woman, father or brother or sister, visits to assure herself/himself of the woman's well-being. Even if conditions are not found to be satisfactory, the girl and her parents accept the marriage hoping for a better future. The women adopt the language and culture of the host society and consider themselves a part of that society. The host society accepts them as wives/mothers/mothers-in-law. Although the word used for them in Punjab/Haryana is said to be 'kudesan' (woman from a foreign land), in my research with families of several such women in three villages of Haryana, I did not hear anyone refer to them by this pejorative term. If the point of view of the men is that they have purchased their wives (more so in UP than in Haryana), the viewpoint of parents is not of having sold their daughters but of having given them away in marriage under difficult conditions. However, this does not exclude the possibility of a category where women are 'bought' with money being transferred to the father, brother or mother. As the Bangladesh cases show, under conditions of extreme poverty and hopelessness parents may delude themselves into believing that they are sending daughters off to a better future than they can provide.

Some Questions Raised

Several sets of questions are raised by the phenomena of these 'new' marriages. One set, discussed above, pertains to their precise nature—do these constitute marriage at all or are they simply another variant in an increasing network of sexual trafficking or buying of wives?

A second, more important set of questions, relates to the robustness of widely held sociological assumptions about rural Indians following uniform and narrowly prescribed behavioural tenets regarding marriage. While sociological research has interrogated the 'fuzzy' or 'fixed' nature of caste and even religion, scholars have not focused on similar diversity and complexity in the domain of marriage and marriage strategies. It is well known that the predominant upper caste ideology of marriage is often violated in actual practice; there is also a necessary gap between the ideal and the actual. Historians have further remarked on a colonial and reformist privileging of upper caste marriage customs leading to an unacknowledged (and unstudied) practice of other marriage forms. Sociologists have pointed to the 'sanskritising' tendencies of upwardly mobile castes which lead to adoption of upper caste diacritical features. However, it is the conditions that allow a diversity of marriages, including ones that are looked down upon and which flout several norms of an ideologically conservative framework, which need to be explored. A related conundrum to be resolved is that conservative caste groups in North Indian society (for instance, Jats and Chauhans), who are extremely intolerant of inter-caste 'love' marriages, are allowing and encouraging a variety of marriages in which the caste and status antecedents of one or the other marriage partner is extremely doubtful.

Several other questions arise when one tries to interrogate these marriages further. How are the matches made? How are grooms/brides identified in these spatially widespread and culturally different locations? Who acts as the go-between? Further, how do the marrying groups/partners overcome linguistic and cultural differences? What are the terms on which women and their progeny are absorbed into the host culture? That such cultural differences are striking is self-evident and illustrated by this simple example: In Rajasthan, the married woman is expected to strictly observe 'purdah', whereas in Andhra it is considered inauspicious for a girl or a married woman to cover her head because only widows do so. How does reconciliation between such widely differing norms take place? Where the entire cultural habitus differs as it does between the north and the south (notwithstanding the commonality of institutions of caste and religion and assuming that people still want to marry within their religion and their caste), how is the divide bridged, negotiated? Are these marriages seen by those involved as conforming to traditional, cultural rules?

Marriage strategies too have to be diversified in the face of the shortage of women. The increasing complexity of marriage strategies among rural families is revealed by one such across-region marriage—between a man from UP and a woman from Bengal. Kallu, the groom, was the youngest among four brothers in a family of marginal low caste landowners. Three of his brothers married women from UP. However, the first two wives of the third brother (Rajendra) died—one from snakebite and the other during childbirth. With two deaths to their 'credit' the family was unable to recruit another locally available UP bride for Rajendra. A bride was arranged for him from West Bengal, through Asha, a Bengali, who had earlier been married into a neighbouring village.

By the time the fourth brother, Kallu, was of marriageable age, the family (his older brothers) was no longer willing to arrange a traditional honourable marriage for him. By keeping Kallu unmarried, his brothers could continue to farm his share of the land. Kallu was keen to escape the neglect that a bachelor in an Indian village inadvertently suffers. Without marriage, a bachelor can keep neither hearth nor farm. With no help from his brothers but permission and encouragement from his mother, Kallu decided to bring a bride from Bengal. Again, Asha came to rescue. It cost Kallu around Rs 8,000 to make the trip to Bengal and bring back his bride, Sushma. Some of this money went to Asha, who undertook to identify the bride, equip her with new clothes and organize the performance of the marriage rituals. Sushma's father is a poor daily wage agricultural labourer, who could neither afford to give away his daughter in a 'dowry marriage' nor pay the expenses of the marriage ceremony. Kallu took care of all expenses (including the village feast necessary to establish the social legitimacy of the marriage). However, he too saved on marriage expenses by marrying away from home and simply bringing back a bride. Asha has arranged several such matches from her own native and neighbouring villages in Bengal with men from UP. Kallu's village has 13 brides from outside—11 Bengalis and two Tamilians.

Does the Kallu-Sushma marriage qualify as a proper marriage (endogamous and hypergamous) and one in keeping with cultural rules? Possibly. The man and woman both belong to a low caste. The man is economically superior as a marginal landowner in addition to holding a job with a labour contractor in Delhi. The girl's father, from a fishing caste, is a landless labourer (both groom and bride claim to belong to the Dhimar caste) and hence inferior in the economic hierarchy. The rule of hypergamy is maintained with the wife-taker remaining economically superior to the wife-giver although caste hypergamy is difficult to establish at such a great distance. Further, regional hierarchy is maintained since UP girls are not given in marriage to grooms from Bengal and girls from Rajasthan are not sent to Andhra Pradesh as discussed later. Through relative economic superiority and the unidirectional aspect of taking and not giving brides, the bride-takers maintain their superiority and hierarchy.

The general presumption in the literature is that the sex ratio was better among the lower castes which have less stringent rules pertaining to status and dowry. A variety of marriage practices (non-dowry, brideprice, exchange marriage) are known to be prevalent among them. The breakdown, by caste, of marriages in the sample from UP for the village in Etah district, however, reveals that across-region marriages are occurring among all castes. Of the 13 such marriages, two are with Brahmins, two with Jats, three with Dhimar, two with Kumhaars, one with an Ahir, two with Telis and one with a Gadariya. In the village being studied in Haryana, the marriages are spread over the castes of Jats, Chauhans, Sainis including lower castes such as Balmikis and Jogis.

A second example reflecting a similar pattern is taken from a detailed report (accompanied by photographs of brides, grooms and their families) from a Telegu newspaper, *Enadu*. Since 1997, 40 marriages had taken place between girls from four blocks of Vizag district (Andhra Pradesh) with boys of various districts of Rajasthan. The couples are from the 'backward classes' and the fathers of the brides claimed that the inability to find grooms in Andhra who would accept the girls without dowry drove them to contract these out of region and state marriages. This explains the supply. On the demand side, why did the Rajasthani boys have to obtain brides from as far as Andhra? The answer again lies in the deteriorating sex ratio. A fortuitous first match (arranged by a Rajasthani man from the Indian army posted in Andhra Pradesh) set the stage for the subsequent marriages between girls from Andhra and boys from Rajasthan. The marriages were performed in Rajasthan according to local customs and traditions. Emphasizing the fact that these were proper marriages, the families said social contacts were being maintained and the girls were happy. To check on whether these were genuine marriages and not cases of girls being sold, the Andhra Pradesh police thoroughly investigated 15 of the marriages and did not come up with any instance of sale.

Primary and Secondary Marriages

Some other distinguishing features of across-region marriages are revealed by the Haryana data. Sociological literature describes a man's or woman's first marriage as being the primary marriage. Any subsequent marriage is considered to be secondary and not of the same status as the first. The secondary marriages are often bereft of ritual and celebration. Several across-region marriages fall into the category of secondary marriages for the men but not for the women. Marriage with a woman from outside his own community is very often the man's second or third (as in the case of Kallu's brother) marriage. The second or third marriage may be contracted after the death of the earlier wife/wives. The women are initially recruited as wives to primarily take care of the household and children from the first wife. Subsequently, they go on to consolidate the marriage by having children of their own. Men may, however, contract secondary marriage even if the first wife is alive but has not produced children or a male child. Evidence from several regions of India shows that such second marriages for men are very common (although a second marriage without divorcing the first spouse is illegal) and have the tacit sanction of the community. Another distinct feature of across-region marriage is that it is not the first brother in the family who faces the prospect of marriage with 'an outsider'. It is usually a lower down (e.g., third, fourth, etc.) brother who is forced to contract marriage with an outsider. Not surprisingly, a boy who is 'less eligible' in local terms (by virtue of lacking substantial property, education, an independent means of income or being handicapped in a physical or cultural manner) will have difficulty in securing a local wife and particularly so in a low sex ratio state. The marriage squeeze ensures that such men will have to look elsewhere. Evidence from rural Haryana and UP reveals that a man's chances of finding a spouse from his own community are severely reduced once he crosses the age of 35. Thus, although unattractive locally, Haryana men are locationally privileged by virtue of belonging to a more prosperous area and are able to draw brides from afar. Men wait until their mid-30 before giving up on a local match; yet the across-region girls they marry are very young. The age gap is even larger for men who are marrying for the second or third time.

Across-region brides are also the third, fourth or fifth daughter in the family. They are generally from extremely poor families of several girls. They may also be from single-parent families or be one of a family of several sisters and no brother. Several of the women revealed that they were married far away because "they had no brother". Among families with several daughters, the first and second may be married off locally, similar to the boys. The third, fourth or fifth are likely to be married off in these dowry-less marriages. Parents continue to worry about the welfare of the daughters given in across-region marriages—this is revealed by their desire to visit their daughter's homes. In several cases, fathers, brothers and sisters of girls stay with the married girl from several weeks to months; the North Indian taboo on hospitality from the daughter's/sister's house does not apply among these communities. The married woman, even if unhappy initially, rarely returns to her natal home permanently. There are some cases though in which the women leave soon after marriage, if they are unable to adjust to the family or culture of their marital homes.

What appears to be of greater significance in across-region marriage is not the fact of marriage being primary or secondary but the birth order of the individuals. Although the men may be socially disadvantaged in other ways (age, appearance, economic viability, etc.), the women are disadvantaged simply by being higher order birth daughters/sisters in poor families. However, the fortunes of the women too vary according to their age and physical appearance. Good looking girls are selected quickly by men and may go to more prosperous families.

Given the better sex ratios in the states from which the girls are coming, why does a poor Bengali or Assamese girl not marry a poor Bengali or Assamese man? One deterrent is dowry; the other puzzle to be sorted out is why local men are unattractive? Unemployment (a correlate of poverty), dependency on alcohol and drugs and idleness are the reasons often quoted by women who are marrying into the more prosperous states.

Marriage Migration and Marriage Distance

Migration studies show that a non-trivial proportion of migration in low income countries, particularly in rural areas, is composed of moves by women for the purpose of marriage. Economists have tried to understand this as part of household strategies that seek to mitigate income risks and facilitate what Rozenzweig calls "consumption smoothing in an environment characterized by information costs and spatially covariant risks" (Rosenzweig and Steak, 1989). Fan and Huang (1998) have linked long distance marriage migration in China to women using this as a strategy to move to economically more advantageous locations. A major concern of sociologists on the other hand has been with the consequences of 'marriage distance' for women. Most groups in Indian society practise a patrilineal form of descent accompanied by patrilocal or virilocal residence by virtue of which a woman almost always moves from her natal home to her husband's home. Studies have examined the role of endogamy and exogamy in restricting or expanding the marriage field (Dyson and Moore, 1983; Libbee and Sopher, 1975; Libbee, 1980; Hyde, 1995). Hyde, in her article on "Women's Village Networks", argues that the relationship between caste status, economic standing, cultural values and marriage distance is complex. She shows that while some studies correlate greater marriage distance with higher caste status and argue that higher castes are able to afford marriages further away enabling them to expand their socio-economic power base, other studies argue the opposite—that indeed the rich need not go far in order to find spouses. Her own study of marriage distance in a multi-caste village in Rajasthan shows a great deal of local variation and the effect of several socio-economic and cultural factors in marriage distances. Several recent studies have also emphasized the importance of a married woman's labour to her natal family. If she moves too far away, her natal family loses her as a source of physical labour and emotional support.

The enormously greater distance in 'across-region' marriages reveals the role of new factors—poverty and the sex ratio—in impacting marriage migration. The networks created by such marriages work separately and in conjunction with rural-urban migration. Women who migrate for marriage, especially to areas where they have no prior caste and kinship links, tend to create marriage networks around themselves. Thus, across-region marriages need to be understood within an approach that combines the economic perspective of marriage migration as household/individual strategies with one that looks at the social implications and consequences of such marriages. If poverty is the push factor sending dependent female members of the household to economically more advantageous locations, are the resulting marital networks in any way useful for the household? Do women have the opportunity to help their natal households and kin? Are they a source of remittances? Do they enable other marriages or facilitate employment for other family or kin members? Several of these questions remain to be explored in greater detail.

Patriarchy and Burden of Adjustment

The burden of adjustment in such marriages is unambiguously on the women who are brought into a culture generally more patriarchal than their own. To begin with, the women have to bridge the sheer cultural chasm that they are faced with. For instance, Sushma, in the example discussed earlier, lived in the village in UP for several years before happier days of relocation to an urban village in Delhi. She had difficulty with the local diet of wheat and bajra which was far removed from her daily diet of bhat (rice). In Bengal, women do not practise purdah (veiling) from their elders and in-laws and are not constrained to exercise restraint on their movements. Hence, the 'ghungat' custom was onerous to adopt and the enforced seclusion difficult to cope with. Verbal communication was made a little easier by the assistance and intercession of the Bengali 'jethani' (husband's elder brother's wife) who translated for her until she eventually learnt Hindi. Even then, her incomprehension of her mother-in-law's orders led to frequent beatings both by husband and mother-in-law. She would have fared much worse without the help of another Bengali speaker in the extended family. Over time, she has successfully acculturated to the marital family, adopting their language and mannerisms while discarding her own. Together with language and other cultural impediments, women face the early period of their marital lives without the solace of being able to pay frequent visits to their natal home. Until they build up local support structures they have only the husband to turn to, whose treatment of them may vary. It is very likely that such women are at the receiving end of more intensified violence in patriarchal cultures where the daughter-in-law is anyway at the bottom of the totem pole.

The cultural divide between the Rajasthani grooms and Andhra brides would appear to be even more insurmountable. Irawati Karve (1965), in her classic work on the Indian kinship and marriage system, showed how far apart the north and the south were on marriage patterns. While southerners prefer to marry within a circle of people known to them (often among relatives) northerners seek strangers as brides and while respecting caste rules, want them from as far as possible (although in the past it was always from within their own cultural zone). So, the southern bride marrying a northerner would find herself in a hostile environment of people unrelated in language, region and culture. Communication with the husband and in-laws would face the Indo-Aryan/Dravidian language divide, to the point of mutual incomprehension. The sense of security provided by marriage within her community is totally missing in this case.

Men also face a cultural divide but deal with it by rarely visiting their in-laws. The in-laws are seen as inferior and sometimes repulsive due to non-vegetarian and other culturally different habits. Many men look for women who know some Hindi before agreeing to the marriage to ease their own adjustment process.

The women face the greater burden of adjustment having been extracted from their local and cultural context. Marriage divests them of their sources of social security, their cultural moorings and they are forced to embrace their husband's culture in totality. Extreme deference ensured through 'purdah' practices, loss of mobility and freedom, loss of social safety networks, loss of cultural practices that made life fun and tolerable is traded for an economically more secure life. The woman thus accepted is torn from her own societal and cultural context; bereft of her 'social body'; it is only her physical self that is considered important for its capability to supply labour—reproductive and other—that is seen as constituting her persona in her marital home.

Marriage, Poverty and Sex Ratio

Thus, extreme poverty and the adverse sex ratio are responsible for bringing about such cross-regional/cultural unions. The girls are from poorer states, poorer districts and poorer villages. For both groom's and bride's parents, the marriages involve less expenditure than a marriage within the community would. Two kinds of expenses are involved in marriages in India—expenses incurred during the marriage ceremony such as feasting, gifts, etc., and the dowry expense. In across-region marriages no dowry payment is made (in fact, the report from Andhra Pradesh explicitly states that the girl's family is 'saved' from dowry). The expenses of an abbreviated marriage ceremony are taken care of by the groom who also spends less money than he might otherwise have in a locally contracted marriage. The men are not necessarily wealthy or even well-to-do although their economic circumstances are better than those of the women.

Marriage enables social adulthood for the woman while allowing the parents to discharge what is still considered to be one of their most important duties. Non-marriage would mean social failure and dishonour within the community. The parents of the girls, being extremely poor, are unable to fulfil the responsibility of arranging within community dowry marriages. With an across-region marriage, the families escape both dowry and marriage expenditure. In Assam, where dowry is not as onerous as in other parts of India, local men are not preferred due to lack of education, early alcoholism and idleness. Poor women from Assam would therefore be looking at marriage migration as a vehicle of mobility to more prosperous areas.

As argued by several sociologists, the scourges of son preference and dowry have spread to almost all regions and sections of Indian society. Although, dowry plagues the southern and eastern regions as well, sex ratios are somewhat better there. The two regions (north and west and south and east) are coping differently with the consequences of adverse sex ratio at one end, and poverty and dowry at the other. In the north, the dowry burden embedded in an overall patriarchal kinship system becomes a death trap for women and girl children; in the south and east, it is forcing families to send their daughters farther for marriage. That these are not entire new trends is revealed by earlier evidence of such marriages between families in Bengal and UP. Punjab, always a female-deficient state, is reported to have 'imported' girls from Bengal for as long as a century! Plains Punjabis also sought 'hard-working' girls from the hills although they chafed at sending their own girls there.

Some Sociological Implications

What are the sociological implications of the pattern described above, if it is a pattern? It is clear that the imbalance of the sexes created in the north and the west with consequences for the availability of marriageable women is being addressed through the 'import' of women from areas with a better sex ratio. What enables this exchange is the poverty of families who are willing to send their girls far away from home. Mediating this is the absence of dowry in such marriages. A surplus of men is logically expected to result in a decrease for the demand for dowry—however, this has to be disaggregated carefully. The low sex ratio situation benefits local women who can now be more discriminating about the men they marry. Eligible men, however, will still be sought after and paid dowries. Not so eligible men will either have to do without dowry (whether they marry locally or outside the community), or remain bachelors. The consequences of large numbers of unmarried men in socially conservative societies need to be addressed. Haryana and

Punjab reportedly have large numbers of unemployed and semi-employed unmarried young men who become victims of drug abuse and pose a threat to women. The consequent need to protect girls expresses itself in the desire of parents to marry daughters off at an early age.

Given the worsening sex ratio, are local women likely to be valued more? Will it lead to preservation rather than destruction of the girl child? At the moment the answers from the field are depressing. The fact that women can be 'imported' from 'elsewhere' prevents society from focusing on the consequences of the shortage. Although the necessity of women's labour, both as unmarried daughter and as daughters-in-law, is clear to the family, the ideology of son preference engenders a cultural misrecognition of women's worth; it constructs women as a dowry burden and as economic free riders. Virilocal residence discourages a woman from laying claim to immovable property, depriving her of the economic security which such an inheritance affords her brother. The demographic transition to a smaller family size in the low sex ratio but affluent states of the north and the west has clearly been at the expense of the female gender. Often, foeticide and the declining numbers of girls are seen by both men and women in low sex ratio states as a positive contribution to controlling family size and bringing down India's population. In an inverted logic, there is a rise in local women's value—due to their scarcity, they will be married to the best men in their own community. There are also reports of men entering dowry-less marriages with poor women of their own community. The valuation of both the local women and the 'imported' women is likely to get redefined under these changing demographic and socio-economic conditions.

The violence that 'outside' women face may be greater than that faced by local women since they do not have access to parents and brothers to appeal to in case of difficulties. Their parents are too far and too poor to offer any kind of help. Nor do the girls wish to return home to become a burden on their poor families. The question of the 'agency' of the migrating bride is something that needs to be explored at every step. Does she accede to the choice of a long distance marriage? Is she helping her family out or does she see it as a strategy for upward mobility and an escape from poverty? Is she making an explicit choice not to marry a poor groom from her own community who might accept her without dowry?

The development of North Indian society shows conflicting and contradictory attitudes towards gender and caste. While the importance of caste in non-marriage interactions is being progressively reduced due to changes in the direction of 'modern' values, newspapers are reporting increasing violence towards rural couples who fall in love and enter inter-caste marriages. These marriages are rejected with vehemence and the 'culprits' treated brutally. Yet, the same society is willing to accept marriages in which the women are brought from 'outside' whose caste status and social background is extremely difficult to ascertain. Only their economic status of being poor and available for marriage is known. What possibly explains the differential acceptability is that inter-caste marriage within a village or between neighbouring villages impacts the local standing of families much more than when one spouse is non-local. Since women are often considered the repository of family or community honour, they are subject to stringent social rules the infringement of which brings about violent punishment. The 'behaviour' of local women has consequences for both their natal and marital families. It further affects the marriage prospects of their siblings. The 'foreign' women, whose origins are somewhat suspect, are measured with a different rod; they are tolerated as long as they try to conform sufficiently to local norms. Bhup Singh, a Haryana male married to an Assamese, was very upset with his wife for bringing her sister and marrying her to a local Chauhan man of much lower status than him. He felt that it would jeopardize his own reputation if he had to associate with socially inferior relatives. If his wife proved herself to be 'socially capable', no one would point a finger at him while their association with less well-to-do relatives would cast his own marriage in a negative light. Meera, the wife, on the other hand, saw her sister's marriage in the same village as extending a helping hand to her own poor family of several sisters.

Intergenerational Change

Given that the ideology of marriage is built upon the set of criteria considered honourable by upper castes, marriages that compromise popular norms and transcend barriers, especially dowry, certainly face greater obstacles in being accepted as 'normal marriages'. The real test of whether such marriages are accepted would rest with the pattern of marriage of the children. Whether women are simply appropriated and assimilated in one generation to contribute to patriarchal patterns of the husband's society or whether they manage to genuinely bring about a change by causing shifts in marriage patterns in the next generation becomes a crucial question.

The marriage prospects of children from across-region marriages may differ for girls and boys. A girl's mixed antecedents can be ignored if her family is well-to-do, and can provide her with a substantial dowry. In the case of boys, having a mother of uncertain social/caste background can become a hindrance to arranging a good match. In patriarchal societies, the male's lineage is important while a woman never continues her own lineage and is in some ways never fully assimilated into the marital lineage either. Her caste status may thus be unimportant for her daughter's marriage. The daughter's status is also not as important as that of the son, since she eventually leaves the family to get absorbed into another lineage. Caste and status hierarchies are relevant for male clan groups; the son's pedigree is hence important and a mixed parentage may lower his worth in the marriage market.

Srinivas, Cohn and others have also considered marriage networks together with trade, religious and political networks for their integrative potential. "Networks of marriage ties are extensive, especially in northern India, where as many as 1,00,000 persons spread over hundreds of square miles may be linked directly and indirectly" (Cohn, 1987). Earlier, marriage networks strengthened caste networks spreading them over a greater spatial area; the nature of social circulation resulting from across-region marriages might in fact turn out to be quite different. These marriages and their networks often cut across caste and class, language and culture resulting in the creation of new links between people in different regions of the country. Such linkages have the potential for generating 'fuzzy' rather than the 'fixed' identities. Earlier, 'fixed' identities were promoted by the colonial state and are now being strengthened by a homogenizing and increasingly communal nation-state. However, one needs to carefully examine the implications of such 'integration' for women who are essentially being incorporated into more patriarchal social structures.

Across-region marriages point to the need to research the wide variety of social patterns made acceptable by adverse conditions of poverty, dowry and the low sex ratio. Most respondents who had brought wives from the eastern states sympathized with the poverty and lack of choice facing families of girls (while not focusing on the fact that they were the beneficiaries of that poverty) in these areas. The long-term unintended consequences of such marriages which perforce break cultural norms and barriers could be shifts in dowry payments, a turn around in the adverse sex ratio and a blurring of distinctions of caste, region and language.

[This article is based on ongoing field research by the author on across-region marriages in Haryana and UP. I am grateful to Rajni Palriwala and Rowena Robinson for helpful comments on the first draft and to Surjit S. Bhalla for discussions.]

This paper was published in *Economic and Political Weekly*, Vol. 39. No. 25, 2004.

References

Agnihotri, Satish (2000). *Sex Ratio Patterns in the Indian Population: A Fresh Exploration*, Sage Publications, New Delhi.

Berreman, G.D. (1975). "Himalayan Polyandry and the Domestic Cycle", in Patricia Uberoi (ed.) (1993). *Family, Kinship and Marriage in India*, Oxford University Press, Delhi.

Blanchet, Therese (2003). Bangladeshi Girls Sold as Wives in North India, Drishti Research Centre, Report for AED, Dhaka.

Cohn, B. (1987). "Networks and Centres", in *An Anthropologist among the Historians and Other Essays*, Oxford University Press, Delhi.

Das Gupta, M. (1987). Selective Discrimination against Female Children in Rural Punjab, India, *Population and Development Review*, 13(1), pp. 77–100.

Das Gupta, M. and Li Shuzhuo (1999). "Gender Bias in China, South Korea and India 1920–1990: Effects of War, Famine and Fertility Decline", in *Development and Change*, Special Issue in Gender, Poverty and Well-being, Vol. 30, No. 3, July, pp. 619–52.

Dumont, L. (1972). *Homo Hierarchicus*, Paladin, London.

Dyson, T. and M. Moore (1983). On Kinship Structure: Female Autonomy and Demographic Behaviour in India, *Population and Development Review*, 9(1), pp. 35–60.

Fan, Cindy C. and Youqin Huang (1998). "Waves of Rural Brides: Female Marriage Migration in China", in *Annals of Association of American Geographers*, 88(2), pp. 227–51.

Hyde, J. (1995). "Women's Village Networks: Marriage Distance and Marriage Related Folksongs", in N.K. Singhi and Rajendra Joshi (eds.), *Folk, Faith and Feudalism: Rajasthan Studies*, Rawat Publications, Jaipur.

Karve, Irawati (1965). *Kinship Organisation in India*, Asia Publishing House, Bombay.

Kaur, Ravinder (2003). "The Marriage Ratio", in *The Indian Express*, August, 25.

Libbee, M.J. and D.E. Sopher (1975). "Marriage Migration in Rural India", in L.A. Kosinski and R. Mansell Prothero (eds.), *People on the Move: Studies on Internal Migration*, Methuen and Co., London.

Libbee, Michael (1980). "Territorial Endogamy and the Spatial Structure of Marriage in Rural India", in D.E. Sopher (ed.), *An Exploration of India: Geographical Perspectives on Society and Culture*, Cornell University Press, Ithaca, NY.

Malhotra, Anshu (2002). *Gender, Caste and Religious Identities*, Oxford University Press, New Delhi.

Mandelbaum, D.G. 1993(1988). *Women's Seclusion and Men's Honour*, The University of Arizona Press, Tucson.

Mazumdar, V. and N. Krishnaji (2001). Enduring Conundrum: India's Sex Ratio: Essays in Honour of Asok Mitra, Centre for Women's Development Studies, Rainbow Publishers, Delhi.

Minturn, Leigh (1993). *Sita's Daughters: Coming Out of Purdah*, Oxford University Press, New York.

Miller, Barbara (1981). *The Endangered Sex: Neglect of Female Children in Rural North India*, Cornell University Press, Ithaca.

Oldenburg, Veena (2003). *Dowry Murder: The Imperial Origins of a Cultural Crime*, Oxford University Press, New Delhi.

Palriwala, R. (1994). Changing Kinship, Family and Gender Relations in South Asia, Women and Autonomy Centre (VENA), Leiden.

—— (2001). "Transitory Residents, Invisible Workers: Rethinking Locality and Incorporation in a Rajasthan Village", in K. Sangari and U. Chakravarti (eds.), *From Myths to Markets*, Manohar Publishers, New Delhi.

Rosenzweig, Mark and Oded Stark (1989). Consumption Smoothing, Migration and Marriage: Evidence from Rural India, *Journal of Political Economy*, Vol. 97, No. 4, August, pp. 905–26.

Sudha, S. and S. Irudaya Rajan (2003). Persistent Daughter Disadvantage: What Do Estimated Sex Ratios at Birth and Sex Ratios of Child Mortality Risk Reveal? *Economic and Political Weekly*, Vol. XXXVIII, No. 41, October, pp. 11–17.

Uberoi, Patricia (ed.), (1993). *Family, Kinship and Marriage in India*, Oxford University Press, Delhi.

Index